MAKING WAVES

MICHAEL REAGAN
MAKING WAVES

with Jim Denney

A
JANET
THOMA
BOOK

THOMAS NELSON PUBLISHERS
Nashville • Atlanta • London • Vancouver
Printed in the United States of America

Published in Nashville, Tennessee, by Thomas Nelson, Inc., Publishers, and distributed in Canada by Word Communications, Ltd., Richmond, British Columbia.

The Bible version used in this publication is THE NEW KING JAMES VERSION. Copyright © 1979, 1980, 1982, 1990 Thomas Nelson, Inc., Publishers.

Library of Congress Cataloging-in-Publication Data

Reagan, Michael, 1945-
    Michael Reagan: Making Waves : bold exposés from talk radio's number one nighttime host / Michael Reagan with Jim Denney.
        p.   cm.
    ISBN 0-7852-7588-6 (hardcover)
        1. United States—Politics and government—1993– 2. United States—Economic policy—1981–1993. 3. United States—Politics and government—1981–1989.
4. Talk shows—United States. 5. Reagan, Michael, 1945–   . 6. Reagan, Ronald.
I. Denney, James. II. Title.
E885.R43   1996
973.929—dc20   96–15763
                                                                                            CIP

Printed in the United States of America.

1 2 3 4 5 6 — 01 00 99 98 97 96

DEDICATION

To the people whose friendship and prayers
were so instrumental in my early years—

Jack and Jacquie Ellena
Art Reichle
The Lobheres
The Tarnutzers

And to
George Green at KABC
who gave me my first chance in talk radio;

and
Jack Merker and Chris Conway
who gave me my first full-time job in radio;

and
The Ballard Family
for seeing something in me
that no other national syndicators saw;

And, of course, to
My wife, Colleen,
who always believed in me.

If not for their faith in me over the years,
I never would have found faith in myself.

CONTENTS

PART THREE
INDISPENSABLE MEN:
REFLECTIONS ON MY FATHER—AND ON
BEING A FATHER

PART FOUR
MAKING WAVES:
WHAT TO DO TILL THE NEXT
MILLENNIUM ARRIVES

ACKNOWLEDGMENTS

My national radio talk show, my Internet website, my monthly newsletter, and this book all have my name on them—but it takes a lot of people to make these things happen. Unfortunately, once you start acknowledging people by name, you invariably leave somebody out. So if I missed anyone, please accept my apology and my gratitude for your help and support.

Thanks go to my friends at various foundations, think tanks, and grassroots organizations who regularly supply me with the solid, quality information that goes out over my airwaves and in this book: Amy Moritz of the National Center for Public Policy Research; Brannon Howse of the American Family Policy Institute; Grover Norquist of Americans for Tax Reform; Tom Schatz of Citizens Against Government Waste; John Goodman of the National Center for Policy Analysis; Frank Gaffney of the Center for Security Policies; Karen Mazzarella and Gary Stewart of Speak Out America; Brent Bozell III of Media Research Center; and Conna Craig of the pro-adoption Institute for Children.

I am deeply indebted to three intrepid individuals for the wealth and depth of insight and information contained in chapters 4, 5, and 6—my good friend (and Bill Clinton's chief accuser) Larry Nichols, and the "Woodward and Bernstein" of Whitewater/Fostergate, Christopher Ruddy and Ambrose Evans-Pritchard. I also want to recognize the generous assistance of the Western Journalism Center.

Thanks to Tom Denney, for the use of his vast library of conservative literature, and to Senator Dan Coats of Indiana, who supplied important information on defense issues.

I especially appreciate the careful critiques of the manuscript by my good friends Bob Phillips, Jeff Jacobs, and Mark Larson. Many of the strengths of this book are due to their perceptive insights—and any flaws or weaknesses that remain undoubtedly occur at places where I failed to heed their advice.

Much of the legwork that helped bring this book into existence was cheerfully carried out by my teammates: Paul Wilkinson and Peter Villar of *The Michael Reagan Talk Show*, Andy Beal of MediaFAX, and Mary Mostert of *The Michael Reagan Monthly Monitor*.

Finally, thanks to Jim Denney, who poured my thoughts onto paper with passion and skill, and to my editor, Janet Thoma, who unerringly guided us through the publishing maze, from conception to completion.

PART 1

ON THE AIR

◆

Talk Radio,
the Dominant Media,
and
the White House

CHAPTER 1

"Live, from the Back of a Winnebago Somewhere in Chula Vista!"

I USUALLY DROVE home with the windows rolled down, the air-conditioner blasting away, the radio cranked up loud, slapping my face to stay conscious. This night, however, was rainy and cold, so I had to keep the windows rolled up. It was stuffy, I was yawning continuously, and my eyelids kept falling down, blocking my view of the interstate . . .

I must have been asleep for a second or two because, the next thing I knew, the car was slewing around in the fast lane, hydroplaning over a patch of I-5 that looked like a lake. The car rotated a full 360 degrees, crossing all three northbound lanes as it spun. I figure the instincts I had acquired as a boat racer probably saved my asparagus that night—I don't remember fighting for control. One moment I was waking up and the car was spinning around, and the next moment I was in the far right lane, nose pointed north again. I didn't bother to stop—I just waved to the surprised-looking trucker who roared past, and kept on going. I mean to tell you, I was wide awake the rest of the way home!

That was back in 1992, when I was just getting my national show off the ground and my whole life was a blur of 262-mile-a-day commutes, late hours, exhaustion—and occasional death-defying thrills! It was a beautiful drive from my home in Sherman Oaks to the studio in San Diego—the gorgeous blue Pacific on the right, Camp Pendleton on the left, breezing through Santa Ana, Laguna, San Juan Capistrano, Dana Point, San Clemente, Oceanside, and finally the radiant city of San Diego.

I quickly became acquainted with every route, alternate route, side road, back alley, and detour between my house and the studio. I kept my radio tuned to KNX, which ran traffic reports every few minutes— and I became unstoppable! One day I might take 5, then jump to the 91, to the 134, to the 101, back to the 5, to the 605, to the 405. The next day, an accident on the 5 might send me down the 134 to the 210 to the 57, down to the 5. Road work on the 210? I'd take the 134 to the 101 to the 5 to the 710, pick up the 405 by Long Beach, and down to the 5. If there was a hang-up down where the 405 joins I-5, then I'd have to get really inventive: 134 to the 210, slide down the 57, jump to the 91 and head east toward Riverside, then south on 15 to the 78 and back over to the 5.

I was only late to work one time, when I got stuck behind a pileup at San Clemente. Even so, I made it on the air. I slid into my chair and behind the mike as the music came up, and nobody in the audience knew how close they came to hearing dead air.

Only one time in my whole San Diego stint did my car ever let me down, and that was late at night, on the way home from doing the show. My radiator blew at a place we affectionately referred to as Checkpoint Charlie, on the I-5 near San Clemente. I called a tow truck, and when the driver asked me where I wanted the car towed, I said, "Sherman Oaks."

"Buddy," he said, "that's eighty miles from here!"

"I know," I replied. It was late, I was beat down into my socks, and all I cared about was crawling into bed.

"That's gonna cost a lotta money," the driver said, scratching his head.

"I know."

"Well," he said, "you mind if we drive by my house so I can tell my wife I'm gonna be late?"

"Fine."

It cost me $300 to get that car towed home. And I'd pay it again.

It was quite an adventure, those first couple years of getting my national show off the ground. It was also the hardest thing I've ever done. The toughest part of all was putting in all those hours and not getting paid. Day after day, I went into the studio, got behind the mike, and told millions of listeners to "smile and dial." And three hours later, I'd walk out of that studio and all I could think was, *How will I pay my bills? How will we buy groceries this week? How will I support my family?* I mean, how many people can say they worked sixty, seventy, eighty hours a week—only to be paid in baseball caps?

What's that? You mean, I never told you about the baseball caps? Well, let me back up a bit and tell you how it all began . . .

A CUSHY JOB

I got my start in talk radio completely by accident back in July of 1983. My wife, Colleen, and I were supposed to have lunch with Kitty, Colleen's best friend from Kansas City. Kitty and Colleen had moved to California together, and Kitty had gotten a job with KABC.

I arrived before Colleen did, and the receptionist said that Kitty was in with Mr. Green—that's KABC's president and general manager, George Green—and sent me on into the office. Kitty introduced me, and the three of us talked for a few minutes.

"Gee, Michael," said George, "you've got a nice personality. Ever thought of doing talk radio?"

I had listened to talk radio from time to time and often thought, *Hey, that sounds like a cushy job—just talking to people on the radio.* So I said to George, "Nobody's ever asked me."

"Well, Michael Jackson's taking Monday off," he said, referring to the number one local talk-show host in L.A., not the moonwalker with one white glove. "Why don't you sit in for him?"

There was no mystery as to why George Green wanted me to pinch-hit on his radio station: I was a novelty. My dad was the president of the United States, and I could warm Michael Jackson's seat for a morning without letting his ratings slide too badly. I thought it would be fun, and I'd get union scale for the gig—not a bad deal. So I said, "Sure!"

I did my first radio broadcast at KABC on July 12, 1983. And that's how I got into talk radio.

In 1988, I went on tour to promote my first book, *On the Outside Looking In.* One of my stops was an interview show on KSDO radio in San Diego. At the studio, I chatted with the program director, Jack Merker, and he was aware of the fill-in job I had at KABC. I told him I was interested in getting a show of my own. "We don't have an opening for a permanent host," said Merker, "but our regular host is going on vacation for three weeks, and we might be able to give you those three weeks. Why don't you send me some tapes of your work?"

The first secret of this business is, *Keep all your tapes.* I sent *copies* of my tapes to Jack, he liked what he heard, and based on that, I was given a three-week guest shot, sitting in for Roger Hedgecock, the number one talk show host in San Diego. A few months later, the general manager, Chris Conway, offered me a contract for a show of my own. I signed the contract and a date was set for the debut of (ta-dah!) *The Michael Reagan Talk Show* on KSDO.

Just days before my talk show was to air, Chris Conway left to take another job, and Mike Shields came in as general manager. Shields had different plans for me: no talk show. I was going to be an anchor in the morning news block. I said, "But I can't read news!"

"What's so hard about reading the news?" asked the new g.m. "Anybody can read what's put in front of 'em."

"I do talk radio," I said. "I don't read copy. If you make me read the news, I'll be terrible."

"You'll take to it like a duck to water."

So they started me out doing morning news in January '89, just a few days before the Bush inauguration. My first morning on the job, they pitched me a curveball. I was on the air during the six o'clock hour and had just finished reading a story when Jack Merker, who was anchoring, said, "We interrupt this portion of the Monday morning KSDO News because we have an urgent call coming in from the White House." I thought, *A call from the White House! My gosh, who could that be?*

Then I heard a familiar voice in my headphones: "Good morning, Mike. This is your old man."

"Dad! This is a surprise! How are you doing?" I was caught totally off guard.

"Well," he said, "things are just fine. How are you doing? I'm a little far away here in Washington to pick up your program, but I just wanted to congratulate you on your first day and wish you well."

We talked for a few minutes about his last visit to Camp David over the weekend, his impending and bittersweet parting from the White House, and his planned return to California, immediately after the Bush inaugural. "Nancy sends her love," he said at last, "and please give our love to Colleen and the children."

"You take care, Dad," I said. "Love you."

"Well . . . love you."

That call was a real special gift from Dad.

"I WANT TO KNOW HOW *YOU* FEEL"

Despite the nice send-off, doing the morning news at KSDO turned out to be one of the worst experiences of my life. Everybody thinks, "Boy, it's got to be easy to be the son of the president. You've got it made!" The fact is, regardless of my last name, nobody would give me a job. So I took the only job I could get—reading the news in San Diego—and I had to leave my family to do it. It ate at me every single day.

I hated the schedule: in bed by nine on Sunday night, get up at two in the morning, and drive two hours from L.A. to San Diego in time to do the news from 5:30 to 9:00 A.M. Once the news was over, I had a day to kill, so I'd hit the golf course or find some other way to stave off boredom. I'd stay over Monday night, get up and do the news Tuesday morning, then drive home to see my family. Wednesday morning, up at two again, drive to San Diego, do the news, kill a day, stay overnight, do Thursday's news, go home to see my family. Fridays, I'd do a round trip to San Diego and back.

To top it off, I was terrible! I had told Mike Shields I'd be terrible, and was I ever! I stumbled over words. I sounded stiff and ill-at-ease. My inflection was flat and unimpassioned. Shields had put me in that slot for the sake of name recognition. It never occurred to anyone to ask, "Can this guy read news copy?" To make matters worse, the guy I was replacing—Ernie Meyers—had been the number one news anchor in the San Diego market. I mean, the guy was an icon! Everybody loved him—and as much as they loved Ernie, that's how much they hated me. People thought I had pushed Ernie out of a job, when in fact he had left because of contractual issues.

In a desperate effort to remake me into a news anchor, Jack Merker hired a diction coach for me. Then, after every show, Jack would send me into an empty studio and have me read the Bible into a microphone for an hour. The theory was that if I could read the Bible with passion and inflection, then news copy would be a breeze. Though I'm sure all those hours of Bible reading did wonders for my soul, they didn't make me a better news reader. To this day, I still have trouble with diction—but that's okay. Now it's part of my persona.

The whole experience was a physical, mental, and emotional meatgrinder. It tore me apart because: (1) the stress was killing me; (2) I was doing a job I wasn't comfortable in, and I was doing it poorly; and (3) I was away from my family so much of the time. My family is the most important thing in the world to me. Perhaps the whole issue of family is so crucial to me because my parents were divorced and I spent so much of my early life in boarding school. Growing up, I had always felt cheated out of time with my father and mother. Now, as an adult, I felt cheated out of time with my wife and children—and I knew they felt deprived of me. Worst of all was the guilt I felt over putting my kids through the same separation, pain, and privation I had resented so much at their age.

After four months, I finally proved to the powers at KSDO that I couldn't read news copy. I had a contract, so they had to do *something* with me. So in June of '89, they gave me my own weekend talk show. It was good preparation for the show I do now, because I did a lot of interviews with politicians and authors. In January of '90, I was offered the weekday afternoon talk show when the previous host left for Chicago. But there was a condition: I had to move to San Diego. My friends, Dennis and Colleen Agajanian, knew some people in San Diego who needed a housesitter, and that worked out great for me. I moved in, started doing my show during the week, and commuted to L.A. on weekends to be with my family.

I did well in that time slot, consistently drawing the number one or two position in the ratings. I've always felt that one of my strengths as a talk show host was that I did my homework. I had a lot of authors on my show, and whenever I interviewed an author, I had *read* the book and I *knew* the book. In fact, one author I interviewed back when I was pinch-hitting for Michael Jackson—CBS newsman Charles Kuralt—told me I was the best interviewer he had ever been on the air with.

Doing the weekday show, however, I discovered I had one big deficiency as an interviewer: I didn't know who I was or what I believed! I didn't know how I felt about different issues. For years, it had never been a problem, because no one ever asked me to think on my own. People didn't want to know what *I* thought; they'd always ask me what my *dad* thought! So it was quite a shock one day when a caller said to me on the air, "I know how your dad feels. I want to know how *you* feel." What could I say?

So it was during my weekday talk show stint that I really became a voracious, avid reader and student of the world scene. I would devour books and periodicals covering all sides of the issues, because I wanted to understand all points of view on every subject. I wanted to have not only opinions but *facts* to back up my opinions. And if the facts contradicted my opinions, I wanted to change and grow. I didn't just want to be "right of center"—I wanted to be *right,* period. To this day, the three hours of output you hear on my show is the product of hours and hours of input, of gathering insight and information, of connecting the dots and discovering the relationships and linkages between seemingly unconnected events.

Having three hours a day on the air, five days a week, gave me room to experiment, try new ideas, and talk to a lot of interesting people. My producer, Marna McClure, one day asked me, "Who would you like to interview?"

"Oh, Jack Kemp," I said.

She gave me a quizzical look, as if I were ribbing her. "C'mon! We're just a small station. Why would Jack Kemp want to be on your show?"

"Because I know Jack Kemp," I said. "Let's call him." So my first interview on my weekend show was with Jack Kemp, via telephone from the pool at his Virginia home.

We snagged some really amazing guests for that show. During Operation Desert Shield, just prior to the start of the war, my friend Roger Hedgecock at KSDO was trying to get the Kuwaiti ambassador to come on his show and talk about the Persian Gulf crisis. The Kuwaiti ambassador kept turning him down. Meanwhile, Marna and I were in a planning meeting and she said, "Who would you like to be on your show next week?"

"The ambassador from Iraq."

"Oh, come on, Mike! You'll never get the Iraqi ambassador! When he talks to the media, he talks to Bernard Shaw on CNN or Ted Koppel on *Nightline.* He doesn't go on a local radio show in San Diego!"

"Call the embassy and see what they say," I said. So she called the embassy and left a message. A few hours later, the embassy called back and told her, "The ambassador would love to do *The Michael Reagan Show.*" We did the show by phone from Washington, and the ambassador gave me a whole hour.

Now, when the embassy of Kuwait heard that the Iraqi ambassador was coming on my show, they did a quick about-face and called KSDO and booked the Kuwaiti ambassador on Roger Hedgecock's show! They weren't going to let Iraq have an hour of airtime on KSDO without getting an hour of their own! So little old KSDO, down in little old San Diego, landed two of the nation's most sought-after interview guests— just hours apart, on the very same day, and smack in the middle of a major international crisis!

MY SAN DIEGO "FAMILY"

The hardest thing about the weekday afternoon show was that I had to move to San Diego and leave my family behind. It was much worse than when I was a news-reader, because I was never home during the week. I was lonely and miserable. In fact, I felt practically *divorced,* seeing my wife and kids only on weekends. I seriously wondered whether our marriage could survive all that separation. It seemed Colleen and I had never really had a chance to be alone together. After all, we had only been married five years when the Secret Service came into our lives in 1980. For the eight years Ronald Reagan was president, we had guys with dark sunglasses and narrow ties hiding in our bushes or following our car wherever we went. We had no privacy! Only when my dad left office did we finally get rid of the Secret Service—but by then, I was working a hundred miles away from my family.

I did my weekday show in San Diego for almost three years, and the one saving grace in my life during that time was a group called Media Fellowship. I had never heard of Media Fellowship until I received an invitation letter from Carol LaBeau, a top news anchor on Channel 10. In the letter, she explained that Media Fellowship was a group of Christians in the TV and radio industry who met once a month for Bible study, prayer, and mutual support. Lonely as I was, that sounded like something I really needed. So I went to a meeting at Carol's home—and was I astonished! There in one room were some of the most well-known faces and voices in the broadcast media of San Diego County!

One reason I was surprised was that I never expected to find so many Christians who were involved in the dominant media. Take it from me, the broadcast business is not exactly a supportive environment for those who live out their faith. In fact, many TV and radio studios are downright hostile to people with religious convictions. Use the name of God in a loud, ugly curse, and you fit right in. But just go up to a coworker and say, "I want you to know I'm praying for you," and *ka-boom!* "Don't you push your religion off on me!" In fact, that was one of the issues a number of the people in Carol's living room that night struggled with: the anti-Christian hostility of the workplace and being hammered on the job for being people of faith and a moral lifestyle.

The public perception of people in the media is that they have it made. They have fame and fortune, so how could they possibly have any problems? When you are a top-rated disk jockey, talk-show host, or news anchor, it's tough going to a nonmedia person and saying, "Would you pray for me? I'm really struggling with a problem." People look at you uncomprehendingly, like, "How can *you* have problems?!" But every person in that room had problems and pain in their lives. Struggles on the job. Money problems. Health problems. Family problems. Loneliness. In that room, no one was a star. All the professional facades were down, and the raw humanity showed through.

We didn't talk shop or politics at these meetings, nor was it a place to network for your next job. It was a place where people came to be ministered to from the Bible, to share themselves and their issues, and to be prayed for and supported. Bob Rieth of Seattle is executive director of Media Fellowship nationwide, and he would come to the San Diego meeting once a month as the "pastor" of the meeting. The people in those meetings became my San Diego "family," and to this day, they are still the closest friends I have. I keep in touch with all the close friends I made in Media Fellowship, including Mark Larson (g.m. at KPRZ in San Diego), Carol LaBeau, and Martha Williamson (the producer of the CBS TV series *Touched by an Angel,* which was nearing cancellation until other talk-show hosts and I began telling the country what a wonderful family show it was). These people still call me and pray for me, and I have lunch once a month with Bob Rieth here in L.A.

For many in the group, Media Fellowship was their church. Highly visible and recognizable people often find it hard to attend a regular institutional church. A story from my father's experience will illustrate why. Around Easter 1988, I was with my dad aboard Air Force One, flying from Washington, D.C., to Point Mugu, the naval air base near Ventura, California, not far from the Santa Barbara ranch. As we were landing, I noticed that Dad's brow was furrowed and he was counting on his fingers, "One, two, three, four, five, six, seven, eight, nine."

I said, "Nine what?"

"Nine months," he said. "Nine months from now, in January, I can start going back to church again."

"What?"

"Well," he said, "ever since the assassination attempt, I have been worried about the danger to people around me." When he said that, I remembered how painful it was for him to know that three other men, including his close friend Jim Brady, were wounded by the same gunman who had targeted Dad for assassination.

"I always wonder," he continued, "What if something like that were to happen in a church full of people? Another thing I'm concerned about is that people should go to church to hear the Word of God. But because I'm the president, when I go to church, I can feel that people have their eyes on me instead of having their ears tuned in to the sermon and the music. People shouldn't be looking at me; they should be looking at Paul's prize, the high calling of God. So I just don't go to church as often as I used to. But in January, when I'm out of office, I'll have more freedom to go to church again."

That's the way it is for prominent people in the media. When they walk into church, heads turn. They become the center of attention, instead of God. And when they leave church, they're hit up for autographs. So it's easier for them to have their "church" in a home than to go to church on Sunday mornings and be a spectacle.

There were other people who practically adopted me and made me feel at home—people like Roger Hedgecock at KSDO, and his friends Michael and Karen Turk. Nothing could replace the family I had left behind in Sherman Oaks, but these good friends and my substitute family at Media Fellowship made the separation a little easier to bear.

I HATE IT WHEN MY WIFE IS RIGHT

As the show grew, I tried to convince Colleen to make the move with me to San Diego. I had really grown fond of playing golf at Torrey Pines, looking out over the blue Pacific and off toward La Jolla as I teed off, and watching the hot air balloons floating over Del Mar. If I just had my family with me, everything would be perfect! But Colleen wouldn't budge.

"I'm not going anywhere," she said. "I don't trust radio. There's no job security in that business."

"You don't know what you're talking about," I argued. "I'm the top-rated host in the market. Things are going great! We'll live there forever! What would it take to convince you we should move?"

"Mike," she said, "when you get a new contract, you show it to me and then we'll pack up and move to San Diego."

After the show had been on the air for two years, it was time to negotiate a new contract. I was feeling pretty good. The show had done well, and the station was promising more money. But while I was negotiating my new contract, something was going on at another San Diego radio station that I knew nothing about. That station, XTRA Mighty 690, a sports-talk outlet with a blowtorch signal, had only one nonsports show—a syndicated political talk show out of New York—and they decided to drop it and go to a 100 percent sports format. Well, the show XTRA dropped had to go somewhere, right? And the station that picked it up happened to be *my* station, KSDO.

Clueless, I walked into the general manager's office, thinking all I had to do was sign on the dotted line and shake hands. Instead, I was told, "Mike, you've got forty-eight hours to pack your bags and get outta town."

I was stunned. "I'm out?" I asked. "Just like that?"

"That's right."

"But why?"

"Dollars, Mike. It's more cost-effective to run a network show in your slot than to produce local programming."

"What network show?" I asked numbly.

"Rush Limbaugh's show."

And that was that. I was history, outta there, unemployed, canned. I *hate* it when my wife is right!

"I'VE JUST BEEN PRAYING FOR YOU"

I immediately began looking for another job doing local talk. I guest-hosted in places like Milwaukee, Seattle, and Dallas, and I got a few job offers. In the end I decided not to move to a new local market. I didn't want to haul my family halfway across the country only to come home one day and say to Colleen, "Pack your bags, honey. I've just been replaced by Rush Limbaugh again."

At the same time, I kept getting calls from a local guy named Jim Ballard. He, his wife, Peggy, and her sons, Mike and Dean, had a new company in San Diego, and they wanted to syndicate my show nation-wide. I didn't want to go with a fledgling company; I wanted to go with the big boys. After all, my name was Mike Reagan—how could they possibly turn me down? Well, I approached CBS, ABC, EFM (EIB), the whole alphabet soup of radio networks, and guess what? They *all* turned me down! No one was interested in giving me a national show—no one, that is, except Jim Ballard. So I went with the only game in town.

On September 7, 1992, we started *The Michael Reagan Talk Show* on Ballard's brand-new American Entertainment Network. The Ballards operated out of San Diego, I was still living in Sherman Oaks, and I sure wasn't going to get Colleen to move to San Diego now! So I was back to commuting 200-odd miles to do my show—and I would continue to do so for the next two and a half years.

My new national show started with five stations. Four of them aired the show on a tape-delayed basis, which meant that four-fifths of my audience didn't know when to call in to my call-in show! The one station that carried the show live—WISN in Milwaukee—preempted the show for football on Monday nights, which meant that one night a week, *none* of my listeners could call in. So I started doing my national show on the assumption that no one was going to call. That was a solid assumption because nobody did!

To keep my early shows from sounding like three solid hours of monologue, the Ballards would go to another room in the building and call me on another line. Jim and Peggy would take turns calling in as "George from St. Paul," "Mary from Atlanta," "Ray from Tacoma," or "Minnie from Houston." When that began to wear thin, they'd arrange to have some of their friends and family call in and pretend to be callers from Orlando or Hartford or Sacramento. Admittedly, the regional dialects my "callers" used were sometimes pretty cheesy—but at least they made the show *sound* like a talk radio show!

Soon, I started to get *real* calls from *real* people in *real* cities around the country—and boy, would I milk those calls! "How's your mother? How's your father? How are the kids?" Today, even though I have plenty of callers, I still prepare for each show as if nobody's going to call. That way, if the phone banks go down, I can do three hours of monologue, no problem.

A lot of people think getting my show onto stations across the country was a piece of cake because my name was Reagan—and to be sure, the name could be an advantage in a few situations. As I told Harry Smith during an interview on the *CBS Morning News,* "The difference between me and other talk-show hosts is that they talk *about* Ronald Reagan; I talk *to* him." Usually, however, my last name was more of a hindrance than an advantage. Since people in the broadcast business *assumed* I was there because of my last name, it was harder to get them to take me seriously. They thought I was just the son of an ex-president, and I didn't have any substance. I had to overachieve on every show just to prove myself to station managers, program directors, and audiences.

For my national show, I commuted from L.A. to San Diego and back every single weeknight. I would prep for the show in the mornings, leave the house at 2 P.M., do the show from 6 to 9, and get back home at 11. At that point, my whole belief system, everything I had always wanted my family life to be—picking my kids up from school, having dinner with them, family prayers at night, family outings—all of that was in the tank. My entire life, it seemed, was spent behind either a steering wheel or a microphone.

To top it off, my syndicator continually operated on the razor-edge of disaster. Perhaps the Ballards assumed that my last name would bring in money by the barrel—but it sure didn't happen that way. For the entire first year, they made nothing; everything that came in went out to pay operating expenses. Even though we had a contract guaranteeing me a salary, oftentimes the money just wasn't there. When I didn't get a paycheck, they at least paid my gas mileage—which helped a lot with a 262-mile daily commute. Still, the contract promised me a certain amount of money at certain intervals, and it wasn't happening. It would have been within my legal rights to walk away from my contract—but where would I go? If the show failed, people wouldn't say, "Mike Reagan's syndicator was undercapitalized." They'd say, "Mike Reagan couldn't cut it in radio"—and because of who my dad was, it would get blown up in the press. I couldn't quit.

Thank God, Colleen was working—though, since she worked on commission, the amount of income varied. Our house—once one of the nicest on the block—was becoming one of the worst-looking. The roof was shot. The paint was peeling. I was really ashamed. It was especially embarrassing because when you're the son of famous parents, everyone assumes you've got a million bucks.

That whole first year, I wondered how long would it be before Colleen finally would have enough of this and decide to leave me. I needn't have worried. I forgot that my wife came from Nebraska, and she was rooted in those great middle-American values. She knew how to hold her family together through tough times, and she was committed to standing by me.

Every night when I came home, hungry and exhausted, I'd find my dinner in the kitchen and my wife in the bedroom. She'd have her glasses on and her red-leather Bible in her lap, and she'd look up at me and smile and say, "I've just been praying for you, Michael."

Then I knew I was home, and everything was okay.

MY NEW "STUDIO"

I look back on those days and find it hard to believe everything I went through to build a national talk show. We started in Carlsbad, about twenty minutes up the freeway from San Diego. One Monday I walked into the studio and was told, "You're not doing your show here anymore."

My jaw dropped. "What?"

"Your syndicators owe us five grand. We told them we're not extending any more credit, so they're gone."

"But I have a live broadcast coming up! Where am I supposed to do my show?"

"We don't know. We just know you're not doing it here."

At that moment, the phone rang. It was for me. Jim Ballard. "Michael," he said, "we've got a new studio for you. It's in San Diego."

"Why didn't you tell me you were changing studios before I got to Carlsbad?!"

"There's no time for that now, Mike. You're going on live in an hour, so you better get down here right away!"

"All right, tell me how to get there."

I wrote down the directions on the back of a business card. Then I jumped in my car and raced down to my new "studio."

I put quotation marks around that word *studio* because my new broadcast facilities were in the empty first floor of a building that was still under construction! It had bare concrete floors, steel beams and girders all around, wires hanging out of the ceiling, sawhorses and tools scattered around, no heat, no air conditioning, and nothing but a bunch of old thrift-shop mattresses around me to absorb the sound. I took one look at the "studio" and said, "You've got to be kidding!"

"Hey," said Jim, "this is radio. No one can see you or your surroundings. All they know is you're a brilliant guy talking on the radio. Knock 'em dead, Mike." You have to hand it to Jim Ballard: The guy refused to be stopped by circumstances.

I put on my headset, sat down behind the microphone, wrapped my coat a little tighter around myself—it was cold in there!—and I was on. "Hi, everybody," I said, same as usual. "Mike Reagan here, you're there. This is where we talk about the issues, get your comments, your concerns about all that is going on in this great big wonderful land that we call the good ol' U.S. of A. So sit back, smile, and dial . . . " And as I sat there talking, huddled in front of the microphone, surrounded by all those mattresses, trying to keep my teeth from chattering as I intro'd the show, I thought, *If the public could only see where I'm doing this show from!*

My listeners had no idea how close we came to being canceled in our first year, just because my syndicator was struggling to pay the bills and get the show off the ground. That's no criticism of the Ballards. They weren't ducking creditors because they wanted to. Fact is, they are some of the most hardworking, enterprising people I've ever met, and they gave 110 percent to make the show a success. I mean, you've got to hand it to Jim Ballard: Within hours of being locked out of the studio in

Carlsbad, he had cobbled together an entire broadcast studio—microphones, radio consoles, phone lines, mattresses, satellite uplink—and he got me on the air without missing a beat! It wasn't elegant, but it did the job. That's classic can-do spirit and know-how—as American as McDonald's hot apple pie!

"YOUR KIDS WILL LOVE THESE CAPS, MIKE!"

One afternoon, I was about to leave home for my mattress-walled studio when my phone rang. It was Jim Ballard. "Hi, Mike. Change of plans."

"What now?"

"We have a new studio. You'll like this place. Acoustical tile instead of mattresses. And it's in Oceanside—closer to your home."

I sighed. "Gimme the address."

So I went to the new studio—it really *was* a studio this time—and I did the show there for the next few months. I never felt very secure, however. I fully expected to get a call any day telling me my next studio was the back of a Winnebago somewhere in Chula Vista.

In addition to radio, my syndicator was involved in producing infomercials, and one of their clients was the National Football League. So even though American Entertainment Network didn't have any money, they had a ton of baseball caps with insignia on them from various NFL teams. Jim Ballard said, "Look, Mike, things are tough for us right now, see?"

"No kidding," I said, trying to remember my last paycheck.

"But there *is* something we can do for you."

"Oh? Well, great. What's that?"

"We'll give you all the baseball caps you want. You can take 'em home to your kids and wear 'em around. They're a twelve-ninety-five value, and they come with insignia of the Forty-Niners, the San Diego Chargers, the—"

"Hold it," I said. "Whoa. Time out. Let me see if I've got this straight. You don't have any money to pay me with, correct?"

"At this particular point in time? No, Michael, we don't have any money."

"So instead of money, you want to pay me . . . in football caps?"

"They're baseball caps, Mike. They just have football insignia."

"No" to Ronaldus Magnus

After I had been on American Entertainment Network for a little less than a year, I began hearing about a letter my dad had written to another talk-show host—a fella by the name of Rush Limbaugh. Maybe you've heard of him? The letter was presented to Rush with great fanfare and hoopla by his TV producer, Roger Ailes (who used to be a media advisor to the Reagan campaign). Rush displayed the letter on his TV show and took it with him when he appeared on the *Donahue* show. On radio, Rush had his announcer, John Donovan, read the letter while patriotic music played in the background. It was quite a production. According to the letter, Ronald Reagan (or, as Rush calls him, "Ronaldus Magnus") was passing on the mantle of conservative leadership and naming Limbaugh the official "voice of conservatism."

For weeks, Rush used this letter on his TV and radio shows, and for weeks people would ask me, "Why did your dad send a letter to Rush Limbaugh? Did he ever give you a letter like that? No? Well, why not?" I didn't have an answer to that. Finally, I had heard that question for about the last time I needed to. So the next time I visited Dad and Nancy at their home in Bel-Air, I asked him about the letter.

My dad looked puzzled. "What letter?" he said.

Then, more important—and more ominous—Nancy said, "*What* letter?" Neither of them knew anything about it.

So Nancy called Fred Ryan, my father's chief of staff, to track down the letter. Fred traced it to one of my dad's secretaries, and she confessed her involvement. She explained that Roger Ailes had composed the letter himself, then gave it to her. She then transferred it to my father's official stationery and placed it in a stack of letters for my father's signature. My father, assuming it was one of the letters he had dictated, signed it with all the other letters in the stack, and the secretary then gave the signed letter to Ailes. Ailes had it matted and framed, then presented it to Rush. To this day, I doubt that Rush even knows how he got that letter—or who actually wrote it.

My dad felt badly about the incident because it created the appearance that he had endorsed Rush while passing over his own son. So he decided to do me a favor. Knowing I was struggling to gain a larger national audience for my show, he had Fred Ryan place a call to Ed McLaughlin at EFM, the syndicator of Rush's show. "President Reagan wishes to thank you for all the kind things Rush says about him on his show," Fred told him. "The president would like to know if it would be possible to hear *two* shows on your network—Rush Limbaugh in the daytime and Michael Reagan at night."

Not long afterward, Ed McLaughlin called me at home, and we talked for a while. Then I met with the president of his company a few weeks later at the National Association of Broadcasters convention in Dallas, where we talked further. In the end, EFM decided not to take my show.

I know some people think I got where I am in this business because my last name is Reagan, or even because of my father's influence. But the one time my dad used his influence on my behalf, it fell flat. Even Rush Limbaugh's network said "no" to Ronaldus Magnus.

So I got paid in baseball caps. In fact, I still wear my San Diego Chargers cap to remind me of what I've gone through. I don't blame Jim Ballard for the struggles we shared. He beat the odds just getting into the syndication game with very little start-up capital. It's a tough business, and Jim and his family hammered together a makeshift launching pad and got me airborne.

It was Jim Ballard who had the idea of doing a proactive talk show with bill numbers, phone numbers, and fax numbers. He wanted to use the show as a way to teach people how to access the Congress, and how to return power back to the state and local levels. Jim actually foresaw what the show would ultimately become, even though I didn't grasp his vision at first.

STUBBORNNESS WITH A PURPOSE

I had found something I really enjoyed doing, and I wanted to make it work, so I just kept plugging. I remembered all the times my mother, actress Jane Wyman, had told me, "You have to pay your dues." I figured that everything I was going through was just part of that. Colleen was earning commissions as a travel agent, and I occasionally gave a speech or two that would enable us to make ends barely meet. Somehow, we survived.

I was able to close off all the fear and financial worry for three hours every weeknight from 6 to 9 P.M. I drove myself to be on top of my game while I was in that studio. I told myself, *I'm not going to fail, I'm not going to quit, I'm not going to lose this show. If I stay focused on this and go through the bad times, then there must be some good times ahead—once I've paid my dues.*

I believe that the magic of success is found in staying unswervingly committed to your goals. You have to stay focused; you have to persevere if you want to succeed. For many years, I didn't know who I was, what I was capable of doing, or what I really wanted to do. When I was in the boat business, people said to me, "What are you doing selling boats? Your mother's the star of *Falcon Crest* and your father's the president of the United States. Shouldn't you be doing something more important than *this*?" Even when I succeeded in business, people looked on it as failure because I wasn't achieving on the same level as my parents.

What people didn't understand was that both of my parents had the same strange quirk: Neither of them believed in nepotism! They actually believed in the work ethic—that a person should rise or fall according to his or her own efforts! Growing up in Beverly Hills, I was the only kid on my block who didn't get everything he wanted for the asking. When I asked my mom for a bike, she said, "You want a bike? Go get a job."

"What do you mean, Mom? I'm only ten years old!"

"I build men," she said. "I don't build boys."

I thought, *What in the heck does that mean?* But I got myself a job. I sold papers in front of Good Shepherd Church. I grumbled a lot, I earned the money, and I bought myself a bike. For years afterward, I wondered why my mother put me through all that.

Now that I'm where I am in talk radio, I understand what she tried to teach me for forty years. If you earn it yourself the hard way, you'll grow up to be a man. If you have it all handed to you, you'll end up forty, fifty, sixty years old, and still be a child.

When I finally figured out what I wanted to do and got into the radio business, a lot of well-meaning people told me, "Give up, Michael. It's never going to happen. You're never going to make it." Some of my best friends said that to me. Those words cut me like a knife—but they were also like a spur to my backside, prodding me to keep going, to prove myself right.

The more people told me to give up, the more I knew I *couldn't* give up. Instead, I focused on excellence. My motto, even in the depths of those tough times, was *Make today's show better than yesterday's.* Someone once defined *perseverance* as "stubbornness with a purpose." That was me. Dogged, unrelenting, bullheaded stubbornness—but with a very clear purpose.

We grew from five stations to nearly a hundred. I regularly broke major news stories that the dominant media refused to touch. From a mattress-lined "studio" in an unfinished building, I interviewed some of the movers and shakers on the national scene. I desperately believed in what I was doing, and I kept pushing and straining and rolling that stone uphill.

Then, in the early spring of 1994, I was approached by a company called Major Networks, which wanted to take over the production and distribution of *The Michael Reagan Talk Show.* Colleen and I talked about it. "You know something, Mike?" she said. "This is the first time in your career you've ever been given a choice about the direction of your life. Every other job you've taken up to this time has been a job you *had* to take." I thought about it and realized she was right. We made a deal over Labor Day, and I started broadcasting with Major Networks in November of '94. (I've since moved to another network, Premiere Radio.) One of my requirements in the negotiation was that we move the show to studios in L.A. At last! No more long commutes!

Suddenly, I was doing my show from a full-featured, high-tech studio in L.A. I was making decent money and being paid in actual U.S. dollars. I was getting the chance to do what I loved in a completely professional way. But like a lot of "overnight success" stories, it had taken a lot of years, a lot of work, and a lot of pain to get there.

MAKING UNDERCAPITALIZED DREAMS COME TRUE

I'll never forget something Marna McClure—the producer of my local show in San Diego—said to me when I left the studio for the last time after being fired. "Michael," she said, "I don't know what's going to happen to you, but if you can unlock all the locked safes inside you, all the different areas of your mind, no one will be able to touch you." I didn't understand what she meant at the time, but her words kept coming back to me over the years.

I think Marna was trying to tell me that I need to bring the person I am and the life I've lived into my show. I believe she was encouraging me to make *The Michael Reagan Talk Show* a show about *experiences,* about *reality,* not just issues and topics. Increasingly over the past few years, I've tried to unlock those safes, take out those experiences, and lay them out for my listeners.

I've discovered something: I don't have to read a book or watch a documentary to know what child abuse is all about, because I was molested by a day camp counselor when I was seven years old. I don't have to go to the library and research issues such as adoption, illegitimacy, divorce, or broken homes, because I was adopted, my parents were divorced, I've lived all those experiences. I don't have to read a paper about growing up in a famous family, and how that can be hard on a child's self-esteem, because I've been there. I don't have to read an article on attention deficit disorder, because I have a son who is ADD. I can talk about all of these *as experiences*—not just issues or topics.

One of the experiences I've unlocked on my show was what happened the day I mentioned to some kids at school that I was adopted. They started jeering and calling me a "bastard." I didn't know what the word meant, so I ran home and looked up the word in the big dictionary in my mother's library. For long afterward I lived in fear that my parents might find out that I was a bastard! If they knew, they might send me away like my birth mother had! For years, that word summed up my self-image: I thought, *My birth mother gave me up for adoption because there's something wrong with ME! My parents divorced because there's something wrong with ME! I was sexually abused because there's something wrong with ME! My mom sent me to boarding school because there's something wrong with ME!* I even believed God was mad at me because I was a "bastard," and it hurts to remember the feelings that clung to me for so many years.

People say that God has a purpose for every life. I don't know what God's purpose was for all the experiences in my life. I don't know why He allowed some of the things that happened to me. But for some reason,

Reagan vs. Reagan

When I started out in talk radio, the hardest thing for me to do was to publicly disagree with my dad. I grew up idolizing Ronald Reagan, and I spent a large chunk of my adult life campaigning for him. My first few months in this business, I talked a lot more about Ronald Reagan's opinions than I did about Michael Reagan's opinions. Then, a caller confronted me and said, "Mike, I already know what your dad thinks; I want to know what *you* think." Suddenly, I realized *I didn't know* what I thought! My father derived his beliefs from his experiences in life. I needed to derive my own beliefs from my own life experiences, not Ronald Reagan's.

Sure, I had disagreed with my dad on issues before. Take the so-called "Tax Reform Act" of 1986. I thought it was a disaster even before my dad signed it into law—but did I tell anybody I disagreed? No way! I didn't tell my dad, and—since I didn't have a radio show at the time—I certainly didn't share my misgivings with a national audience. And what did that tax bill do? For one thing, it did away with Investment Retirement Accounts—IRAs—so it in effect raised taxes on investments. And the changes it brought in the tax laws affecting real estate and lending institutions helped produce the S&L crisis of the late 1980s. I was right about that bill in 1986—but I didn't have the guts to voice my opinions, so what good did it do?

In 1991, an issue arose that brought me to a critical threshold in my talk radio career. That issue was the Brady gun control bill, named for James Brady, the White House press secretary who was wounded during the March 1981 assassination attempt on my father. The Brady bill was strongly opposed by Republicans and the NRA, and strongly promoted by Democrats and Jim and Sarah Brady's lobbying group, Handgun Control, Inc. In 1991, Ronald Reagan went public with his support of that bill.

You have to understand this about Ronald Reagan: He was deeply affected by the memory of speeding away in the presidential limousine while his longtime friend, Jim Brady, and two law enforcement officers lay writhing in their own blood on a Washington sidewalk. Brady was left partially paralyzed and wheelchair-ridden, and his speech and memory patterns have been permanently damaged. Dad has always felt responsible for Jim Brady's suffering, and it was largely out of that sense of guilt that he supported the bill.

But could I publicly oppose my father on the air? That was a tough barrier for me to cross. Ronald Reagan is a conservative icon. I didn't know if my audience would accept me disagreeing with a position taken by my dad. Yet I knew I had to cross that threshold if I was to maintain credibility with my audience. I couldn't just be a lockstep Republican. I had to be honest with myself and with my audience. So I voiced my opposition, and I was gratified and relieved that I could clearly, cogently explain *why* I disagreed with my famous father on a given issue. Best of all, my audience accepted my disagreement! I knew then that I was no longer just the son of the president. I was respected for my opinions, based on my own life experiences.

Then there was the case of Nancy and Ollie. Nancy Reagan has never been a great fan of Oliver North. In a 1988 interview, Barbara Walters asked Nancy if she agreed with her husbands assessment of Oliver North as "a hero." Nancy shook her head and stated flatly, "No!" And I understand why Nancy Reagan feels that way. She is convinced that Oliver North usurped the authority of the president, ran a rogue operation, and mired the Reagan White House in a demoralizing scandal—and she is convinced that Ollie lied when he said my father knew about the operation.

Then you come to 1994. Oliver North is running for the United States Senate against Charles Robb—a Democrat incumbent who has voted with Bill Clinton 95 percent of the time. Robb is also the candidate who has denied alleged extramarital affairs and drug use, then later admitted receiving nude back rubs from a beauty queen and being at parties where lines of coke were laid out (though he insists he never snorted). Robb also denied—then later admitted—knowing about an illegal tape of an opponent's cellular phone calls. Now, let's assume for a moment that Nancy Reagan is right, and that Ollie North is a liar. Clearly, an even stronger case can be made against Robb. So, if we assume that Ollie and Chuck are both liars, which liar should we support?

North entered the race as a decided underdog—yet by September 1994 he had cut Robb's commanding 13-point lead to zero—they are running neck and neck. In October, a month before election day, Ollie pulled slightly ahead of Robb in the polls. That's when Nancy Reagan let Ollie have it. Referring to Iran-Contra in an appearance with PBS interviewer Charlie Rose, Nancy said, "Ollie North has a great deal of trouble separating fact from fantasy. He lied *to* my husband and lied *about* my husband, and kept things from him that he should not have kept from him." Her statement was repeated all over the media—and the North campaign never recovered from it. On November 8, Robb defeated Ollie with 5 points to spare.

By inserting herself into the controversy, Nancy gave a backhanded endorsement to the liberal incumbent senator over the conservative wannabe senator. I found fault with her statement at the time because I knew it would lose a very important senate seat for us. Whether I agreed or disagreed with her assessment of Ollie North was irrelevant. What mattered was putting conservative Republicans in charge of the legislative branch of the government. Who would do a better job defending the Reagan legacy and conservative principles in the Congress? Oliver North——or a liberal tax-and-spend Democrat? Nancy Reagan would have better advanced the goals and principles of Ronald Reagan by saying nothing at all about Ollie North—and I said so on the air.

And then there's that massive new office complex on Pennsylvania Avenue. At 1.9 million square feet, sporting a $656 million price tag, it's the biggest, most expensive federal building in Washington, D.C. (the Pentagon is the only federal building that's bigger, and it's over in Arlington, Virginia). Because the rents in this albatross will be 25 percent higher than comparable private sector office space, it will never be fully occupied. If anything ever symbolized outrageous big-government wasteful spending, this monstrosity is *it*. Originally called the Federal Triangle Project, it is now going to be called—you guessed it!—the Ronald Reagan Building and International Trade Center.

I had already been attacking the Federal Triangle Project on my show for three or four years when the suggestion arose in the

Congress of naming it after my dad. What was I supposed to do? Support a boondoggle just because they put my dad's name on it? Pork is pork is pork, whether it's Democrat pork or Republican pork. Fact is, I denounced the project even *more* vehemently because I felt this wasteful white elephant was an insult to my dad's name!

Then I got a call from a friend who heads a major conservative think tank in Washington, D.C. This think tank had also actively opposed the project. "Mike," said my friend, "Fred Ryan called on me the other day"—Fred was then my father's chief of staff—"and he said Ronald and Nancy Reagan are both in favor of naming the building after him. They feel that conservatives groups are slowing things down by attacking the project, and they want us to stop."

"What?!" I said, flabbergasted.

Until that moment, I hadn't realized Dad and Nancy were in support of the project. But as I thought about it, it made sense. After all, Nancy would like to see Ronald Reagan's likeness added to Mount Rushmore! So would I, in fact—but it just ain't gonna happen. So Nancy figured having Ronald Reagan's name on a mountainous office building would be the next best thing.

Sorry, I can't go along with it. Here we have a bloated federal spending project, typifying all that Ronald Reagan ever hated about Washington, D.C.—and people want to name it after him! Make it a monument to him! Hey, even conservative legislators, even conservative talk show hosts, even Ronald Reagan's own family would have to love it, right? Well, not *this* Reagan! So once again, I had to take a public stand in opposition to something that Dad and Nancy favored. But that's okay with me, it's okay with Dad and Nancy, and fortunately, it's okay with my listeners.

I say if you really want to honor Ronald Reagan, you rip the building out of the ground and name the *hole* after him! After all, *that's* what Ronald Reagan really stood for: less government spending, less government waste, less government, *period*. If we have to name this monstrosity after someone, please–*puh-leeze!*—don't name it after Ronald Reagan! Instead, name it after someone who truly stands for wasteful spending and big government. Someone like Dan Rostenkowski. Or Dick Gephardt. Or Bill Clinton. Or better yet, why not carve *all* their faces on it—and call it Mount Wastemore!

Hey, I just call 'em as I see 'em.

this is where I'm supposed to be. He allowed a burden to be placed on my shoulders, a burden I didn't think I was strong enough to carry—but I'm finding out He thought I was. And maybe one of the reasons I went through what I did is so that—on the air, in my books, wherever I am—I can bring some insight and comfort to other people who are going through similar experiences.

That's why I wanted to open this book by telling you how *The Michael Reagan Talk Show* came into being. My show isn't something that was hatched in some corporate boardroom. It started as a severely under-capitalized dream, and it was hammered on the anvil of adversity, and tempered in the crucible of desperation. It's nothing less than a miracle that I'm on the air today—a miracle that owes as much to my wife's faith and the prayers of committed friends as it does to my own sweat and dogged determination.

The show is still changing and growing—as am I. Every weeknight, between 6 and 9 P.M. Pacific time, you're listening to Mike Reagan going to college, getting an education, finding out about himself. When I look back on all the painful corners of my life—including the painful struggle of building my radio show—I don't think, "Oh, woe is me!" I think, "What a life! What an adventure! Man, that hurt—but it was also exciting!"

So what are you trying to build with your life? What kind of adversity and desperation are you feeling right now? I just want you to know that—if my own experience is any indication—*you can make it.* Look for the excitement around the next corner. Got a roadblock in your way? Check the traffic reports and find an alternate route. Is your life spinning out of control? Keep a steady hand on the wheel, get turned in the right direction, and keep moving forward. Is life paying you in baseball caps? Wear your cap proudly, stay focused on your goals, and whatever you do—

Don't quit!

CHAPTER 2

If the Press Doesn't Want the Job, I'll Do It

IN 1994, I was invited to appear at the National Association of Editorial Writers Convention in Phoenix. During one panel discussion, the print journalists on the panel began raking talk radio hosts over the coals, complaining about how irresponsible we are, what rabble-rousers and bomb-throwers we are, and on and on. I listened patiently for a few minutes; then it was my turn.

"If we in talk radio are such rabble-rousers," I responded, "then what are you? I guess everyone in this room writes for the *National Enquirer,* right?"

"Hey! We're respected journalists!" they objected stiffly. "You can't lump us in with the supermarket tabloids!"

"And I'm a respected talk-show host," I said. "You can't lump me in with the shock jocks and rabble-rousers. We have irresponsible people in my business, and you have irresponsible people in yours. Don't condemn me because of what the shock jocks do, and I won't condemn you for what they print in the *Enquirer.*"

"Well," said one journalist, "you talk-show hosts are directly responsible for the loss of the healthcare plan this year. Don't you feel some guilt for misrepresenting the healthcare issue and causing millions of Americans to be medically worse off than if we had passed the bill?"

"Wait a minute," I said. "Can I just ask a question? How many of you have actually read the Clinton healthcare plan?" In a roomful of about two hundred people, one hand went up.

"Hold it," protested a person at the other end of the dais. "That wasn't a fair question. Here's a fairer question: How many here either read the healthcare plan themselves or appointed a staff member to read it on their behalf?"

About six hands went up. I said, "There you are. Out of all the people in this room, only half a dozen hands went up. Yet you tell me I'm not doing my job. You are the ones telling the public that the Clinton healthcare plan is wonderful! And hardly any of you actually read the plan!"

There was an uncomfortable silence in the room.

"Well, you know what?" I continued. *"I read the Clinton healthcare plan.* All 1,342 pages of it. In fact, I not only read it, I made it available to my listening audience. I sent it out *free* to anyone who requested it, so that they could read it too, and so that my listeners and I could discuss it intelligently on the show. Not even the president of the United States gave away copies—but I did! None of you in the press made the text of the healthcare plan available to the public—but I did!

"Because people could read it with their own eyes, they were able to see that the actual plan and the plan the president talked about were two different things. I ask you: Did I deprive millions of Americans of healthcare—or did I help save the country from a disastrous mistake?"

Another uncomfortable silence.

"So don't come down on me," I concluded. *"I was doing your job."*

The room erupted in an uproar! "Whoa!" they said. "How dare you!" But I had made my point, and the people in that room had no answer for it.

I do the job that Dan Rather, Peter Jennings, Tom Brokaw, the *Washington Post,* the *New York Times,* and all their brethren and sisteren in the dominant media are *supposed* to do but *fail* to do. I hear what they refuse to hear, read what they refuse to read, report what they refuse to report, and then I comment on it and offer my perspective.

YOU HEARD IT HERE FIRST!

Why are so many newspapers seeing their circulation shrinking of late? And why are the major networks declining in viewership and influence? Why has the radio talk-show business become so big in recent years? I'm convinced it's because a growing segment of the public feels ill-served by the dominant media. People know they are not getting all the information they need. They sense that what they *do* get is heavily filtered and distorted. Feeling let down by the print and broadcast press, millions have turned to talk radio as an alternative source of information.

One of our Ohio affiliates requires its local talk-show hosts to listen to my show before doing theirs. Why? Because they get so many calls from their listeners about the issues I bring out on my show! These local hosts are scratching their heads and saying, "Where does Mike Reagan get all of his stuff?"

The First Lady of the United States, Hillary Rodham Clinton, will tell you where she thinks I get my stuff. In an interview on Friday, March 24, 1995, she claimed that all of us in the talk radio industry—Rush and Mike and Liddy and Ollie—get what she called "marching orders" from some sinister fax machine deep in the bowels of Republican National Committee (RNC) headquarters. And you know what? I really do get faxes from Washington, D.C. I get 'em from the RNC, and I get 'em from the DNC—the Democratic National Committee. I get 'em from Richard Strauss, the White House media liaison for radio talk-show hosts. If anything, the Democrats outfax the Republicans two-to-one. Sure, I get propaganda from all sides—but do I march to the beat of anyone's drum? No way! Yes, I'm a Republican (I have to be; it's in my dad's will!) but that doesn't mean I never praise Democrats or rake Republicans.

Over the years I've had a lot of Democrats on my show—not just conservative Blue Dog Democrats like Billy Tauzin (now a Republican), but moderate and liberal Democrats. I've had Senator Paul Simon from Illinois on the show, because he and I were on the same side of the Balanced Budget Amendment. I've had Gary Condit from California on the show to discuss his support of the unfunded mandates bill. I've had Gloria Allred on the show, talking about the O.J. Simpson trial. When liberal Democrats do good things, I air it—and when Republicans do bad things, I hold their feet to the fire till they sizzle. I call 'em as I see 'em, and my listeners know it. People trust what I say on the air because I'm not in anybody's hip pocket.

People also trust what I say because I give accurate information. I do my homework. I read seven or eight newspapers a day. I piece together the various accounts of the day's events, and I read between the lines and connect the dots. You can bet that if you only read one news account of a given event, the image you get will be distorted, incomplete, and skewed. But if you read five or six different accounts of the same event, some of the pieces of the puzzle begin to fall into place. Next, I call up people I know in the State Department and the Congress. I also get thirty to forty "heads-up" faxes from acquaintances, friends, and listeners (along with those "marching orders" that Hillary is so worried about).

And that's what I do on *The Michael Reagan Talk Show*. I go to reliable sources and knowledgeable people. I drive down the side roads and back alleys of the stories that the dominant press only examines from the overpass. I get the information nobody else gets, and I put it out to people along with bill numbers, fax numbers, phone numbers, and addresses, so my listeners can get involved.

The ladies and gentlemen of the ruling news establishment could do the same job if they wanted to. They just don't want to. Why not?

I would suggest five simple reasons:

1. The press is cowardly.

There is a price to pay for bucking the liberal elite in this country. ABC News White House correspondent Brit Hume found out the hard way. At a White House press conference introducing Supreme Court nominee Ruth Bader Ginsburg, Hume asked what most reasonable people would consider a tough but fair question: Noting that the choice of Ginsburg, after the withdrawal of Judge Stephen Breyer over nanny-gate problems, suggested "a certain zig-zag quality in the decision-making process here," Hume asked, "I wonder, sir, if you could kind of walk us through it and perhaps disabuse us of any notion we might have along those lines. Thank you." It was a policy question—certainly not a personal attack on either Clinton or Judge Ginsburg, and it was courteously stated. But Bill Clinton didn't like the question.

"How you could ask a question like that after the statement [Judge Ginsburg] just made," the president responded icily, "is beyond me." Then he growled a surly "Thank you" and stamped off the podium. Ever since then, Brit Hume has been frozen out of the information loop at the White House. He found out that this president could be very vindictive and intolerant, First Amendment or no First Amendment.

The Washington Pravda

The *Washington Post*—the newspaper that beheaded the Nixon presidency and whose name was once synonymous with the term *investigative journalism*—has deteriorated into a cozy little propaganda arm of the Washington establishment. Yes, the *Post* and the equally tilted *New York Times* still set the national news agenda, and yes, all the news agencies in America still face east and kowtow to Ben Bradlee every day. But Jeff Cohen of Fairness and Accuracy In Reporting (FAIR)—a liberal watchdog group that is certainly no friend of conservatives and talk radio—called it right when he said that the *Washington Post's* "anti-establishment image is one of the most absurd myths in journalism today. It has been an instrument of state power for many years."[1] As an "instrument of state power," the paper no longer deserves to be called the *Post*. A more fitting name would be the *Washington Pravda*.

In early 1994, the *Post* had a chance to publish Mike Isikoff's exclusive, hard-hitting, well-corroborated story on Bill Clinton's sexual harassment of Paula Corbin Jones—yet the *Post's* national editor Fred Barbash arbitrarily killed the story, resulting in a shouting match between Barbash and Isikoff. After his story was spiked, Isikoff resigned in disgust. Paula Jones—who never wanted to take the president to court—was forced to file suit against Clinton (just under the statutory deadline) in order to get the press to sit up and take notice.

Later that year, the *Post* spiked another huge Clinton-related piece, the story of drug smuggling and arms running through the Mena airport in Arkansas in the 1980s. Written by Sally Denton and Roger Morris, massively corroborated, cleared by lawyers, and destined to give not only Clinton but also the Republicans and Ollie North a black eye, the story was killed at the last moment by managing editor Robert Kaiser.

It's a sad thing to see what the *Post* has become. The *Post* could have once again made journalism history by delving into the arcane and dirty doings of the Clinton administration—a White House so brazenly corrupt it makes all of Nixon's men look like a bunch of Boy Scouts. Instead, the newspaper that was lionized in *All the President's Men* chose the role of unindicted co-conspirator in the multiple scandals of the Clintonistas.

To underscore the point, President Clinton sent a chilling message to the press corps at his very next press conference by taking a question from a reporter from an in-flight magazine. All the reporters in the room wondered, *Where did this guy come from?* But they got the message: Brit Hume was replaced by some nobody from an airline magazine. The president was letting it be known: "This can happen to you. Ask me one tough question, and it'll be your last. You'll never be called on in a press conference. You'll never interview me on a morning news show. I will punish you." Ever since, the entire White House press corps walks on eggshells and operates from a base of cowardice because they don't want to be brit-humed by the president of the United States.

What is the result?

The much-vaunted "people's right to know" is abridged—not by the government but by the press itself. The Clinton administration has been rife with stories that the press would have covered like a cloud—*if* the subject of those stories had been Ronald Reagan, or George Bush, or Newt Gingrich. But instead of putting these stories on the front page where they belong, the self-censoring liberal media either buries these stories on page 27D—or ignores them altogether.

Prime example: the death of Vincent Foster. As you'll see in Chapter 6, there is a mountain of mysterious evidence surrounding the July 1993 death of this White House lawyer and close Clinton friend. If you only get your information from the dominant media, you have probably never heard that there are *three different official versions* of how Vince Foster died and where his body was found. For some reason, the national press doesn't think that's newsworthy.

On June 26, 1995, White House aide Deborah Gorham gave closed-door Senate testimony stating that she moved sensitive National Security Agency (NSA) documents from Vince Foster's office to a safe in the office of Foster's boss, Bernard Nussbaum. The press never bothered to ask: What was Vince Foster doing with National Security Agency files in his office? Why didn't investigators ask a single question about those files during Senate hearings? What's going on here? Considerations of state secrecy and national security never stopped the press during the Reagan-Bush years—but reporters are strangely lacking in professional curiosity these days.

You may wonder where I found out about these events. Well, I didn't read about them in the *Washington Post* or in the *New York Times* or in the *Los Angeles Times.* I didn't see it covered on CBS, ABC, NBC, or CNN. No, I had to pick up an overseas newspaper, the *London Sunday Telegraph,* to find out what's happening in my own country! And that's just plain wrong. The reason we have a First Amendment in this country is precisely so that we can learn about the events going on in our country from our own newspapers.

But it's not going to happen. The American press has been cowed into silent submission by the political establishment.

2. The press is ignorant.

Too many reporters simply refuse to do their homework. Sometimes, the results of their ignorance can be funny and relatively harmless. For example:

On June 8, 1995, baseball legend Mickey Mantle underwent transplant surgery to replace his cancerous liver. As the surgery was in progress, the hospital called a press conference and a hospital spokesman made a statement. The surgery was proceeding well, said the spokesman, and the liver donor had also donated seven other organs for transplants in other patients. At this point, one reporter asked, "Is the organ donor still alive?"

Okay, we're talking about the medical status of a sports hero, so a little ignorance in this case does no great harm. But what if the story being reported by the press has to do with the medical status of the entire country—if, for example, the press is reporting on the Clinton healthcare plan? Now the stakes are significantly higher. What if the press is reporting with equal ignorance about the economy and the federal budget? Or what if the press is spewing nonsense about our national defense? Imagine the potential damage to our national interests if our only source of information on a major war is a spigot full of journalistic hogwash!

Case in point: On January 27, 1991, NBC News aired a Gulf War special called "The Realities of War." The air war against Iraq had been going on for nine days, and the ground war was weeks away. There was considerable apprehension in the country and in the Congress about the conduct of this war. There was scare talk of thousands and thousands of soldiers returning in body bags before it was over. It was in this tense climate that NBC's "Scud Stud" reporter, Arthur Kent, sent back a satellite report from Saudi Arabia on the progress of the war. In a conversation with NBC anchor Faith Daniels, Kent said, "Saddam Hussein is a cunning man. Nowhere does he show that more clearly than on the battlefield, when he's under attack."

Faith Daniels replied, "And that, Arthur, really seems to be this administration's greatest miscalculation."

"That's right, Faith," said Kent, adding that Saddam was "ruthless. But more than ruthless. In the past eleven days, he's surprised us. He's shown us a capable military mind, and he still seems to know exactly what he's doing."

At a crucial moment in history, as our military is poised for a ground assault in a distant part of the world, we find the esteemed ladies and gentlemen of the press *not* reporting facts, but reporting opinion, mongering fear, and undermining morale. Kent and Daniels were just plain wrong. Compare their assessment of Saddam Hussein with the actual outcome of the war and General H. Norman Schwarzkopf's assessment of Saddam Hussein on February 27, 1991: Saddam, he said, "is neither a strategist, nor is he schooled in the operational art, nor is he a tactician, nor is he a general, nor is he a soldier. Other than that, he's a great military man."

The press was wrong about that war because it didn't do its homework on defense and military issues. Today, the press is just as ignorant of the real issues and the real facts in such crucial areas as economics, defense, education, healthcare, crime, and foreign policy. As citizens we deserve better information than we get from the media.

3. The press is biased.

Reporters and editors deny that bias has anything to do with their news judgment. They claim to be utterly objective. Yeah, right. The majority of decision makers in the press have their agenda—a liberal agenda—and this agenda shapes not only their editorial commentaries but their news reporting as well. I know this from personal experience.

My first book, *On the Outside Looking In,* was published in 1988, near the end of my father's second term as president. There had already been a couple of those "my-parents-were-so-horrible-and-that's-why-I'm-all-screwed-up" books written by children of famous parents, and the word was out that my book was another entry in that genre. To be sure, *On the Outside Looking In* was an honest book and not everything in it was flattering to my parents or to Nancy Reagan or, for that matter, to myself. But it was not a "get-even" book, and my father and the first lady were completely behind me. In fact, they issued a press release expressing their support for me and my book.

One of the people who got a copy of that press release was Dan Rather of CBS News. But Rather doesn't do stories that don't support his left-leaning agenda—and he's not one to let the facts get in the way of his point of view. So he ignored my dad's press release and, in March 1988, did a two- or three-minute hit piece on me and the Reagan family. In his story, I was pictured as the Billy Carter of the Reagan family. Rather had clearly never read a page of the book, though he had been furnished with advance copies. Instead, he went to someone who was supposedly a "Reagan family friend." This person was such a good friend of the family that he or she chose not to be identified. Rather asked, "What do you think of Michael Reagan's book?" This "friend" borrowed the line my father had used with devastating effect in the Reagan-Mondale debates, "There he goes again." And that's how they ended the piece.

Rather knew that the president and first lady had issued press releases saying they had read the book and were 100 percent supportive of it and of me. I know Dan Rather had a copy of that press release, but he didn't refer to it in the story. Instead, he dishonestly portrayed *On the Outside Looking In* as an embarrassing attack on my parents. Rather is part of a growing journalist cult that operates on the premise that point of view is more important than truth.

Those who promote the political and social agenda of the left know that the news media today has become the propaganda arm of the liberal establishment. "The media have been our best friends in this fight," said Susanne Millsaps, executive director of the Utah branch of National Abortion Rights Action League.[2] What fight was she talking about? The fight to keep abortion legal, of course. The people of the press, she went on to say, "claim objectivity, but I know they're all pro-choice."

For years, journalists have vehemently denied that there is any such thing as media bias. "No way, no how, no sir!" they chorus. "We're professionals, we're objective, we set all our personal feelings aside and only report the facts!" Uh-huh. Well, we conservatives remember how, for example, the Republican Contract with America was derided and belittled in the press—not just in the editorial pages but in the hard-news pages of the press. And on April 17, 1996, a Freedom Forum poll was released that confirmed with hard numbers what conservatives already knew to be true. While the Contract with America produced genuine legislation (some of it signed, some vetoed by President Clinton) in such areas as legislative reform, welfare reform, defense spending, tax cuts, and an honestly balanced budget, *only 3 percent* of journalists in the Freedom Forum poll considered the Contract to be a "serious reform proposal"; *fully 59 percent* viewed it as an "election-year ploy."

The Freedom Forum survey, which was conducted by the Roper polling organization, polled 139 journalists and produced numbers that—even for those of us who already believed in a major leftward media tilt—are nothing less than shocking. According to the survey, only 7 percent of journalists voted for George Bush in 1992, while fully 89 percent of journalists voted for Bill Clinton (in the general population, Clinton received 43 percent of the vote). A mere 2 percent of reporters in the poll labeled themselves as conservative, and only 4 percent are registered Republicans. By contrast, 91 percent label themselves liberal or moderate; 50 percent are registered Democrats and 37 percent are independents. It's important to note, by the way, that the Freedom Forum is a liberal First Amendment foundation, so you can't accuse the poll of being cooked up by conservatives.

Despite these amazingly lopsided findings, Elaine Povich, a former Capitol Hill reporter and author of the Freedom Forum report, denies that the poll confirms a liberal bias in the media![3] And that's part of the problem. People in the media can't see their own bias even when it stares them right in the face. Understand, the word "bias" doesn't necessarily mean that reporters *deliberately* skew the news (although, in some cases, I believe they do). "Bias" is simply the mindset, the worldview, the sum total of beliefs and prejudices through which they filter and reflect the day's events. The problem is not always so much that they *willingly* distort the other side of the issue, but that they can't imagine there even *is* another side of the issue.

We all have our biases. I have mine, you have yours, and the ladies and gentlemen of the press clearly have theirs. I freely admit my worldview. I put it on display for fifteen hours every week. I'm honest with myself and with you about where I'm coming from. But liberal journalists live in a state of denial, claiming to do what is humanly impossible: viewing the world through filtered, tinted distortion lenses and reporting what they see with total clarity and objectivity.

4. The press is lazy.

In August 1995, just as the House was convening hearings on the Waco disaster, the *Washington Post* published a front-page story, claiming it had obtained a letter written by House Speaker Newt Gingrich to the National Rifle Association (NRA). In the letter, Gingrich promised that no gun control legislation would pass as long as he was Speaker of the House. The *Post* story was written as if the newspaper had scored a major journalistic coup, uncovering a sinister secret document and establishing a previously unknown relationship between Republicans and the NRA. Within hours, the *Post*'s "discovery" of the Gingrich letter became the lead story on major TV and radio newscasts.

Immediately, Rep. Charles Schumer of New York—the White House's point man in the Waco hearings—was denouncing the Gingrich-NRA connection. And in various speeches and interviews throughout the day, President Clinton declared that the letter "reveals who's in control of Congress," meaning the NRA. But the real question raised by this story is: Who's in control of the *Washington Post*?

The fact is, the *Post* allowed itself to be used as a propaganda mouthpiece for either the Clinton White House or Chuck Schumer (or both). The *Post* knew this letter was not a "smoking gun," nor was its "discovery" the result of bold investigative journalism. In fact, the NRA had widely disseminated this letter in its national advertising! The NRA was trumpeting the letter, not hiding it! Not only had portions of the letter appeared in the May issue of the NRA's official journal, the *American Rifleman,* but the full text of the letter had been posted for all the world to see on the NRA's Internet bulletin board since January 28—one day after Gingrich wrote it and six months before the *Post* "broke the story"! Is this the closest the *Post* can come to a "gotcha" scoop these days?

Clearly, the *Washington Post* did not make a *news* decision to publish the letter. They made an *ideological* decision to go along with the White House-Chuck Schumer spin-doctoring on Waco. The blatant (though unspoken) message behind the *Post*'s nonstory story was, "See everybody? The NRA runs Newt Gingrich and the Republicans. The Waco hearings are nothing but an NRA-Republican plot to embarrass the administration." That's not news. That's front-page editorializing—grubby, lazy, dishonest journalism at its worst.

Another demonstration of the laziness of reporters is the fact that they are often so late to the party! A lot of people were surprised and pleased that Sam Donaldson—the noted investigative reporter, sheep-rancher, and farm-subsidy recipient—finally did a hard-hitting piece on the FBI's persecution of Randy Weaver and the execution of his wife and son at Ruby Ridge, Idaho. I wasn't pleased. After all, the Ruby Ridge debacle took place in August 1992, but Sam Donaldson took up the story in September 1995. By the time his piece aired on ABC's *PrimeTime Live,* I had been talking about Ruby Ridge for three years. *Three cotton-picking years!* Where were you, Sam? Face it: This is not exactly Pulitzer-class spadework.

5. The press is a panderer.

Sure, we all know the media panders to ratings and sensationalism, especially during the TV ratings sweeps. As the saying goes, "If it bleeds, it leads." Amid the endless, sensationalized parade of death, mayhem, and sleaze that passes for "news" on our TV screens and front pages, there is very little attempt to make sense of all that is going on in this great and wonderful land that we call the good old U.S. of A.

But when I say, "The press is a panderer," I'm not so much referring to the way the media panders to the prurient interests of its audience. That's shameful enough, but I'm even more concerned about the way the press panders to the liberal elite. There was a time when investigative reporters used to go undercover to get the truth. They don't go undercover anymore; they just get between the sheets. They cozy up and snuggle up and outbid each other for the privilege of flacking for the liberal powerbrokers. You tell me: How much courage and journalistic integrity does it take to rewrite press releases from the Clinton White House and the Democratic National Committee, then pass it off as news?

Case in point: In September 1995, I received a press release from the House Democratic Leadership Communications—an office run by Congressman Dick Gephardt of Missouri. The subject of the press release:

Medicare. As part of the general Democrat effort to portray Republicans as mean-spirited old Scrooges who only care about tax cuts for the rich, Gephardt claimed that planned Republican cuts in Medicare were totally unnecessary, according to the trustees of the Medicare Trust Fund. "A $270 billion cut in Medicare is not needed," said Gephardt, blithely ignoring the fact that Republicans had proposed a *reduction in the rate growth*—not a cut. (Under Gephardt & Co., the cost of Medicare had been doubling every seven years; under the Republican plan, it would double every ten years. Medicare costs still grow under the Republican plan, but at a slower rate.)

"Far from being a sudden crisis," Gephardt continued, "the situation in the Trust Fund has improved over the past few years. So what has caused some members of Congress to become concerned about the fund? Certainly not the facts in this year's Trustee's Report, that these members continually cite. The Report found that predictions about the solvency of the fund had improved by a year. The only thing that has really changed is the political needs of those who are hoping to use major Medicare cuts for other purposes." In other words, evil, greedy Republicans only want to take Medicare funds away from the sick, aged, and needy so they can give a tax cut to the rich.

Many broadcast and print news organizations across the country took the Gephardt press release and rewrote it as a hard news story, repeating the congressman's assertions as fact. Gephardt banked on the fact that the press doesn't check facts cited by liberals—and Gephardt was right. The press only checks facts cited by conservatives. But you know what? *I checked Dick Gephardt's facts*—and I found out that he left out the most important facts of all!

I went to the Trustee Report that Dick Gephardt cited in his press release, and I found the page and paragraph he was quoting from. It read: "The most critical issues, however, relate to the Medicare program. Both the hospital insurance trust fund and the supplemental medical insurance trust fund show alarming financial results. While the financial status of the hospital insurance program improved somewhat in 1994 *[that's the line Gephardt referred to—but he left out the rest of the sentence]* the hospital insurance trust fund continues to be severely out of financial balance, and is projected to be exhausted in about seven years."

What's this? The fund will be exhausted in seven years? This is exactly the passage Gephardt refers to when he claims there is "no sudden crisis" looming in the Medicare system—yet this passage actually says Medicare is headed for complete disaster if we don't act now to save it! The Republicans are on the right track—and Gephardt is lying about it! Yet the press printed Gephardt's assessment without even taking the simple step of going to the document and looking it up.

Shame on you, Congressman Gephardt! You thought no one would check the Trust Fund Report to see if you are telling the truth. But I check these things, Congressman. *Believe me, I check!*

Medicare is headed for certain collapse by the year 2002 unless Republicans are successful in their attempts to slow the runaway growth of this program. Dick Gephardt knows this is true, and he misleads the public about it. The dominant media would know it too if they would bother to check the facts instead of just rewriting press releases.

Where do you find the truth in America today? You find it in the alternative press, such as the *American Spectator, National Review, Investor's Business Daily,* Paul Rodriguez's *Insight* magazine, plus a few mainstream sources such as the *Washington Times* and the *Wall Street Journal.* You find it in the investigative reporting of Christopher Ruddy, David Brock, and a handful of other intrepid journalists. You find it on C-SPAN. And you find it on *The Michael Reagan Talk Show* and in my *reagan.com* website on the Internet. You won't find it, however, on CBS, ABC, NBC, or CNN or that liberal birdcage-liner that lands on your front porch every morning.

The founding fathers placed the First Amendment at the very beginning of the Bill of Rights because they understood that government can't be trusted; it needs to be independently monitored. The founding fathers never imagined the day would come when the press would abdicate its First Amendment rights and simply turn a blind eye to the excesses and sins of government. If the dominant media doesn't want the First Amendment anymore, if today's editors and reporters don't care about using their constitutional freedom of the press to dig for the truth, to find the real stories, and to inform people of what's truly going on in America, that's just fine with me.

I'll do their job for them.

CHAPTER 3

Whose Hate Talk?

WHAT THIS country needs is more hate talk. We need more hate talk on the radio, more hate talk in the Congress, more hate talk in our churches, more hate talk in our neighborhoods.

You think I'm kidding? I'm absolutely serious.

By way of explanation, let me take you back to April 19, 1995. You know what I'm talking about. That was the day a massive fertilizer bomb exploded outside the Alfred P. Murrah federal office building in Oklahoma City. Instantly, the entire face of the building was ripped away. The bodies of 164 people—including 19 children—were eventually pulled out of the rubble. Within days, two suspects, Timothy McVeigh and Terry Nichols, were charged with the crime.

But they weren't the only ones charged with this crime. I was blamed for this crime, too. So was Rush Limbaugh. So was Ollie North. So was G. Gordon Liddy. The tragic deaths of all those people were laid at the feet of conservative radio talk-show hosts. Who charged us with this crime? The president of the United States and his friends in the dominant media.

Now, the president's charges didn't come right away. In fact, during the first five or six days after the bombing, President Clinton made a real effort to remain presidential. He actually seemed to want to help America heal. He invited children to the White House and talked with them about their fears. He went out to Oklahoma City and took part in the memorial service for the victims. Most of us in talk radio got behind the president and supported his efforts to calm the nation's fears and heal the nation's divisions. I may be critical of Bill Clinton on a lot of issues, but during those days I expressed unqualified support for his efforts. Most important of all, the entire nation was coming together in this time of national sadness; we all felt it.

But you know, it's hard for Bill Clinton, the Perpetual Campaigner, to wear the mantle of presidential leadership for very long. The mantle keeps slipping off. He's so busy *running* for president, he forgets to *be* the president. There he was, having to act presidential for almost a whole week after the Oklahoma City tragedy; finally the strain just got to be too much for him.

So, in a speech to a group of educators in Minneapolis—just *one day* after the memorial service for the victims!—the real Bill Clinton came forth. He went on the attack. Complaining about all "the loud and angry voices" on the nation's airwaves, President Clinton said that radio "is too often used to keep some people as paranoid as possible and the rest of us all torn up and upset with each other. They spread hate, they leave the impression by their very words that violence is acceptable. . . . I never want to look into the face of another set of family members like I saw yesterday."[1]

DOES THIS SHOW SPEW HATRED?

Who were the "they" Clinton referred to? Who were these "loud and angry voices" that, according to Clinton, *really* caused the bombing in OKC? He didn't say! In a very calculated and carefully crafted way, Clinton used vague language and code words to fix blame on some unnamed "they" who were stirring up hate and violence in America. And at that precise moment, the healing of the nation stopped, and the division of the nation recommenced. Suddenly, we were no longer one grieving nation; it was "us" versus "them," those who spread hate and violence by their words. By carefully avoiding names, Clinton left it to the media to speculate on exactly who he was talking about. And right away, of course, the media started naming—you guessed it!—*talk-show hosts.*

The very next morning, I was awakened before six by a call from a friend on the East Coast. It seemed Bryant Gumbel was bandying my name around on NBC's *Today* show, accusing me and other conservative talk-show hosts of causing the deaths in OKC. Because the show came on three hours later on the West Coast, I was able to get up and watch it. Here's how Gumbel intro'd the segment on "hate radio":

> The bombing in Oklahoma City has focused renewed attention on the rhetoric that's been coming from the right and from those who cater to angry white men. While no one is suggesting right-wing radio jocks approve of violence, the extent to which their approach fosters violence has been questioned by many observers, including the president. Right-wing talk-show hosts Rush Limbaugh, Bob Grant, Oliver North, G. Gordon Liddy, Michael Reagan, and others take to the air every day with basically the same format: detail a problem, blame the government or a group, and invite invective from like-minded people. Never do most of the radio hosts encourage outright violence, but the extent to which their attitudes may embolden and encourage some extremists has clearly become an issue.

I was amused that Gumbel tossed Ollie North in there with the rest of the spewers of "hate talk," since North had only been on the air a couple of weeks by that time. The rest of us "right-wing radio jocks" had been busily creating a climate of hate and violence for years; Ollie was a new kid in the "hate talk" business.

After watching the segment, I picked up the phone and called Gumbel's office at NBC in New York. "This is Michael Reagan," I told Gumbel's assistant. "Mr. Gumbel just named me on the air as a purveyor of violence and hatred. I would like to invite him to come on my radio show so that we can discuss his views. I'd like to know what he thinks I do on my show that encourages hate. I'd like to know where he gets his information and if he has ever actually listened to my show. This won't be an ambush; it'll be a conversation. I'll make plenty of time available so we can have a real discussion."

Gumbel refused my invitation. He wouldn't come on the air and defend his statements because he didn't have the truth on his side. He'll only talk when he's all safe and protected in Studio 1A.

Later in the day, I issued a news release demanding that the president clarify his remarks of the previous day, and I sent a copy of that news release directly to the White House. In that release, I said the president should either name me as one of the "loud and angry voices" or say clearly, "I wasn't talking about Mike Reagan." After all, it was clear from what Bryant Gumbel had said on the *Today* show that the president's words had inspired a growing climate of hate directed at me and others in my profession—and I feared it was just a matter of time before a Ryder truck, reeking of fertilizer and diesel fuel, pulled up in my driveway!

The White House never issued the clarification I demanded but did send White House deputy chief of staff Mark Gearan to my show (via telephone from Washington) to defend Clinton's remarks. My first question to Gearan was, "What have I ever said on my show that would cause the president or people in the press to believe that I'm one of those who inspires people to run out and take over the government?"

Gearan deflected the question, saying that the president was really just talking about "the general civil discourse in society today. . . . We need to move beyond some of the reckless speech and hateful speech that exists too much, in his view, around society."

I pointed out that, in the past, when President Clinton had spoken out against the media—as when he laid into Rush Limbaugh during a call to a St. Louis radio station from Air Force One—he always singled out talk radio. Given Clinton's record of attacking talk radio, wasn't he making a veiled but calculated attack on my industry? Certainly, the president fully expected media pundits to affix the names of specific talk-show hosts to the president's unnamed "they."

"Mike," Gearan responded, "I can't explain why the news analysis [targeted talk radio] and why your name was bandied around . . . but I think what we need now, rather than trying to further divide the country, is a reasonable discussion about those that are in a position, whether in office or in radio or television, or have an opportunity to converse with the American public. [They] need to be mindful that words have consequences. And that's what the president was saying, that people need to be mindful of that. We are all for the First Amendment, freedom of speech, but with that freedom comes a responsibility, and what the president urged . . . is for people, when they see instances of what they view as reckless speech and hateful speech, that they should speak out against it. And I think most Americans agree with that."

I pressed Mark on the question that really bothered me: Certainly, the president, in making his blanket accusation, had to have somebody *specific* in mind. Who exactly were these unnamed "loud and angry voices"?

"Well," said Gearan, "in the specific instance when the president spoke, he had seen the *60 Minutes* report—Leslie Stahl's report—where the militias used short-wave radio—"

What?! Whoa! Hold it! Time out! Was Gearan serious? Did he *really* expect us all to believe that when Bill Clinton denounced "things that are regularly said over the airwaves today," he was talking about extremist nuts, broadcasting from their basements on Radio Shack short-wave transmitters? Does America *regularly* listen to these beyond-the-fringe amateur broadcasters? Are we supposed to believe that Clinton would, with his vague language, tar the entire talk-show industry when his *real* target was a bunch of kooks with audiences that numbered in the *dozens*? It was as if Bill Clinton had gone duck hunting with an atom bomb: Sure, he may have knocked off a few ducks, but the ducks weren't the only ones who felt the heat!

As the clock wound down to the commercial break, I put a final question to Gearan. "Mark," I said, "you've listened to *The Michael Reagan Talk Show*. You know me. You hear me back there in Washington. Does this show spew hatred?"

"Michael, I have to tell you," he began. "This is—uhhhh—I—I don't think it's appropriate for the administration to get into naming names. And anyway, that was not the president's point. He was speaking beyond that. Certainly, from my point of view, from the limited times I've been on your show, you allow people the opportunity for other points of view to be expressed. That's what's important. And as long as talk radio and all other forms of the media allow for the open exchange of ideas, that checks the facts, that does it in a responsible way, that's what we're seeking to do."

"Mark," I concluded as the bumper music came up, signaling the break, "thank you very much."

THE BLAME BUSINESS

Of course, the media attacks against talk radio didn't diminish after that. For the next couple of weeks, they intensified. The president had dropped a cudgel, and the dominant media eagerly picked it up and began using it to bludgeon their hated opponents in talk radio. After all, for the past few years, talk radio had been eating into the media's ratings and readership; talk-show hosts made print and broadcast reporters look bad by reporting the stories they had ignored; talk radio had broken the information stranglehold of the liberal media. Talk radio can devote hours of detailed, thoughtful attention to issues and events that the dominant media only skims over with headlines and sound-bites.

Suddenly, the president had legitimized any and all attacks on talk radio, no matter how ridiculous—because, after all, the president himself had just implied that talk radio had caused all those tragic deaths in Oklahoma! Instantly, no stretch, no leap, no overblown fantasy was considered too absurd by the press. Columnist Carl Rowan appeared on CNN's *Inside Washington,* charging that conservative opposition to affirmative action was somehow linked to the Oklahoma bombing. "I'm absolutely certain," he said, "that the harsh rhetoric of the Gingriches and Doles creates a climate of violence in America. We're talking about Americans who have been told that affirmative action means that blacks have stolen everything from white guys."

Other liberal scribes were quick to add their two cents' worth. Molly Ivins put it bluntly in her newspaper column: "Do I think the climate of hate speech, hate radio and hate politics contributed to the torn, tiny bodies in Oklahoma City? I know they did."[2]

William Raspberry stated his belief that not only hate speech but what he frankly called *innocent* speech ought to be chilled! "Talk-show hosts . . . need to understand that their words, no matter how innocent or rhetorical or satirical they may in fact be, have the power to push certain people over the edge, into violence."[3] If talk-show hosts aren't even allowed "innocent" words, much less rhetoric or satire, what's left? Apparently, Mr. Raspberry just wants all of us in talk radio to shut up and go away.

Like so many in the media, Anthony Lewis wrung his hands over the "climate" that talk radio created, observing, "The Oklahoma City bombing has made us think again about hateful speech and how to deal with it. . . . Major leaders of opinion . . . bristled at the suggestion that their rhetoric had something to do with Oklahoma City, and of course it did not in any direct sense. But what about the climate that their words helped to create?"[4]

The Uncle We Hate and Fear

A survey conducted in mid-March 1995 found that *only 15 percent* of Americans have "a great deal of faith" in the federal government. That is a full thirty percentage points *below* the 45 percent level of confidence reported in a 1975 Gallup poll—immediately following Watergate and the resignation of Richard Nixon! Why are Americans so disillusioned with their government these days? Pollsters Peter Hart and Robert Teeter, who conducted the telephone survey of 1,003 people for the Council on Excellence in Government, say that the people they talked to expressed frustration and anxiety over the high degree of government intrusion into every corner of their lives. During the past two decades, the public outlook has changed from optimism to extreme cynicism and even fear.

During the week following the Oklahoma City bombing, President Clinton made a series of statements, including, "We must stand up against those who say, 'I love my country, but I hate my government.' . . . Who do these people think they are?" Who, indeed? Is it possible to hate your government while loving your country? Aren't your country and your government one and the same?

Well, first we have to define our terms. What exactly do we mean by the word *government*? Depending on the context, that word can mean many things:

• The word *government* can refer to the founding principles that define America—our Declaration of Independence and our Constitution. Certainly, these are a part of our government, and they are worthy of our respect and our careful stewardship. Of course, anyone who wants to is free to criticize even these documents. It's a free country, and those documents are the reason we are free.

• The word *government* is sometimes used to refer to "we, the people." As Lincoln said, the government of the United States of America was designed to be a government "of the people, by the people, and for the people." That's a wonderful ideal, but let's face it: There is an entity that exercises power over our lives, that can be intimidating by its very size and power, and to which we pay our taxes; that entity is called "the government," and it often acts apart from our will and our best interests. That entity is supposed to serve the people and be accountable to the people, but it is not "we, the people." When that governmental entity gets out of control, then it is up to us, the rightful government, the vast collection of individuals called "we, the people," to reassert our rightful authority and rein in the oppressive governmental entity.

• The word *government* can also refer to our political and legal institutions—the president, the Congress, and the Supreme Court. The people who occupy positions of power in these institutions may not like being criticized, but they often richly deserve it—and the people have not only a right but a duty to speak out when their representatives in the institutions of government fail to govern well. Anyone (including the president) who tries to chill dissent against these three branches of our government is behaving in an un-American way.

• The word *government* can also refer to the bureaucracy— the bureaus, agencies, programs, and offices that are often staffed by people who have little motivation or inclination to be helpful, efficient, or even courteous to taxpayers. Many bureaucrats, of course, are fine, dedicated, hardworking people—but the bureaucracy as a whole seems fiendishly designed to reward laziness and incompetence while punishing ingenuity and diligence. Obviously, not even the worst bureaucrats deserve to be wiped out by a fertilizer bomb—but the word "bureaucrat" is not (as Bill Clinton once declared) a "hate" term, nor should bureaucrats and bureaucracies be considered above criticism.

Every few years, when the president and the Congress can't agree on a budget, we experience what's called a "government shutdown." What does that mean? Certainly, the founding documents and the laws of the government don't shut down. And what about the executive and legislative branches of government? Do they shut down? No. If anything, they become busier and louder than ever! So what actually shuts down in a "government shutdown"? The bureaucracy! Do we pledge allegiance to the bureaucracy? Do we send soldiers into battle to defend the bureaucracy? Do presidents put their hand on the Bible and swear to protect and defend the bureaucracy? No way! So when we talk about "the government," we need to be clear on what we mean.

Once we have made it clear exactly what "government" we are talking about, it becomes obvious that, yes, it is possible to love your country (the principles that define America and make her great—the Constitution, the flag, the people comprising this "nation under God") while fearing, distrusting, and criticizing your government (pandering politicians; tax-and-spend liberals; door-busting, tank-driving feds who shoot first and ask questions later; heavy-handed bureaucrats who use federal power to crush dissent; the IRS, the BLM, the BATF). There are reasons that people who once loved and trusted Uncle Sam now fear and even hate him. Instead of continually making Uncle Sam more threatening and intimidating where average citizens are concerned, we would do well to find ways of making ol' Uncle Sam a little more cuddly!

"In a nation that has entertained and appalled itself for years with hot talk on the radio and the campaign trail, the inflamed rhetoric of the '90s is suddenly an unindicted co-conspirator in the blast," wrote Richard Lacayo.[5]

Those who fret about the possibility that talk-show hosts might create a "climate" of hate and violence should ask themselves how responsible it was for ABC, NBC, CBS, and CNN to run and rerun—relentlessly, daily—edited footage of the police beating of Rodney King during the 1992 trial of the L.A. cops. They should ask themselves if the blood of the fifty-eight people who died and the 2,400 who were injured in the subsequent rioting isn't on the hands of the major news organizations. But the press will never submit itself to that kind of self-examination. They're in the blame business, not the responsibility business.

INCITE—OR INFORM?

People tend to have very short memories, and they think that events like Oklahoma City are totally unprecedented in our times. Unfortunately, America's history is checkered with stories of people who have taken it upon themselves to use violence in order to achieve change or make a statement. In fact, one of the earliest recorded cases in which terrorists used a truck bomb to attack a building occurred in New York City in 1920. They didn't have Ryder trucks in those days, so the terrorists used a horse-drawn wagon. They piled lead weights around the bomb, then parked the wagon next to the J. P. Morgan bank building. At around noon, the bomb exploded, sending hot lead shrapnel into the crowd, killing thirty people and injuring more than a hundred. The perpetrators were never found, but, like Bill Clinton, J. P. Morgan was quick to name scapegoats for the crime: He blamed Jews and Catholics.

Now, I ask you the same question I asked Mark Gearan: What have I done on my show to light the fuse in Oklahoma? Is it "hate" to say that the government is too intrusive, that the bureaucracy is too big, that taxes are too high and federal spending too extravagant? That's not hate. That's fact. Is it "hate" to document instances where Bill Clinton has been untruthful with the American people, where liberal legislation has targeted individual freedom, and where government agencies such as the Bureau of Alcohol, Tobacco, and Firearms (BATF), the FBI, the Environmental Protection Agency (EPA), and the IRS are out of control and destroying the lives of innocent people? That's not hate. That's fact.

If you were to come into my studio and watch me do my show, you wouldn't see a guy ranting and raving and foaming at the mouth. I don't do attack. I don't do shock. I don't do character assassination. *I do information.* I have newspaper clippings, magazines, faxes, and all sorts of information stacked up around me and ready to dispense during my nightly three-hour chat with America. Admittedly, a lot of that information is not welcomed by the left. Sometimes, hearing the truth sounds like an attack. It may even sound like "hate speech," but it's not.

And what is "hate speech," anyway? Is "hate speech" something that only comes from the right? Are liberals incapable of hate?

It seems to me that some of the *worst* hate speech in this country has been advanced by people such as Bill Clinton, Dick Gephardt, and Tom Daschle. I think it is hate speech to accuse Republicans of being racists and Nazis for wanting to end affirmative action. I think it is hate speech to accuse Republicans of wanting to see children and old people die, simply because the Republicans are trying to balance the budget, save Medicare, and slow the growth of spending programs. It is the worst kind of hate speech to depersonalize your opponents and caricature them as monsters and demons instead of engaging them in an honest dialogue about the issues.

In the same column I cited previously, Molly Ivins refers to militia members as "belly-creeping dimwits," a "racist, hate-mongering bunch of cockroaches," and "scum." She lumps all conservatives together as a "poisonous stew of gun nuts, racist right-wingers, and religious zealots" who, when "heated by paranoia and lies" on talk radio, "finally exploded" in Oklahoma City.

I ask you, are those hateful words or what? In other columns, she has referred to Congressman Bob Dornan as "a well-known crackpot," to Pat Buchanan as "a nativist boob," and to Newt Gingrich as "the draft-dodging, dope-smoking, wife-divorcing, deadbeat-dad" (she later admitted most of those descriptors were false but claimed she was just "trying to meet the standards of accuracy" set by talk radio; the divorce part, at least, is true). I don't know about you, but I really can't hear the love in Molly's voice when she says stuff like that.

I'm still trying to figure out why conservative talk-show hosts who discuss issues and help people understand and affect their government are full of "hate," while liberal ad hominem attacks should be deemed the absolute quintessence of civil, reasoned discourse. I'm not saying liberals shouldn't go right ahead and spew their guts out. Unlike liberals, I still think this is a free country. But face it: Liberals who attack conservatives with such obvious venom, then turn around and moan and gripe about "hate speech, hate radio, and hate politics" are just exposing themselves for the blatant hypocrites they are.

During this liberal pile-on, there weren't many Republicans leaping to the defense of radio talk shows. But there was one, Congressman Larry Craig of Idaho, who made a very strong statement—one of the most reasoned and sensible statements of that tragic hour, the kind of statesmanlike communication one wishes the president engaged in. Here's an excerpt from Congressman Craig's April 1995 press release:

> Make no mistake, those who executed this bombing are outlaws of the worst kind—misguided and sick people hiding behind some cause so they can inflict human suffering on people they don't even know. But "they" in this case doesn't include everyone in America who opposes govern-

ment excess. It doesn't include people who choose to exercise their constitutional right to assemble, right to free speech, right to keep and bear arms, to practice responsible civil disobedience, or to disagree with the federal government. Neither the ultra-right nor the ultra-left, neither conservative radio programs nor liberal media are guilty of this crime. The criminals who did it are responsible.

Those who would use this act of barbarism to lay blame on their political or ideological enemies do every citizen of this nation a great disservice. They are attempting to place the blame somewhere other than on the shoulders of the criminals themselves—not because of their grief, but because of callous political self-interest. It also shows they have a shallow understanding of what makes our country great.

In this nation, the rights of the individual come first. The guilty must be found, tried, and punished. The rights of the innocent must be preserved. In this nation, ideas and beliefs are not crimes. God forbid that they ever will be.

Amen! The message that needs to get through to all these whining, thin-skinned liberals is simple: "Grow up, already! We're all adults here, and you'd better learn to take the rough-and-tumble of debating ideas like adults—not like sniveling little kids." If some fool takes it upon himself to blow up a building, you catch him and you slap him down hard. But you don't slap the people who are engaged in a dialogue to try to save this country from creeping socialism. Violence and speech are separate issues.

As Supreme Court Justice William J. Brennan Jr. observed in the case of *The New York Times v. Sullivan* in the 1960s, the reason we have a First Amendment is so that we can enjoy "uninhibited, robust, and wide open" speech. President Clinton should be inviting that debate, not trying to close it down.

NO LIDDYISMS ON MY SHOW

Understand, I'm not saying that everyone in talk radio is a model of good judgment, reason, and respectability. There are some very strange, extreme, and even irresponsible things being said on talk radio. And most of them are being said by G. Gordon Liddy. But that's Liddy; that's his persona. I use my microphone to inform and motivate; Liddy uses his microphone as a cattle prod—*buzz-buzz, shock-shock!* And that's not a criticism of Liddy, just an observation. I have always defended Liddy's right to shoot off his mouth; I even defended Liddy in a debate with Tom Leykus on *CBS This Morning,* and I was one of many talk-show hosts who voted that Liddy be given the Freedom of Speech award by the National Association of Radio Talk Show Hosts—as an endorsement not of his words but of his right to say them.

Everyone in this business has a shtick, and Liddy's shtick is to keep his audience off-balance with the things he says. Liddy's the Watergate burglar who held his hand in a candle flame until the skin crackled just to convince recruits for his undercover operation that he could take the pain. He's the guy who, when Nixon aide Jeb Magruder offhandedly remarked that it would "be nice if we could get rid" of columnist Jack Anderson, took it as an order for an assassination. (Magruder had to tell Liddy that it was a casual remark, not a command.) Most recently, Liddy's the guy who, as a nationally syndicated talk-show host, described the most effective way to shoot a federal agent who is invading your home without a warrant or warning. If you listen to Liddy, you have to expect the unexpected.

But you won't hear any liddyisms on my show. You'll never hear me encourage anyone to shoot federal agents under any circumstances whatsoever. I'll tell you why: A very close member of my family worked for the federal government at one time. In fact, he held the top job in the government. On March 30, 1981—less than three months into his first term—Ronald Reagan was shot on a street in Washington, D.C. So before people say, "Mike Reagan spews hatred against the federal government," or "Mike Reagan shares responsibility for the Oklahoma City bombing," they should remember where I come from. I've seen a member of the federal government, a member of my family, lying wounded in a hospital bed because of some fool with a gun.

Now consider this: Prior to the time Ronald Reagan was shot, there was a lot of anti-Reagan hate speech going on. There was anti-Reagan hate spewing from the print media, the electronic media, the Democratic party, and the Hollywood left. Did I blame any of those groups for the bullet in my father's chest? Did I accuse these "loud and angry voices" on the nation's airwaves of "creating a climate of hate" against the president and leaving the impression that violence is acceptable? Did I blame Jodie Foster, because the sick little would-be assassin was trying to impress her by offing the president? No. I blamed the guy who pulled the trigger. It was *his* idea and it was *his* action.

Of course, that was a different time. These days, if someone commits a crime, we have to find a scapegoat to blame (preferably a *right-wing* scapegoat). We have to find out who "inspired" that crime, who created a "climate of hate."

DEMONIZING THE RIGHT

Bill Clinton and Molly Ivins and all the people like them on the left know better. They know talk radio isn't about "hate." They want to demonize people like me because we spotlight the liberal agenda. If I put out false information on my show, there are plenty of listeners who can instantly pick up the phone or crank up the fax machine and set me straight. That's something you don't have with the dominant media, either print or electronic.

The next time Dan Rather or Peter Jennings puts out a lie or a distortion, just try picking up the phone and see if you get through. And when the newspaper gets a story wrong, what's your redress? If you're lucky, a correction may appear in a half-inch box on page J-19. Or you can write a letter, which may or may not be printed in edited form three weeks later when it no longer matters. But in talk radio, the quality of the information you get is very good because errors are usually detected and corrected in a matter of minutes.

Now, try as hard as he might to deny it, we all know what President Clinton was up to in his Minneapolis speech: He was demonizing talk radio. And so were his friends in the dominant media and the Congress. Ever since he was elected, Bill Clinton & Co. have been looking for ways to neutralize dissent. They tried to revive the old Fairness Doctrine, which would have enabled the government to tell radio stations what kind of content to carry. The Fairness Doctrine was beaten back—and rightly so, since the First Amendment doesn't guarantee "fair speech," it guarantees *free* speech!

Next, they tried to sneak an anti-lobbying bill through Congress with a number of hidden provisions that would have profoundly affected talk radio. For example, it would have classified *The Michael Reagan Talk*

Show as a "lobbyist" because I give out fax numbers and bill numbers and tell people how to affect their government—and that would have put me and a lot of other talk shows out of business. Fortunately, that bill also died a much-deserved death.

The liberals in the government and the liberals in the media each have their own reasons for demonizing talk radio. The media's reasons are simple: They're afraid of competition. Since the rise of talk radio, thousands of people have been tuning out TV news and canceling their subscriptions to newspapers and newsmagazines—and that means less prestige, less power, less influence, and less ad revenue for the liberal press.

And make no mistake: Bill Clinton had reasons for demonizing talk radio that had absolutely nothing to do with feeling the pain of the grieving Oklahoma City survivors. In politics, there is *always* a reason for everything that happens. Always. Nothing happens by accident. Politics is a mind-game, an artform, and, above all, a profit-making business. When President Clinton took to the stage in Minneapolis while bodies were still being pulled from the rubble in Oklahoma, he did so for very basic political reasons: to bring dollars and power back to the Democratic Party.

The Democrats have been scared to death of talk radio ever since November 8, 1994, when both houses of Congress fell into Republican hands. The liberals saw not only their power slipping away but their money as well! Before the election (according to Federal Election Commission statistics), corporate political action committees (PACs) divided their ten million dollars in annual contributions equally between the two major political parties. But after the Republican landslide, corporate PACs shifted their loyalties dramatically: From November 9 to December 31, Republicans received *an astounding 89 percent* of corporate PAC donations!

Money is the mother's milk of politics, and when the Democrats saw all that beautiful money sloshing to the other side of the aisle, they went into hysterics. They knew that talk radio had been a major player in the election—but how could they neutralize talk radio without running afoul of that pesky old First Amendment? Answer: Start slinging blame. If you're successful, you can bottle up the opposition and become a powerful fat-cat liberal once more!

A Deaf Ear to the Left

President Clinton says we should all speak out against reckless speech wherever we find it. Strangely, however, there's a whole lot of hate talk and violent speech that President Clinton doesn't seem to hear. Maybe there's something wrong with the hearing in his left ear; perhaps that's why he can only hear "hate talk" if it comes from the right. I mean, there has to be something wrong with his hearing or he'd be able to hear the hate talk from his own vice president, Al Gore. It was Gore, you recall, who once referred to "the extra-chromosome Right Wing"—a horribly insensitive remark, given the fact that an extra chromosome is the cause of Down's syndrome and other forms of mental retardation. Gore once referred to Ollie North as "a liar, a hypocrite, and a disgrace to the Marine Corps," and he regularly hammers Republicans—those who represent the mainstream in America—as "extremists."

There's nothing wrong with *my* hearing in *either* ear. I've had right-wing callers who have said hateful things about President Clinton—saying, for example, that something terrible should happen to him. In a heartbeat, I pull the plug and those hate-callers are gone from my airwaves. I don't tolerate it for an instant. But unlike President Clinton, I can also hear hate speech from the left. Some examples:

• "This is the essence of angry white men, taken to some fanatic extreme, and I will grant you that. But it's the same kind of idea that has fueled so much of the right-wing triumph over the agenda here in Washington." (*Washington Post* reporter Juan Williams on CNN's *Capitol Gang,* February 23, 1995, linking the Oklahoma bombing to the Republican-led Congress.)

• Newt Gingrich is a favorite target of haters on the left. A typical comment: "Let's face it: to most African Americans, Newt Gingrich is one scary white man," wrote *Time* correspondent Jack E. White in the January 19, 1995 issue. And Bryant Gumbel handed this opening to Dick Gephardt in a *Today* show interview on January 4, 1995: "You called Gingrich and his ilk, your words, 'trickle-down terrorists who base their agenda on division, exclusion, and fear.' Do you think middle-class Americans are in need of protection from that group?"

• "A lot of people are afraid of you. They think you're a bomb-thrower. Worse, you're an intolerant bigot." Character-assassin Sam Donaldson to Newt Gingrich on ABC's *This Week with David Brinkley,* November 1994. And on July 5, 1995, Paula Zahn fired this torpedo at Pat Buchanan during an interview on *CBS This Morning*: "You've got political enemies out there calling you an isolationist, a bigot, you're anti-gay, and some even go as far as saying that your social stands are reminiscent of Nazi Germany. How are you to win them over?"

• And where in the world does Jesse Jackson get his information? In a meeting with *Chicago Sun-Times* editors in December 1994, he said, "The Christian Coalition was a strong force in [Nazi] Germany. It laid down the suitable, scientific, theological rationale for the tragedy in Germany. The Christian Coalition was very much in evidence there." That was a neat trick, seeing as "the tragedy in Germany" took place in the 1930s and 1940s, and the Christian Coalition wasn't founded until 1988. And Jackson didn't stop there. Later that same month, he appeared on British television and said, "In South Africa, the status quo was called racism. We rebelled against it. In Germany it was called fascism. Now in Britain and the U.S., it is called conservatism."

• Oh, yes. As every good liberal knows, all Republicans are evil racists—which is why it's okay to hate Republicans. As *Chicago Tribune* columnist Clarence Page so thoughtfully and factually observed on the *McLaughlin Group,* October 15, 1995, "Most of the KKK has joined the Republican Party." Former NBC reporter Bob Herbert railed against the "insidious and blatantly racist strategy" of the evil, enemy Republicans in his *New York Times* column, September 22, 1995: "For urban dwellers, and especially the poor, the Republican party as currently constituted is the enemy—the source of endless destructive, mean-spirited and racist initiatives."

• A commentator on National Public Radio's *All Things Considered* openly wished for the death of Supreme Court Justice Clarence Thomas. "I hope his wife feeds him lots of eggs and butter, and he dies early, like many black men do, of heart disease.

Well, that's how I feel. He's an absolutely reprehensible person!" The words of Julianne Malveaux on April 28, 1994. This is the same woman who, in a *USA Today* column, once supported 1992's Los Angeles riots, which killed 58 people, saying, "Pat Buchanan calls those who hit the streets 'looters and lynchers.' President Bush calls them 'criminals.' I call them 'freedom fighters.' . . . I not only accept the rebellion in Los Angeles, I identify with them."

• And one of Malveaux's NPR colleagues, Nina Totenberg, offered these loving thoughts regarding Senator Jesse Helms on CNN's *Inside Washington,* July 8, 1995: "I think he ought to be worried about what's going on in the Good Lord's mind, because if there is retributive justice, he'll get AIDS from a transfusion, or one of his grandchildren will get it." Thank you for sharing that with us, Nina.

• On March 21, 1995, Congressman John Lewis (D-Georgia) said of Republicans (paraphrasing Reinhold Niebuhr's famous quotation about the Nazis), "They're coming for our children, they're coming for the poor, they're coming for the sick, the elderly, and the disabled." Congressman Sam Gibbons (D-Florida) has also likened Republicans to Nazis.

• Representative Pete Stark (D-California) once called a black cabinet official in the Bush administration "a disgrace to your race," and called a Republican congresswoman "a whore for the insurance industry."

THE RIGHT WAY TO HATE

At the beginning of this chapter, I said that we need more "hate talk" in this country—not less. And I'm absolutely serious about that.

The problem is that people hear that word *hate* and automatically assume that it is a bad thing. In fact, the right kind of hate is a virtue. Check it out: The Bible says that if you want truly to obey God, you have to "hate evil"—and that we should hate the things that God hates: "Pride and arrogance and the evil way and the perverse mouth I hate," says Proverbs.[6] "Hate evil, love good; establish justice," adds Amos.[7] "Abhor

[hate] what is evil," says Romans, "cling to what is good."[8] Hate—the right kind of hate—is a virtue! And there's far too little of this kind of hate in the world today.

Too many people are content to occupy the mushy middle between good and evil. They are unwilling to take a stand, to hate evil, to love good, to establish justice. They're afraid to speak out boldly, to say without equivocation, "This is evil; this is something we all should hate." They're afraid to suggest that there might actually be stark contrasts of white and black, good and evil, in the world; for them, everything must be painted in shades of gray.

The world needs more people who are willing to step out of the mushy middle and take a stand: *Hate what is evil, cling to what is good.* There is enormous power for good in the right kind of hate. Ronald Reagan hated communism because of the death, misery, and enslavement it brought to millions of people. In 1981, he gave a speech in which he denounced the Soviet Union as an "evil empire," and he predicted that the hated evil empire would end up "on the ash heap of history." Liberals and moderates gasped in horror! What a hateful thing to say! Won't the Soviets be offended?

Yet, because of the righteous, holy hate of Ronald Reagan—a hate that was directed not at people but at an evil empire, an evil idea, an evil and totalitarian system of government—his prediction ultimately came true. The evil empire *has* been consigned to the ash heap. The lesson of history is clear: *Hate what is evil, cling to what is good.*

We need that kind of hate today. We need to hate such social evils as the welfare state, affirmative action, abortion, class warfare, race warfare, runaway crime, runaway government spending, runaway taxation, teen pregnancy, the spread of AIDS and other STDs, attacks on religious freedom, terrorism, and political oppression. We don't hate these social evils because we hate people, but because we care about people and want to liberate them.

You might say, "Hold it right there, Mike! Welfare and affirmative action aren't social evils!" My response: However well-intentioned these programs may have been in the beginning, we now have conclusive evidence that affirmative action perpetuates racism and that welfare destroys initiative, disintegrates families, maintains poverty, promotes ignorance, and keeps people enslaved and beholden to an uncaring government bureaucracy. These programs are also used by unscrupulous politicians to buy votes in order to maintain a dependent-class power base.

If you say you want to eliminate affirmative action or the welfare state, liberals scream, "That's hate, that's racism!" No. That's *compassion.* What I really hate is to see anyone, regardless of race, addicted to government programs. No one ever became successful or achieved their dreams by standing in line for a government check.

So if you tune in my show, you'll hear the right kind of hate talk, the kind that hates evil and truly cares for people, the kind that wants to lift people up and show them how to become the best they can be.

Hate what is evil, cling to what is good. That means you call 'em as you see 'em—even when you see that the evil is coming from your own side of the aisle. If you've listened to my show for any length of time, you know that it is not a one-sided, fiercely partisan, Republicans-only show. You've heard me "hate what is evil" when the Republicans have sided with bad legislation, when Republican leaders have covered up the independent audit of House finances, or when Republicans betrayed the Contract with America or the Balanced Budget Amendment. I make a point of holding *everybody's* feet to the fire—liberal or conservative, Democrat or Republican.

You've heard me "cling to what is good" in the Democratic Party. You've heard Democrats—including *archliberal* Democrats such as Barbara Boxer and Paul Simon—praised or interviewed on my show when they've introduced good legislation that I could get behind. You've even heard Democrats guest-hosting my show when I'm away! Instead of clinging to ideology or party distinctions, I try to hate what is evil and cling to what is good.

CLINTON-BASHERS AND REAGAN-BASHERS

You might respond, "Don't tell me you don't do the wrong kind of hate talk on your show, Mike! I've heard plenty of Clinton-bashing on your show!" Yes, you've heard me argue with President Clinton's policies, his words, and his actions many times. You've heard me talk about Bill and Hillary's murky dealings in Arkansas. You've even heard me refer to Bill Clinton as an "empty suit." Is that hateful? I don't think so. "Empty suit" is a metaphor, a word-picture describing the way Bill Clinton conducts his presidency: no core values, no firm beliefs, no charted course—just a blow-dry image and a pollster to steer by. His only vision for America is to take the country deeper into socialism. I consider the liberal vision for American an evil thing, and I will never apologize for it.

If disagreeing with President Clinton constitutes Clinton-bashing, then okay, I'm a Clinton-basher. But I only bash in the realm of policies, actions, and ideas—plus those personality traits (such as lying and faithlessness to his wife) that spill over into his public conduct. If a man can't be trusted to be true to his family, how can we expect him to keep faith with the American people? That's relevant.

I believe I'm much more fair to this president than the Reagan-bashers of the press ever were to Ronald and Nancy Reagan. And I'll tell you something else: I pray for Bill Clinton. Every week, I meet with my prayer group at church and one thing we always pray for is the leadership at all levels of our nation. I pray that God will watch over this man, change his heart, and give him wisdom to make sound decisions for our nation and to provide moral leadership. Frankly, I don't see any sign of change, but I don't believe prayer is ever wasted, and I am keeping the faith. Personally, I don't think it's possible to pray for someone and hate him at the same time. I can honestly tell you that, even though I hate much of what he does and says as president, I don't hate Bill Clinton the human being.

I try to only hate what is evil and cling to what is good. Can the haters on the left say the same?

The Larry Nichols Files

L ESS THAN two months after Vince Foster's death, Larry Nichols was on my show, claiming that Vince Foster did not die at Fort Marcy Park. People in the dominant media and in the White House said Larry Nichols was a liar. The record shows that the White House was lying and that Larry Nichols has been correct in every assertion he has made. Today, he is in demand on many local and national talk shows, but I feel honored to know that I put Larry Nichols on national radio when no one else would give him the time of day.

Who is Larry Nichols? He's the former marketing director of the Arkansas Development Finance Authority (ADFA), an agency set up in the 1980s by then governor Bill Clinton, supposedly to provide money for housing and business development in the state. According to Larry, he discovered after joining ADFA that not all of the money was used for the stated purpose of the agency. Instead, ADFA was used to launder drug money that came into Arkansas through the Mena airport (when planes took Contra arms shipments to Nicaragua, they came back through Mena loaded with drugs). The drug money was used to buy ADFA bonds, and the money from the bond sales was turned right around and "loaned" to the people with drug connections. ADFA was also a source of enormous amounts of cash for Bill Clinton's campaign and personal use. According to published statements by Nichols, gobs of ADFA money went to Clinton's numerous girlfriends.

Larry acknowledges that, at first, he fell right in with the excitement and sordid pleasures of being a Clinton insider. He has firsthand experience with the party-hearty lifestyle of the Clintonistas, which included money, drugs, booze, and women. He claims firsthand knowledge that Bill Clinton not only inhaled but regularly abused marijuana and cocaine.

When Larry began objecting to some of the obviously fraudulent loans being issued by ADFA, he was fired and smeared, accused of misuse of long-distance telephone and air freight services. In September 1991, he turned around and filed suit against Clinton and ADFA for defamation and wrongful termination. The state of Arkansas secretly "dismissed" his suit, using a phony court order, illegibly signed by a "special judge" who did not exist.

Since then, Larry Nichols has taken his case against Bill Clinton to the public via a series of videos, a widely distributed "plaintiff's exhibit book" filled with documentary evidence of his charges, speaking engagements, and appearances on talk radio. When I first began talking to Larry about having him on the show, I was skeptical of a great deal that he had to say. So much of it seemed flat-out incredible! I made him prove every word before we went on the air. In time, I found that some of the things that seemed so incredible at first were only the tip of the Arkansas iceberg.

"I WILL TELL THE TRUTH"

Larry Nichols is one of the most courageous, straight-up human beings I have ever known. In 1994, after making a series of charges regarding Don Tyson, chairman of Tyson Foods, Inc., on my show and a few other talk shows, Larry received a letter from Don Tyson, which is reprinted below (from *Nichols vs. Clinton: Plaintiff's Exhibit Book* by Larry Nichols):

Dear Mr. Nichols:
   A disturbing report has come to my attention. You are being quoted in a publication called "For the People News Reporter" dated June 27, 1994 as having talked to a talk show host named Chuck Harder on June 9, 1994 on something called "For the People Broadcast."
   The "News Reporter" quotes you as having said on the radio, "Don

Tyson was in the middle. He has been. He used his chicken trucks to haul cocaine."

If you said this, it is obviously slander, libel and defamation of the most vicious sort.

I am compelled to ask you, "What do you have to say for yourself?"

Did you say these things?

Do you claim you were misquoted?

Do you have any justification for spreading these vicious lies, if you weren't misquoted?

Do you have anything you want to show me to justify your conduct?

Will you publicly take it back and admit it is not true?

Will you apologize to me and my company?

Are you aware that "For the People" is broadcast into many states, some of which have criminal libel and defamation statutes?

Do you realize you cannot with impunity destroy people's reputation without cause anymore than you can destroy their lives and property?

Will you give me the courtesy of a definitive reply?

> Yours truly
> Don Tyson
> Chairman

Larry did indeed give Mr. Tyson the courtesy of a definitive reply. In a widely distributed open letter, Larry wrote:

Dear Mr. Tyson:

If you're wondering whether I have said what you asked in your letter, I have, and will continue to do so. You asked why, but you should know the answer. It's because it's all true.

So that you understand why I'm doing this, it's because of your friend, Bill Clinton. You've used him to build your company at the expense of Arkansas, and you plan to do the same for America.

I've enclosed a couple of documents from the Arkansas State Police files and other agencies. These are already all over the nation. I will tell the truth about you and Bill Clinton.

So that you know, people from the FBI, the Arkansas State Police and the Drug Enforcement Agency have told me not to mess with you because you have the money and power and would have me killed. You're now on notice. Fire the shot whenever you want; I can't stop you. I can only tell you to call ahead of time and get my schedule. It may be tough to fit you and yours in between talk shows. But I'm sure something can be worked out.

Let's do lunch.

Love, Larry

Since then, there have been beatings, trumped-up jailings, and major assaults on his reputation and credibility. Shortly after the Oklahoma City bombing, he was in San Bernardino, California, for a speaking engagement. As he got out of his car, he was rushed by camera crews from ABC News, CBS's *60 Minutes,* and other news organizations, clamoring for a statement. "What can you tell us about your nephew, Terry Nichols, and his arrest in connection with the bombing in Oklahoma?" "When was the last time you spoke with your nephew?" "What did Terry Nichols say to you about the bombing?"

Larry told the reporters he didn't know Terry Nichols, was no relation to Terry Nichols, and had never spoken to Terry Nichols. "How many times has he called you?" they asked, as if they didn't even hear him. Finally, Larry asked them for their source. One of the reporters went back to his news van and returned with a wire feed that claimed that "anti-Clinton activist Larry Nichols is the uncle of alleged Oklahoma bomber Terry Nichols." The interesting thing about this wire copy was that, unlike all other wire copy you see, it had no origin—it didn't say Associated Press, Reuters, Washington Post, or anything else. It just had a date and a libelous story. The question is, who in this country would have the clout to put out a false story on the national wire services without indicating a source?

"That night," Larry recalls, "ABC affiliates on the West Coast ran a fifteen-second story showing my picture—one of those pictures in which I looked like a hoodlum—alongside a picture of Terry Nichols. Under my picture was a caption that said, 'Anti-Clinton activist, uncle of Terry Nichols,' and under Terry's picture, it said, 'Suspected Oklahoma City bomber.' That graphic stayed on the screen for all but the last two seconds of the story; then the announcer said, 'Larry Nichols, however, denies he is related to the bombing suspect. . . . Turning to other news—' And the clear impression was left with millions of people that I was somehow tied to that bombing in Oklahoma City. And you can't sue them, because they stuck that little disclaimer in there at the end."

A STRING OF FIRSTS

By my count, Larry Nichols has broken more than thirty major stories on *The Michael Reagan Talk Show*. For some reason—perhaps because Larry is the only guy out there with the courage to put the truth out and take the heat for it—information keeps coming to him. It comes by phone and by fax, it lands on his doorstep, it comes to him from sources within the White House, the Justice Department, the Starr investigation, and elsewhere. More than once, I've told him on the air that if he ever steered me wrong, I wouldn't have him on the show again. I've had Larry Nichols on my show again and again, and he has never once steered me wrong.

When you hear Larry on my show, listen closely, because he speaks with care and precision. He has never said (as some people claim) that Vince Foster was murdered; he'll tell you flat-out, he doesn't know how Vince Foster died. But he does know beyond a shadow of a doubt that Vince Foster did not die in Fort Marcy Park. Read Chapter 6 and you'll know it, too. Meanwhile, here are a few of the revelations and predictions Larry Nichols broke for the first time nationally on my show—all of which have been strongly substantiated or proven true:

- He predicted the indictments of Whitewater figures Web Hubbell, Neal Ainley, and Arkansas governor Jim Guy Tucker weeks or months before those indictments were handed down.
- He predicted that friend-of-Bill, Rose-Law-partner-of-Hillary, and associate attorney general Web Hubbell would go to jail—and he made that prediction on my show *two years* before Hubbell was even indicted.
- He broke the story about the shredding of documents at the Rose Law Firm—which was later confirmed by testimony before congressional committees.
- He broke the story about Bernie Nussbaum, Patsy Thomasson, and Maggie Williams removing documents from Foster's office—and we were talking about it on my show months before anyone in the press was talking about it. That story, in large part, led to Nussbaum's resignation.

- He released the Secret Service memo on my show—the now famous memo that clearly says that Foster was found dead *in his car,* not on the grass in the park (to understand the full implications of that memo, see Chapter 6).
- He broke the story about big-time Clinton contributor Dan Lasater's trafficking in narcotics—and about the political strings that were pulled to get Lasater a full and complete pardon.
- He broke the story about Arkansas chicken mogul Don Tyson being investigated for trafficking in narcotics since 1973.
- He broke the story about campaign contributions that Bill Clinton made to himself in his gubernatorial races—contributions Clinton couldn't possibly afford ($120,000 cash in 1982, for example). Where did he get the money? Larry Nichols also uncovered the fact that while campaign contribution lists for other Arkansas political figures can be found going back to 1948, *all official copies* of Bill Clinton's campaign finance records prior to 1992 have been destroyed (Larry, however, has a set that *escaped* destruction, and he has made them public).
- Larry announced on my show that the Arkansas Development Finance Authority—a state agency set up by Bill Clinton—was used for laundering drug money.
- Larry brought forth a lot of new information on gun running, drug running, and money laundering in Mena, Arkansas, during the Contra supply operation in the 1980s.
- Larry broke the story of the Helen Dickey phone call on my show—a well-documented account that dramatically conflicts with the White House account and raises the crucial, even impeachable question of "What did the president know and when did he know it?" (See Chapter 6 for the full story.)
- Larry broke the story of the "safe house" within short walking distance of Fort Marcy Park where Vince Foster was found dead— the house leased in Vince Foster's name and where he may have actually died.
- He broke the story of a Drug Enforcement Agency (DEA) report in which an informant claims that, while Bill Clinton was governor of Arkansas, he and a number of Arkansas officials flew to Dan

Lasater's 17,000-acre Angel Fire resort in New Mexico aboard a private plane owned by Don Tyson. Two underage Mexican prostitutes were brought across the border to serve as the evening's entertainment. When one of the prostitutes, age sixteen, died of a cocaine overdose, Clinton aide Patsy Thomasson flew back to Mexico aboard the Tyson plane and disposed of the body in a dumpster alongside a Mexican runway. After we put the story on the air, a reporter at the *Wall Street Journal* tried to break down the story by claiming there was no such place as Angel Fire, New Mexico. As usual, Larry was able to produce documentation and photographs proving the existence of both Angel Fire and the DEA report.

"I'm not a prophet," says Larry Nichols. "I'm not clairvoyant. I don't guess. I *know,* because I was with these people who are doing these things. I was there. I was in the middle of it. I know what I saw. I know what I was a part of."

"GOD'S GOT ME IN A PICKLE"

If you ask Larry if faith in God has gotten him through the harrowing experience of the past few years, he'll tell you, "If you were me, don't you think you'd *better* believe in God? I guess you can say I've got the classic case of foxhole religion. At some point, even tough guys and scumbags like me have to believe in a higher being. And I just really believe that for some reason, God's got me in a pickle, and I don't know whether he's mad at me and he's punishing me or he likes me and he's helping me.

"I can't quote you Scripture and I don't think it's right to run around acting holier than others. You've gotta know, I just can't cut it on my own, with everything that's happened to me. People come up to me and assume I'm a Bible authority, which I'm not. They say, 'Well, you said that Jesus is your Lord and Savior,' and I say, 'That's right,' but if you come up and ask me what it says in Luke 59:2, well, I don't have a clue what you're talking about."

There is one prediction Larry Nichols has made on my show that has not yet come to pass, as I write these words. Since early 1995, Larry has been predicting that Kenneth Starr's grand jury would hand down an indictment of the first lady, Hillary Rodham Clinton. Before completing this book, I checked back with Larry to see if he stands by his information. "That one's still coming," he replied.

CHAPTER 5

The Arkansas Flu

THEY CALL it the Arkansas Flu.

It is highly contagious, and it strikes without warning. Its victims die horribly and violently—usually from suicide or a mysterious accident. Victims usually show few symptoms or warning signs, though some have reported feelings of paranoia—a sense of being watched or followed— shortly before they died. The Arkansas Flu is no respecter of persons; it has taken the lives of people ranging from anonymous young women to investigative journalists to a top White House official. The list of those who have succumbed to the Arkansas Flu includes (in chronological order):

Suzanne Coleman was killed on February 15, 1977, and her death was ruled a suicide. Arkansas state trooper Larry Patterson and other troopers who were on Bill Clinton's security detail at that time say that she had an affair with Clinton, the then attorney general for the state of Arkansas, and that she was alleged to have been pregnant with Clinton's child at the time of her death (the allegation was never proven). She was killed by a gunshot to the head. No autopsy was performed.

Danny Casolaro was an investigative reporter who died on August 9, 1991, in a Sheraton hotel in West Virginia. Casolaro, who had previously been credited with some excellent reporting on Iran-Contra and other scandals, had gone to West Virginia to meet a witness offering information. Casolaro was found dead in a bathtub, and his death was officially ruled a suicide. How did he supposedly kill himself? He was found in the bathtub with a plastic bag over his head, and his wrists were slashed—not once, but multiple times, again and again. There was blood spattered all around the hotel room. In the course of his suicide, he apparently put up quite a struggle with himself.

"Casolaro had interviewed me a few times shortly before he died," recalls Larry Nichols. "He was working on the Contra connection to all of this. When we were talking, he sent me a bunch of his notes, and he said he was scared. All of a sudden, I didn't hear from him anymore, and later I heard he was dead."

Casolaro was embalmed before the autopsy was performed, which is not the best way to preserve evidence in a potential homicide investigation. The death of Danny Casolaro remains a mystery to this day.

C. Victor Raiser III, national finance cochairman of the Clinton for President campaign, died in a plane crash (along with six other people, including his son) on July 30, 1992. Raiser was en route to Alaska for a fishing vacation at the time of the crash, and the cause of the accident has never been determined.

Paul Tilly, who died in September 1992, was a top Clinton campaign strategist and political director of the Democratic National Committee. He died of "unknown causes" in his hotel room in Little Rock, and no autopsy was ever performed.

Paula Grober died on December 9, 1992. She was Bill Clinton's speech interpreter for the deaf, and she had worked closely and traveled extensively with Bill Clinton since 1978. She was killed in a single-vehicle car accident, and there were no witnesses.

Vince Foster, deputy White House counsel in the Clinton administration, died on July 20, 1993. His death was ruled a suicide, despite an overwhelming number of glaring inconsistencies. More on his story in the next chapter.

Jon Walker was an investigator with the Resolution Trust Corporation. At the time of his death on August 15, 1993, he was looking into the murky goings-on between the Clintons, the MacDougals, Madison

Guaranty Savings, and a land venture called Whitewater. How did Jon Walker die? It seems he just sort of fell off the top of the Lincoln Towers Building in Arlington, Virginia. Must have been suicide. Sure, that's what it was.

Jerry Luther Parks, who died on September 26, 1993, was the owner of American Contract Services, which provided security for the Little Rock office of the Clinton for President campaign and transition headquarters. One Sunday evening, about two months after the death of Vince Foster, Jerry Parks was driving home from church when he stopped at an intersection to make a left turn. In broad daylight, a white Chevrolet pulled up behind Parks. One of the two men in the car jumped out, approached Parks' car, and unleashed a hail of gunfire. Parks was hit seven times as he tried to get out of the car to defend himself with his own gun. He died sprawled in the street.

Parks's relationship with Bill Clinton went back a number of years, and he had actually kept files on what he considered to be a pattern of illicit activities conducted by the then governor. Parks told his family that he had difficulty getting repaid for substantial out-of-pocket expenses he had laid out as head of Clinton's private security detail, and he had been trying to collect that money from the White House for months. According to reporter Christopher Ruddy, the White House privately told Parks that the funds that were to have been paid to Parks were embezzled, and Parks was asked not to make the matter public, since it would embarrass the president. About six months after the inauguration, and shortly before Vince Foster died, Parks got his money.

It's not known what he planned to do with the files he kept on Clinton. Perhaps he intended to use them as leverage to get the money he was owed, or perhaps he planned to sell them to the tabloids. We'll never know. A few weeks after Parks was paid, his house was burglarized, and, according to Parks's wife and son, the files were among the items taken. After the loss of the files and the death of Vince Foster (whom Parks knew personally, and who had once recommended Parks for a job), Parks became extremely fearful. He would take different routes home every night, he worried about someone planting a bomb in his car, and he carried a gun even when he went to check the mailbox.

Did He Inhale ... or Did He Snort?

An interesting sidebar to the Jerry Luther Parks story involves Parks' wife. According to Ambrose Evans-Pritchard of *The London Sunday Telegraph*, Mrs. Parks managed an upscale apartment complex in Little Rock in 1984, while Bill Clinton was governor. Mrs. Parks told Ambrose that during that time, she was instructed by the owners of the complex to "take care of" a visitor who would be coming to the apartments—and not ask any questions. The "visitor," as it turned out, was Clinton's brother, Roger, who took up residence in the "corporate suite," the bedroom of which was on the other side of a thin wall or partition from the manager's office where Mrs. Parks worked. The governor's brother occupied the place for about two months in the summer of '84—shortly before Roger Clinton was arrested and convicted on cocaine charges.

Mrs. Parks reported hearing sex-and-drug parties going on in Roger Clinton's apartment—the sound carried easily through the thin wall. "On quite a number of occasions," said Ambrose, citing Mrs. Parks' account, "Bill Clinton would come. They'd park the governor's limo at some far corner of the complex, and he'd stroll over, usually in the afternoons, and join in. Usually, it would be him and Roger—and girls. She said some of the girls were very young. . . . She told her husband, who worked for a private security company, and was a former police officer. He started—ostensibly for her protection, and maybe for other purposes—taking notes and [conducting surveillance] from their third-floor apartment across the courtyard—noting who was going in and out and so forth. He kept a dossier on it."

When the governor went into the bedroom with one of the girls, said Mrs. Parks, she could hear everything. Being a self-described born-again Christian, Mrs. Parks was so disgusted she had to leave her office. On one occasion, said Ambrose, she entered the suite when it was unoccupied and found "all the paraphernalia of cocaine. There were bits of cocaine sprinkled on the furniture, and no attempt had been made to cover it up."

In July 1993, the Parks home was broken into and the apartment surveillance files Jerry Parks had been keeping on Clinton

> were stolen from the bedroom dresser, along with files Parks had amassed on Clinton's affair with Gennifer Flowers and other activities. Parks himself was ambushed and died in a hail of gunfire two months after the burglary. Was Jerry Luther Parks murdered because of what was contained in those files? Mrs. Parks and her son, Gary, are convinced he was.
>
> The rest of us, as Ambrose Evans-Pritchard concludes, can only look at the evidence and wonder.

Despite eyewitnesses to the killing, it has never been fully investigated, no suspects were ever arrested, and no motive was ever officially determined.[1] *Pittsburgh Tribune Review* reporter Christopher Ruddy has termed the police follow-up to Parks's murder "a cover-up."

Ed Willey, an attorney and Clinton fund-raiser, died on November 30, 1993. Cause of death: gunshot wound to the head. His body was found in a wooded area in northern Virginia. The death was officially ruled a suicide.

Herschel Friday, an Arkansas attorney and a member of Bill Clinton's campaign finance committee, died in the crash of a small plane at his privately owned airstrip in Arkansas on March 1, 1994. Interestingly, both Friday and C. Victor Raiser III, who died seventeen months earlier, were involved with Clinton campaign finances and both died in private plane crashes.

Kathy Ferguson died on May 10, 1994, and the story of her death should have been on the front pages of every American newspaper the very next day. Instead, the dominant media totally ignored the story until Larry Nichols and I brought the story forward on my show. Only then did the Associated Press and a few other news organizations call me and ask to know more about Kathy Ferguson.

Who was Kathy Ferguson and why is her death so important? She was the wife of Danny Ferguson, the Arkansas state trooper who was Bill Clinton's most trusted bodyguard and procurer of women. You've heard of Danny Ferguson: He is Bill Clinton's codefendant in the Paula Corbin Jones sexual harassment case. (Danny has publicly admitted that he asked Paula Jones to go to Clinton's room and that he escorted her in the elevator and left her at the door of the room.) At the time of her death, Kathy and Danny Ferguson were divorced, and Kathy was engaged to a police officer named Bill Shelton.

Shortly before her death, Kathy Ferguson confided to several friends that while attending a function at the governor's mansion in Little Rock, she was cornered in the kitchen by then governor Bill Clinton. According to the sworn affidavit of one friend, Sherry Butler, Kathy said that Clinton "pinned her to the counter." Kathy Ferguson also told Butler that she was convinced everything Paula Jones alleged about Clinton was true and that she "wouldn't put anything past Bill Clinton." Another of Kathy's friends, Dr. Samuel T. Houston, in a sworn affidavit, testified that just one day before Kathy died, she commented to him, "I wish I didn't know what I know" concerning the activities of her ex-husband, Danny Ferguson, in service to Bill Clinton.

What did Kathy Ferguson know that she wished she didn't know? In part, she knew what several Arkansas state troopers came forward and told: that their duties on behalf of Bill Clinton included procuring women for the then governor. But that wasn't all she knew. Kathy died in mid-1994, long after Clinton was elected president, and after many of his sexual indiscretions had been either publicly alleged or convincingly documented. What else did she know that she wished she didn't know?

Kathy Ferguson died in her Sherwood, Arkansas, apartment and was found by her fiancé, Bill Shelton. Death came as a result of a single gunshot to the head. When the coroner arrived at 12:45 in the wee hours of the morning of May 11, he found her body sitting on the couch, slumped to the right, her head spattered with blood, a .38 caliber handgun on the floor. Strangely, the spent casing of the bullet was sitting in an ashtray on a table to the right of the body. Another interesting detail: The coroner found a note on the coffee table which referred to problems in the relationship between herself and Shelton, but it was not a "suicide note" per se (even though that's what the autopsy report calls it). In fact, it was actually more of a farewell note, and the coroner's report observes that "clothes on the couch and packed in a plastic bag suggested she was planning on leaving"—*not* killing herself!

The autopsy report indicated that the bullet had entered her head slightly above and behind her right ear, and exited her left front temple.

Dr. Houston, however, in his sworn affidavit, says that six nurses closely examined Kathy Ferguson's head at the open-casket funeral and all six agreed that what they saw was a mirror image of what the autopsy report stated: The smaller entrance wound was behind her left ear and the larger exit wound was on the right temple—not behind the ear, but well in front of it, causing the right eye to be tugged out of its proper position. The significance of this fact is that Kathy, being right-handed, was unlikely to have shot herself behind her left ear. That would have been a very unnatural position.

Just a month after Kathy Ferguson's death:

Bill Shelton died on June 12, 1994. His body was found slumped over Kathy's grave, a supposed suicide note next to the body. Exactly as the autopsy report declared Kathy to have been shot, Bill Shelton was shot just behind the right ear.

There are other documented cases of the Arkansas flu on the record, but these are enough to make a person stop and think: What is the common thread linking all these deaths? What caused this epidemic called the Arkansas flu?

Acknowledgment: The phrase *Arkansas flu* was coined, I believe, by political satirist J. Jordan Cannady, writing in the September-October 1994 issue of *Slick Times.*

CHAPTER 6

Vince Foster: The Mystery Unravels

I F YOU had ever visited Vince Foster in his White House office, you would have seen a framed, faded picture, over forty years old. It was taken at Miss Mary's kindergarten in Hope, Arkansas. Three of the five-year-old boys in that picture would one day grow up to work in the White House together: Bill Clinton, president of the United States; his chief of staff, Mack McLarty; and Vince Foster himself, deputy White House counsel. *That* is how close Vince Foster has been to Bill Clinton throughout most of his life.

So it seems strange that after Vince Foster died, Bill Clinton turned out to be a very poor friend to his lifelong buddy. The president certainly didn't pull out all the stops in trying to find out why his friend died. In fact, Clinton scarcely seemed curious. Instead of ordering the FBI to conduct a pains-taking and thorough investigation of the Foster matter, which he easily could have done, Clinton stood by and allowed the park police to bungle the investigation. The park police are competent enough for their principal assignment, which is to act as security guards for our national parks. But they are clearly over their heads when confronted with a high-profile homicide or suicide with major political and national security implications. Because of Bill Clinton's puzzling lack of interest in seeing the Foster case solved, the death of the president's trusted advisor and boyhood friend was investigated not by the Justice Department (the parent entity of the FBI), but by the Department of the Interior!

Just a day or two after Vince Foster died, President Clinton stated publicly that it would "remain a mystery" why his friend died. I thought at the time that it was a strange statement for Bill Clinton to make. How could the president know at such an early stage of the investigation that the reasons for Foster's death would remain buried forever? How could Clinton know that investigators would not turn up clues—a note, a tape recording, some piece of evidence to suggest a reason for his friend's apparent suicide? Wasn't Bill Clinton even curious enough to *hope* that the mystery would be solved? Or—and this is the most troubling question of all—did Bill Clinton actually *want* Vince Foster's death to remain a mystery?

I'm not saying I think Vince Foster was murdered or that the president of the United States had anything to do with his death. Actually, I tend to believe Vince Foster killed himself (though not in Fort Marcy Park where his body was found). The point is, I don't agree with the president's view that the death of Vince Foster *must* remain a mystery. And I certainly don't think it *should.*

Since President Clinton made that strange statement, much of the mystery concerning Vince Foster's death has begun to unravel—no thanks whatsoever to the media establishment in America, which has turned a blind eye to the mass of disturbing evidence in this case. Though deputy White House counsel Vincent W. Foster Jr. was the highest ranking government official to die by violence since John F. Kennedy, the press has been strangely uninterested in the many inconsistencies surrounding his death. The vast majority of the investigative journalism in the Foster case has been carried on by just two reporters: Christopher Ruddy of the *Pittsburgh Tribune Review* (formerly of the *New York Post*) and Ambrose Evans-Pritchard of the *London Sunday Telegraph*. Important spadework has also been done by David Brock at the *American Spectator,* John Crudele at the *New York Post,* and Mike Isikoff, who was forced to leave the *Washington Post* so that he could write the truth about Bill Clinton.

Talk radio has also played a major role in pulling back the veil from the Foster mystery. Many of the most startling revelations in the Foster case and related Whitewater matters have come not from a newspaper but from the appearances of Larry Nichols on my national show.

One thing is sure beyond a shadow of a doubt: *Vince Foster did not die in Fort Marcy Park.* As you are about to see, the evidence in the Foster case is so compelling, so overwhelming that even the O.J. Simpson jury would be convinced! Foster may have died by his own hand or the hand of another; that is yet to be determined. But however he died, for whatever reason, he unquestionably died elsewhere and his body was moved to the park.

FOSTER'S LAST DAYS

Piecing together the information turned up by Nichols, Ruddy, and Ambrose Evans-Pritchard, I've assembled a step-by-step sequence of known events surrounding the strange death of Vince Foster. Read it. Then you tell me: How did he die? And, more important, *why* did he die?

May 13, 1993
Some observers believe the Travelgate scandal is linked to Vince Foster's death. Maybe, maybe not. In either case, here are the salient facts:

Without advising FBI director William Sessions, the White House summons FBI agents to investigate the White House travel office, then loudly publicizes its supposed "cleanup" of the travel operation. It soon becomes apparent that the White House may have used the FBI for political purposes, attempting to smear the reputations of seven innocent people in the travel office, some of whom had worked there for more than three decades. The reason for discrediting them: to oust them and make way for Clinton cronies (including Bill Clinton's cousin, Catherine Cornelius) to take over the office.

Of the seven, five are later rehired, one retired, and one—travel office head Billy Dale—is indicted on two shaky counts of embezzlement as a White House face-saving move. Over the next eighteen months, Dale racks up $500,000 in legal fees while government prosecutors try to make the case stick; in November 1995, the White House is embarrassed when the jury—after one hour of deliberation!—finds Dale innocent on both counts.

After years of denial, Hillary Rodham Clinton's involvement in the scandal is confirmed when a long-suppressed memo by White House aide David Watkins is released during Senate hearings in October 1995. The memo, dated May 14, 1993, shows Hillary demanding the removal of the old travel office staff. "We need these people out—we need our people in," she is quoted as saying. "We need the slots."

Another key player in the Travelgate affair is Vince Foster, the White House official who called in the FBI.

Late June to early July 1993

Vince Foster purchases a special, highly sophisticated alarm system for his home in Georgetown. His wife, Lisa, notes that he seems stressed and anxious. Only forty-eight years old, Foster has always been in excellent health. Now, however, she notices that he continually rubs his hands together in a compulsive way. He complains of severe heart palpitations, high blood pressure, and insomnia. It is important to note—as any competent psychologist or psychiatrist will tell you—that these are symptoms of *anxiety* or *fear*, not suicidal depression.

July 12-18, 1993

During the week before his death, Foster's sister arranges for him to be seen by a psychiatrist in the Washington area to treat his sleeplessness and other symptoms. She instructs the doctor not to take notes because Foster's symptoms may be related to his top-secret work with the government. Foster, however, does not go to the doctor. He goes to a different kind of professional: James Hamilton—a Washington criminal attorney. According to Lisa Foster's recollection, Vince goes to him for advice on how to deal with the Travelgate scandal and potential congressional hearings.

The weekend of July 17-18, Vince and Lisa Foster drive to the eastern Maryland shore, supposedly for a brief vacation. According to the Fiske report, the Fosters just happen to stumble upon Web Hubbel at the palatial estate of Michael Cardozo, head of Bill Clinton's legal defense fund. Hubbell later tells investigators that the weekend consisted of nothing more than tennis and poolside chats.

Monday, July 19, 1993

FBI director William Sessions is fired by President Clinton just one day before Vince Foster dies. There are two possibilities: (1) the timing of the Sessions firing is coincidental, or (2) the timing of the Sessions firing is intended to thwart an FBI investigation into a crime that is about to occur.

Whether the firing was intentional or coincidental, there is no question that the Sessions firing compromises the investigation into Foster's death.

Months later, in a handwritten letter to Christopher Ruddy, Sessions pointedly observes, "The relationship between the White House and the FBI at the time of Mr. Foster's death should be looked at in the context of known events that had political implications. . . . The White House and Justice Department were clearly in a politically awkward position with the FBI 'Travelgate' investigation in July 1993—when Foster's body was discovered." Sessions himself concludes that, because of his firing, the Foster investigation is "compromised from the beginning."[1]

Though the timing of the Sessions firing may well have been coincidental, it is interesting to compare this event with the Travelgate firings and the Clinton Justice Department's unprecedented mass firing and replacement of all thirty-two U.S. attorneys nationwide in early 1993, which was almost certainly designed to mask the fact that Clinton wanted to install his own handpicked flunky, Paula Casey (a Clinton campaign worker and former law student of Bill's), as U.S. attorney in the Little Rock office. Casey became a useful tool in that office, where she personally quashed numerous criminal referrals from the Resolution Trust Corporation regarding fraudulent Whitewater loans, check-kiting, phony tax deductions, and the diversion of money from Madison Guaranty depositor accounts to Bill Clinton's political campaign. The Clintons clearly have a history, both in Arkansas and in Washington, of moving "unfriendlies" out of sensitive "slots" and replacing them with "our people" in order to consolidate control and head off investigations.[2] The Sessions firing, just the day before Foster dies, may be innocent—but it gives off a familiar and unsavory aroma.

Foster's schedule the day before his death contains a couple of unusual items. First, Foster's friend, Marsha Scott—a woman he has known for twenty years—meets with him behind closed doors for about ninety minutes to two hours. Scott is later interviewed by investigators and asked what she and Foster talked about. Amazingly, all she can remember from the entire lengthy conversation is that Vince Foster said he and Lisa had a "good weekend" at the Cardozo estate.

The second item concerns the evening of the nineteenth. After Foster's death, President Clinton was asked by a reporter about any recent conversations he might have had with Vince Foster. First, the president denied having any recent conversations with Foster . . . then he suddenly recalled having a conversation but couldn't recall the details . . . and finally he remembered that he had invited Foster over to the White House screening room to watch a movie. Foster declined the invitation. The movie was *In the Line of Fire*, in which Clint Eastwood portrays a Secret Service agent attempting to thwart a political assassination. Clinton recalls that he and Foster continued talking for about twenty minutes and agreed to meet on Wednesday to discuss unspecified "organizational changes."

Tuesday morning, July 20, 1993
Vince Foster has a busy morning. He spends about ninety minutes in the office of the White House counsel, talking with Bernard Nussbaum. The subject of their discussion is not known.

Also that morning, Foster has a phone conversation with Brantley Buck, the Rose Law Firm partner who is conducting an internal investigation of Web Hubbell's billing practices. He also receives three calls from Jim Lyons, a Denver attorney hired by the Clintons to issue an audit of their Whitewater investment. Lyons is planning to fly from Colorado to Washington to meet with Foster the next day. Also on Foster's calendar for the following day: His sister is coming to the White House, and Foster is planning to give her a tour of the presidential mansion.

(Incidentally, it is also this morning that Arkansas judge David Hale is served with a search warrant by feds investigating the Whitewater-related Madison Guaranty Savings and Loan.)

Tuesday afternoon, July 20, 1993
During the noon hour, Foster lunches on a cheeseburger, fries, and a Coke in his White House office. After lunch, Foster walks out of his office and remarks to Linda Tripp, executive assistant to Bernard Nussbaum, "There are still some M&Ms in the candy tray if you want them. I'll be back." Far from seeming depressed, he actually appears jovial as he departs. The last person known to have seen Foster alive

is a Secret Service guard who observes the White House deputy counsel leaving the West Wing at about 1:00 P.M.

Sometime between 1:00, when he left the White House, and 6:00 P.M., when his body is found, Foster dies. An autopsy examination of Foster's stomach contents later finds food that "might have been meat and potatoes," consumed about two to three hours before his death. If the so-called "meat and potatoes" were in fact the cheeseburger and french fries he had for lunch (as seems likely), then Foster probably died between 2:30 and 3:30 P.M., maybe as late as 4:00.

From the time he leaves the White House until the time his body is discovered—a period of about five hours—his whereabouts are unaccounted for. It seems incredible that in all that time, he phones nobody, speaks to nobody, is seen by nobody. As we shall see, the evidence indicates that *somebody* knows what happened to Vince Foster during those five lost hours.

Approximately 5:30 or 6:00 P.M., July 20, 1993

White House employee Helen Dickey places a call to the governor's mansion in Little Rock, Arkansas, asking to speak to Governor Jim Guy Tucker. Arkansas state trooper Roger Perry, who is working the security detail at the mansion, takes the call. Helen Dickey is very upset on the phone. She tells Roger Perry that Vince Foster had gotten off work, gone out to his car in the White House parking lot, and shot himself. Perry asks her to repeat the information; then he calls the residence and relays the information to Governor Tucker through Mrs. Tucker. The phone call lasts about ten minutes.

Both Vince Foster and Helen Dickey are well known to Perry from their Little Rock days. Foster, Hillary Rodham Clinton's Rose Law Firm partner, was a frequent visitor to the governor's mansion. Helen Dickey lived in the governor's mansion, working as Chelsea Clinton's nanny. Trooper Perry finds the news of Foster's death so shocking that as soon as he has relayed the message to Mrs. Tucker, he calls his friend, fellow trooper Larry Patterson. Patterson's recollection of the time of Perry's call can be pegged to his regular schedule: He has just gotten off work and arrived at his apartment. The phone is ringing as Patterson is coming in the front door, so the call from Perry—who calls not more than about ten minutes after receiving the call from Helen Dickey—takes place between 5:00 and 6:00, Arkansas time.

After Perry calls Patterson, he calls another friend, former Arkansas State Police director Lynn Davis, who fixes the time of Perry's call at no later than 6:00 P.M., Arkansas time. Working backwards to when Helen Dickey first called Perry, you arrive at a time window of between 5:30 and 7:00, Washington time (the troopers remember it as being closer to the earlier figure but allow that it could have been as late as 6:00 Arkansas time, 7:00 Washington time). So these three witnesses, all of whom are reputable and have given sworn affidavits, establish a time of about 5:30 to 7:00, Washington time, for the Helen Dickey call. The earliest figure is fifteen minutes *before* Foster's body has even been discovered and reported to the police; that latest figure is a full ninety minutes before the park police claim to have reported the news to the White House. In the matter of when the White House knew that Vince Foster was dead, somebody is clearly lying.

It should be noted that Helen Dickey disputes this account. She claims in an affidavit that she heard about Foster's death a little after 10:00 P.M. and placed the call to the governor's mansion a few minutes later, at close to 10:30, Washington time. Helen Dickey's version, if true, could have been easily substantiated, except that the phone logs were conveniently "erased" by a "computer glitch." What about phone company logs? The White House now claims that *all* of Helen Dickey's White House phone logs are protected under the umbrella of "national security." Obviously, Helen Dickey must be one heck of a high-powered nanny— perhaps even a *cabinet-level* nanny—to possess state secrets with "national security" implications.

But the fact is that Helen Dickey's version can't possibly be true. Dickey and whoever is coaching her have made a major blunder in concocting a much later time for her phone call: She says she spoke to Trooper Perry at about 10:30, Washington time. But by that time, Perry was no longer on duty, and this fact is established by contemporaneous duty logs. Larry Nichols notes that Dickey's affidavit is not properly notarized, nor is it dated, meaning it is not a valid affidavit—a probable hedge against a perjury charge.

"It's just the way Clinton's people work," says Nichols, who was a Clinton insider when Clinton was governor. "Now she can lie on the affidavit without risking jail time for perjury. They just tell her, 'Sign this—it really doesn't matter in a court of law.'" However, Roger Perry, Larry Patterson, and Lynn Davis have also given sworn affidavits that fix the much earlier timeline for Helen Dickey's call—and their affidavits are legally sworn, notarized, signed, and dated. Most important, their affidavits don't contradict reality and insult reason like Helen Dickey's bogus story does.

The timing of the Helen Dickey call—which was first broken on my show—is one of the most intriguing and important facts in the Vince Foster mystery. Here we have, as Larry Nichols says, "a little, lowly employee at the White House"—yet she knows Vince Foster is dead even before the park police have identified him, possibly even before his body has been discovered by a passerby! If the little, lowly nanny knew about the death at 5:30 or 6:00 P.M., from whom did she hear it, and how did that person know? If Helen Dickey knew, then it's a foregone conclusion that higher-ups knew—which raises the old question, "What did the president know, and when did he know it?"

As Larry Nichols has said on my show, "You have the key to the Vince Foster death in Helen Dickey."

Approximately 6:00 P.M., Tuesday, July 20, 1993

At a maintenance facility in Turkey Run Park, about two miles from Fort Marcy Park, park employee Francis Swann is sitting on the tailgate of his truck with a coworker, having a beer after work. A white van pulls up and the driver—later described by Swann as a heavyset white man in his mid-forties, dressed in work clothes like a utility worker—rolls down the window of the van and calls to Swann. "There's a dead body by the cannon up in Fort Marcy," says the man. "Will you call the park police?" Then the man drives off, apparently not in any hurry. Without noting the license number or getting the man's name, Swann goes to a pay phone and dials 911.

It will be nine months before the identity of the man in the white van is learned by investigators. Today, he is publicly known only as CW (for "confidential witness"), and he places the discovery of the body at about 5:45 P.M. (Interestingly, though the Robert Fiske investigation had no luck in turning up CW, the witness was brought forward by talk radio, on the *G. Gordon Liddy Show.*)

The "Safe House" on Dogwood Street

A revelation Larry Nichols made on my show underscores the significance of the fact that the north entrance to Fort Marcy Park was not secured. He has uncovered the existence of what he calls a "cat house" or "safe house" on Dogwood Street in Merriewood on the Potomac, which abuts Fort Marcy Park. The house is located only two to three hundred feet from the north entrance, which is nearest to where Foster's body was found. Nichols speculates that this house may be where Foster spent some of those missing five hours. "I'm not saying Foster died in that house," says Nichols, "but it's a possibility that should be explored. We know for a fact that the body was moved from *somewhere* to that park, and the house on Dogwood is certainly a handy possibility." The lease on the house was jointly in the name of Vince Foster and another prominent Arkansas attorney who set up an office in Washington, D.C., when Clinton was elected president.

The house rented by Foster was frequented, according to Nichols, by Foster, Hillary Rodham Clinton, and other people in the administration. Larry Nichols should know. "It's the same arrangement we had here in Arkansas, when I was on Clinton's team," he recalls. "We had houses that we rented where we could go and have wild parties and do women and drugs and stuff, and the media couldn't find us." Larry has turned over all documents and photos pertaining to the "safe house" on Dogwood Street to the Kenneth Starr investigation.

From about 6:15 to 8:45 P.M., Tuesday, July 20, 1993
The park police investigation at Fort Marcy Park.

George Gonzalez, a Fairfax County, Virginia, paramedic is the first emergency worker to see Foster's body. He finds Foster lying on his back amid dense brush on a steep hill or berm, with his head almost reaching the crest of the hill. Foster's body is laid out neatly, facing straight up, arms straight down at his side, legs perfectly straight—almost, Gonzalez recalls, "as if it was ready for the coffin."

VINCE FOSTER: THE MYSTERY UNRAVELS

Gonzalez and others at the scene note that there is only a very small trickle of blood apparent from the nose and mouth. (Later analysis of the path of the various blood tracks on Foster's face, as shown in Polaroid closeups taken before the body was removed, indicate Foster's head was moved in at least four different directions *after* he died.) There is a small bullet hole (entry wound) in the back of his mouth, and a large exit wound in the back of his head, indicating at first glance that Foster shot himself in the mouth—yet there is no puddle or spatter of blood or bone on the ground beneath or around the body, as would be expected. Though the autopsy will show that bone and tissue are missing from the back of Foster's head, the missing material is nowhere to be found at Fort Marcy Park.

The scene is so neat and bloodless, in fact, that when it is time to remove the body, emergency medical service worker Kory Ashford is able to cradle Foster's head in his arms while placing the body in a body bag—without wearing gloves and without getting any blood on himself. It does not impress him as a suicide by gunshot, because he has seen many such suicides, and they invariably tend to be messy and bloody. When Ashford writes his report at the station, he classifies it as a homicide.

Normally, a gunshot to the mouth causes sudden, profuse bleeding—a massive, messy backsplatter, to be gruesomely frank. A gunshot to the brain is unlikely to instantly stop the heart; as the heart continues to beat, the blood—a liquid under pressure—gushes out through the wound. The amazingly small amount of blood that was observed means that Foster was almost certainly dead when the shot was fired. This does not necessarily mean he was murdered, since he could have died of a heart attack, a drug overdose, carbon monoxide poisoning, or suffocation. But it is virtually certain that, however Foster died, he didn't die from that gunshot wound. Instead, the gunshot seems to have been fired to prevent investigators from noticing the *real* cause of death, whatever it was.

The gun in Foster's hand is an antique .38 Colt revolver assembled from two different guns, as shown by two different serial numbers on the weapon. The serial numbers are later traced, and it is learned that the original guns were sold in Seattle in 1913. Questioned by investigators, no one in Foster's family recognizes the gun as belonging to him. Chris Ruddy describes it as the kind of gun police call a "drop gun," an anonymous gun left at a crime scene to mislead investigators. It is found still in Foster's hand, the thumb resting in the trigger mechanism. This is rare in suicides, where the violence of the gunshot—involving both the recoil of the gun and the reflexes of the body—usually causes the gun to be thrown as far as twenty feet from the body.

If the gun was fired inside Foster's mouth, there should have been blood all over the gun; the weapon, however, is immaculately clean. There are two rounds in the cylinder, one fired, one unspent. Later exhaustive, repeated searches turn up no matching slug at Fort Marcy Park, nor any matching ammunition in Foster's office or his two homes. Amazingly, though the gun is found in Foster's hand, there are *no fingerprints* on the gun.

The telltale pattern of gunpowder residue shows that Foster's hand was positioned on the gun in an extraordinarily awkward and unwieldy fashion: Both index fingers were high on the gun frame, in front of the cylinder gap, and neither hand was on the pistol grip. The easiest and most stable way to hold a gun is with the right-hand fingers wrapped around the pistol grip, and Foster did not do that. "It doesn't make any sense," San Antonio medical examiner Vincent Di Maio told reporter Chris Ruddy. "It would be such an awkward way, you'd have to contort yourself to do this. It is not consistent with suicide." And retired Army ballistics expert Dr. Martin Fachler said, "If you ask is this an indication of foul play, I have to say, yeah, maybe it is."[3]

Another intriguing aspect of the whole matter of the gun is the fact that the first two people to see the body of Vince Foster in the park—the "confidential witness" (the driver of the white van) and the paramedic, Gonzalez—both say there was *no gun in Foster's hand* when they arrived.

From the moment they arrive on the scene, the park police begin to violate every rule of police procedure in such cases. Standard police procedure is to treat every apparent suicide as a homicide until proven otherwise. The park police fail to do so. In fact, park police investigator Cheryl Braun later admits that the death was determined to be a suicide—open and shut—even before detectives had inspected the site where Foster's body was found! Other gaping holes in the initial investigation:

• Photographic evidence and reports made by the park police have been destroyed or lost, and what remains has been shielded from public view.

• The park police lead investigator had never handled a homicide before.

• The park police did not even test the gun to see if it would fire before concluding their investigation. To this day, there is no proof that the gun in Foster's hand made the wound in his head, nor is there any proof that the gunshot wound in Foster's head was the cause of his death. In fact, most of the evidence indicates otherwise.

• The crime scene was never fully secured. The north entrance to the park on Chainbridge Road was left open, and there are eyewitness reports of people who came and went via that entrance while the investigation was in progress. In fact, Chris Ruddy reports that park police were not even aware that there was a rear entrance to the park—an entrance that was much closer to the body site then the front entrance.

• Four different people searched Foster's pockets, yet no keys were found on his person while his body was at the park. No keys were found in Foster's car, a 1989 Honda, which was in the parking lot. Yet, despite the fact that Foster couldn't have driven to the park without keys, the park police concluded he committed suicide. Where did the keys finally show up? At the hospital morgue where Foster's body was taken! In fact, a check of his pockets at the morgue turned up not one but two sets of keys.

How could four investigators have missed *two* sets of keys in Foster's pockets? They couldn't have. The answer to the puzzle may lie in the fact, contained in the Fiske report, that two White House officials, William Kennedy III and Craig Livingstone, went to the morgue to identify the body. Soon after the officials left, the keys were found in Foster's pockets. The mystery of the keys is eerily reminiscent of the twenty-seven-piece "suicide note" discovered in Foster's briefcase after previous searches found the briefcase empty.[4]

• Investigators did not go door-to-door in the neighborhood around Fort Marcy Park, asking if a shot was heard, until *two years* after Foster's death. *Two years!* No one heard the supposedly fatal shot, even though there are a number of homes within three to four hundred feet of the scene and even though there were a number of people in the park throughout the afternoon.

• Investigators failed to retain critical evidence, such as Foster's personal belongings. Instead, his papers, his pager, and other personal effects were returned to the White House the day after his death—and before they could be analyzed by police or the FBI.

• Foster's clothes were sent to the FBI for analysis. The FBI found carpet fibers on his suit jacket, shirt, pants, tie, belt, underwear, socks, and shoes. The fibers were of various colors—white, gray, tan, red, green, and blue. He also had blond hairs all over his clothes and his body; whose blond hairs were they? And why would he have carpet fibers on both his outer clothes and his inner clothes? Did he roll around on a carpet while still alive? Did someone roll his body around on a carpet while searching his body, looking for hidden documents or hidden microphones or who knows what else? Was his body rolled up *inside* a carpet for transport to the park? Amazingly, the FBI made no attempt to match those fibers to carpets at the White House, or in Foster's home, or anyplace else—nor did the FBI examine Foster's car to see if any matching fibers could be found in the driver's seat (indicating he drove himself to the park) or, more ominously, in the trunk.

• Investigators found no trace of soil on Foster's shoes, even though he supposedly walked seven hundred feet from the parking lot to the place where he allegedly killed himself. Foster's glasses were found nineteen feet away from his head. Investigators theorized the glasses were thrown by the violent recoil of his head from the force of the gunshot, but that is physically impossible—especially given the fact that there are no other signs of a violent reaction to the gunshot (his body was neatly laid out, and the gun was still in his hand). The lack of soil on the shoes and the location of the glasses are not consistent with a suicide theory, but they could easily be explained by a theory in which Foster's body is physically carried to the park (say, by two men) and the glasses are thrown or accidentally dropped during transport.

• Statements were taken from several witnesses who were in the park shortly before the body was discovered. One couple parked in the space next to Foster's Honda observed two men—one an unkempt, long-haired, blond man who stood at the front of Foster's car, with the hood of the vehicle raised; the other, a dark-haired, possibly shirtless man who sat behind the wheel of Foster's car. When the couple was shown how their statement was written up by park police investigator Cheryl Braun, they were shocked by what they read. The report stated that the witnesses had observed not one car (Foster's) but *three* cars—Foster's, plus a second car with a shirtless man who drove away, plus a third car that pulled in later, with a long-haired driver who raised his hood, then took a walk, then left. It was not at all what the witnesses said they saw. Instead of an ominous picture of two men who were bothering Foster's car and may have been his killers, we have an extraneous story of two irrelevant motorists who happen to wander into the parking lot! The park police let the erroneous Braun report stand uncorrected and refuse to make Officer Braun available for comment. The Fiske report makes no mention of the witness statements, and neither the Fiske nor Starr investigations has ever contacted these witnesses.[5]

Tuesday evening and night, July 20, 1993

According to the July 21 White House press briefing, the White House is first notified of Foster's death at 8:30 P.M. That notification is received by Lt. Woltz, a uniformed Secret Service officer, from Lt. Gavin of the park police. Unaccountably, Woltz does not relay the information to any member of the Clinton administration until 9:15, while President Clinton is being interviewed on the *Larry King Live* broadcast on CNN.

This timeline does not jibe with the testimony of park police officers. Investigator Cheryl Braun, for example, claims she found Foster's White House I.D. in his car at about 7:00 P.M. She immediately relayed a message to Lt. Gavin through another officer; when she found the message had not gotten through, she called Gavin personally at about 7:30, advising him that the White House should be informed.

But Gavin claims it was another park police investigator, John Rolla, who informed him of finding Foster's White House I.D. Rolla explicitly claims he found the I.D. in Foster's car *after* the body was removed from the scene, at about 8:45. This is clearly contradictory, since it places the identification of Foster as a White House official at a point in time *after* the White House says it was informed of Foster's death! And John Rolla has other credibility problems. The phone number of a Secret Service officer was found in his notebook, and immediately following that entry was the address and phone number of—are you ready for this?—none other than Vince Foster! When questioned in his deposition as to why he had been carrying Foster's address and number around with him,

Rolla became nervous and defensive, claiming he had no idea how those entries got into his notebook.

Of course, none of these confused official timelines jibes with the account of the Helen Dickey phone call, which probably took place at about 5:30 or 6:00 P.M. It also seems that the White House timeline is contrived to make it appear that the White House was not notified of Foster's death until Clinton was on the air with Larry King. One wonders: If the nanny knew Foster was dead, how could the president *not* have been informed?

According to the White House timeline, chief of staff Mack McLarty notifies Hillary Rodham Clinton of Foster's death at 9:40 P.M. (she is in Little Rock). After Hillary is notified, three White House officials enter Foster's office and begin rummaging through Foster's desk and file cabinets. The three officials are White House counsel Bernard Nussbaum, Hillary's chief of staff, Maggie Williams, and special assistant to the president Patsy Thomasson (who ran the bond business of Clinton crony and convicted cocaine distributor Dan Lasater while Lasater was in prison for more than two years). They remove files related to Whitewater and the Clinton's personal finances. A handwritten loose-leaf diary belonging to Foster is also removed and hidden from investigators for almost two years by Nussbaum; in April 1995, over a year after his resignation from the White House, he turns a photocopy of the diary over to the Starr investigation.

The rummaging in the dead man's office continues long into the night, and what emerges from both public testimony and the "deep throat" sources of Ruddy and Nichols is a picture of a White House staff that was more panic-stricken than grief-stricken following the death of Vince Foster. Ruddy, in a March 9, 1994, story in the *New York Post,* states that three separate White House sources describe Clinton aides scrambling "like cats and dogs" to get into Foster's safe.[6]

In addition to cleaning out Foster's desk and file cabinets, Nussbaum is obsessed with obtaining the combination to Foster's safe, according to Chris Ruddy. Because Foster has taken the extraordinary step of not sharing the combination with anyone, not even his secretary, it is a matter of hours before the combination can be located (probably through the Office of Administration, which Patsy Thomasson runs). When it is finally opened, sometime before dawn, a number of documents are removed and turned over to David Kendall, Bill and Hillary's personal attorney; the safe is opened again the following afternoon and more documents are removed. The frenzied scramble to open the safe—where the most sensitive and politically damaging documents are likely to be stored—underscores the appearance that the White House staff are engaged in a cover-up—which is a felony called obstruction of justice.[7]

One of the ironies of the situation is that Hillary Rodham Clinton and Bernard Nussbaum first met when both were serving as Democratic legal aides for the Senate Watergate hearings in the summer of 1973. Perhaps their Watergate experience taught them an important lesson: *Don't be a dope like Nixon! Send everything to the shredders!*

In September 1993, less than two months after Foster's death, Larry Nichols comes on *The Michael Reagan Talk Show* and reveals that Nussbaum, Thomasson, and Williams broke into Foster's office and removed documents. Not only does the White House deny Nichols's claim, but Nussbaum appears on ABC's *This Week with David Brinkley* and on CNN, calling Larry Nichols a liar and a discredited conspiracy nut. Yet the story refuses to go away. Finally, in December 1993, the White House admits that, yes, aides did enter Foster's office, and yes, papers were removed, and yes, some of those papers did pertain to the Whitewater scandal, and yes, the White House did lock out the Justice Department investigators so that they could not examine Foster's office. By the time Nussbaum resigns in March 1994, it is clear who has been telling the truth all along.[8]

When the documents are finally turned over to investigators (under an extraordinary subpoena, negotiated by Nussbaum, that shields the papers from public scrutiny), we can only wonder if these are the same papers that were in Foster's office. Have some been shredded? Have some been doctored? Have some been faked? Important evidence from Foster's office—such as his appointment book and the index to all his files—simply vanished that night and has not been seen since. If the Clinton White House had nothing to hide, it could have demonstrated that fact by simply leaving everything intact, exactly as Vince Foster left it, until investigators had completed their task. Instead, Nussbaum & Co. went into the office of a possible homicide victim and tampered with a secondary crime scene, removing documents and obliterating evidence in a case with vast political implications. Every action taken by the White House during the long, frenzied, mad-scramble night of Foster's death absolutely screams cover-up.

Wednesday, July 21, 1993

White House officials publicly express shock and astonishment over Vince Foster's (apparent) suicide, and everyone—including President Clinton—says that Foster had not behaved unusually and no one suspected that Foster was depressed or despondent. Clinton refers to him as "the Rock of Gibraltar." Foster's Rose Law Firm partner Web Hubbell tells the FBI, "I did not notice Foster acting differently in the days or weeks before his death." Clinton, Hubbell, and others in the White House will later change their stories and describe Foster as being very "down" and "depressed" shortly before his death.[9]

Throughout the day, investigators from the park police and the Justice Department are given only restricted access to Foster's White House office. Investigators are allowed to view only documents that have been prescreened by Nussbaum. One of the reasons cited is "national security." This conflicts with the fact that Patsy Thomasson, who spent the night pawing through Foster's files alongside Nussbaum and Maggie Williams, had not received a security clearance (probably in part because of her close ties to cocaine distributor Dan Lasater) and was only able to work in the White House on a temporary pass. Nussbaum insists on being present when park police investigators question any member of the White House.

Thursday, July 22, 1993

Hillary Rodham Clinton is at her mother's home in Little Rock, where she has been since before Foster's death. During the first forty-three hours after Vince Foster's death, Hillary engages in seventeen phone conversations with Susan Thomases, a New York attorney and unpaid consultant to the Clintons. Considerable speculation centers around a flurry of phone calls involving the first lady, leading up to the time the Justice Department tries to gain access to Foster's office to conduct the investigation. The appearance that Mrs. Clinton was orchestrating a "stonewall" of the Justice probe seems unavoidable.

Here are the bare-bone facts: Late Wednesday, Bernard Nussbaum had made an agreement with deputy attorney general Phillip

B. Heymann to allow the Justice Department access to Foster's office. Now, early Thursday morning, Maggie Williams arrives early and confers with Nussbaum. After they talk, Williams calls Mrs. Clinton in Little Rock at 7:44 A.M., Washington time. According to phone logs, they speak for seven minutes. At 7:58 A.M., Hillary calls Susan Thomases in Washington. That conversation lasts three minutes. Just one minute later, Susan Thomases pages Nussbaum at the White House—bang-bang-bang, three calls in rapid succession. Then, minutes later, Nussbaum unilaterally reneges on the agreement with Heymann and the Justice Department, and he bars the door to Foster's office. Yet everyone involved denies that Hillary sent instructions to Nussbaum (via Thomases) to keep investigators out of Vince's office. Instead, we are supposed to believe that this flurry of phone calls was nothing but a lot of hearts and flowers and fond memories of good ol' Vince.

Monday afternoon, July 26, 1993

Almost a week after Foster's death, associate counsel Steve Neuwirth is inspecting Vince Foster's briefcase. He turns it upside-down, and a lot of little pieces of paper—fragments of a supposed suicide note—come fluttering out of it. The note has been torn into twenty-seven pieces; a twenty-eighth piece—supposed to contain Foster's signature and possibly a date—is missing. Nussbaum, David Gergen, and President Clinton all examine the note. No one is able adequately to explain why the briefcase, which had been searched and turned upside down several times before, should suddenly be found to contain these note fragments. Significantly, investigators later find no fingerprints anywhere on the note—only an unidentified palm print. It is impossible to tear a piece of paper into twenty-eight pieces without leaving latent prints—unless, perhaps, you are wearing plastic gloves.

As independent homicide expert Vincent Scalice later points out, the note is not a true suicide note because it lacks several ingredients almost always present in a suicide note. The note, says Scalice, "doesn't mention final departure, death, farewell to loved ones, or harm to oneself." Foster does not leave any message of goodbye to his wife of twenty-five years, nor to his three college-age children. The note is nothing more than a laundry list of regrets about working in Washington,

D.C., and concludes, "I was not meant for the job or the spotlight of public life in Washington. Here ruining people is considered sport."

Not long before his death, Foster had told his wife, Lisa, he was considering resignation. She had suggested he make a "resignation list," a list of reasons why he felt he should resign his White House position, in order to clarify his thinking. The twenty-seven-piece "suicide note" reads exactly like such a list.

One of the biggest blows to the depression/suicide theory of Foster's death later comes in October 1995, when three forensic experts hired by the financial newsletter *Strategic Investment* make independent analyses of the twenty-seven-piece note and conclude it is a forgery. The three experts—thirty-five-year veteran NYPD homicide expert Vincent Scalice, Oxford University's Reginald Alton, and forensic and handwriting expert Ronald Rice—compared the note against twelve certified samples of Foster's handwriting, and all three concluded the note could not have been written by Foster. Alton described the note as the work of a "moderate forger, not necessarily a pro, somebody who could forge a check." The panel, according to reporter Stephen Robinson, concluded that the handwriting looked like Foster's, but close examination showed that the letters were not formed in the same way that Foster wrote. "For instance," said Robinson, "Mr. Foster wrote the letter *b* with a single stroke, while the forger used three separate strokes. The forger was unable to recreate Mr. Foster's confident counter-clockwise loops or circles."[10]

Accepting the experts' assertion that the note is a forgery, it is easy to imagine a scenario whereby someone rifling through the papers in Foster's office desk might come upon Foster's handwritten "resignation list" (perhaps in his loose-leaf diary) and use it as a template for tracing a "suicide note." Why was the note torn into twenty-eight pieces? Try it yourself: Tear a sheet of paper into twenty-eight equal pieces and you'll have a bunch of fragments that are larger than a postage stamp, but considerably smaller than a business card—large enough to reassemble into something legible, but with enough tears to partially destroy many individual strokes and loops in the writing. Thus, an amateur forger might tear up the forgery in order to mask any deficiencies in his (or her) work. Why was the twenty-eighth or "signature" piece missing? Perhaps because Foster didn't bother to sign his "resignation list," or maybe because an attempt to forge the signature was so obviously poor that the forger felt it safer to discard the twenty-eighth piece. The forgery explanation provides the only plausible theory as to why the note was torn in pieces.

Tuesday evening, July 27, 1993

The White House turns over the pieces of the note to the park police—thirty hours after the note was first discovered in the briefcase.

THE INVESTIGATIONS

Autopsy and Initial Investigation

A seventy-five-year-old coroner—Dr. James Beyer, deputy chief medical examiner for Northern Virginia—performs the autopsy on Foster's body, declaring the death a suicide. Beyer has previously ruled at least two known homicide cases as suicides. In a 1989 case, Beyer concluded that a man named Tim Easley had killed himself by stabbing himself in the chest, despite obvious defensive wounds on the man's hand. The case was later reopened, and the dead man's girlfriend confessed to the murder. In a 1991 case, Beyer reached a conclusion of suicide in the death of Tommy Burkett, who died from a gunshot to the mouth, much like the Foster case. Dr. Beyer failed to notice the man's broken jaw and torn ear, evidence of a severe struggle. Only when Burkett's family had the body exhumed and examined by an independent expert was the case reopened.

In statements to investigators, Dr. Beyer makes conflicting comments regarding X-rays taken during the autopsy. At one point, he says that X-rays showed a single bullet track through the head, and that there were no bone fragments inside the skull. When he is unable to produce the X-rays for FBI investigators, he says that no X-rays were taken because the X-ray machine was not working at the time of the autopsy.

The Fiske Investigation—June 1994

Special prosecutor Robert B. Fiske Jr. releases his conclusion that "the evidence overwhelmingly supports" a determination of suicide in the Foster case. Fiske is quick to sign onto the "depression theory" as a motive for Foster's "suicide." As evidence, Fiske cites Foster's "obvious" loss of weight. Medical records, however, indicate that Foster actually *gained* weight during his brief stint at the White House, from 194 pounds when he joined the administration to 197 pounds at his autopsy.

The motives Fiske officially lists for the supposed suicide are flimsy and unbelievable: Foster was "deeply depressed" over three critical editorials in the *Wall Street Journal* and by the scandal of the White House travel office.

Other major flaws in the Fiske report include:

- The matter of Foster's death was exempted from the grand jury probe of Whitewater, meaning that no one was interviewed under oath on this issue. Why should this one matter—arguably the most critical Whitewater-related issue of all, since it involved the death of a high government official—be exempted from grand jury scrutiny?
- The Fiske report is riddled with errors regarding the timeline, the crime scene, and witness testimony. The report claims a large pool of blood was found under Foster's head, even though not a single person at the site made any such report. In fact, several witnesses clearly expressed surprise at *not* finding blood on the ground.
- The Fiske report ignores eyewitness reports that there were people at the scene who may well have been involved in transporting Foster's body.
- Fiske never bothered to have maintenance worker Francis Swann (who called 911) identify the "confidential witness," the man in the white van who apparently discovered Foster's body in the park.
- The "confidential witness" claims the FBI badgered him to alter his testimony on important factual matters, including the location of the body.
- The Fiske report claims that the FBI sifted a half ton of soil at the body site, looking for the missing bullet and other evidence; the soil-sifting never took place.

The Starr Investigation

On August 4, 1994, Robert Fiske's reappointment as special prosecutor is turned down by a three-judge panel. His replacement is Kenneth

W. Starr, a Washington attorney who served as solicitor general under President Bush and a judge on the U.S. Court of Appeals in Washington, and who has been mentioned on more than one short list of potential Supreme Court nominees. The rebirth of the Whitewater probe under Starr begins on a promising note. Starr reopens the Foster case and assigns assistant U.S. attorney Miquel Rodriguez, a highly respected, aggressive prosecutor, to lead the grand jury probe. But the investigation quickly runs into trouble.

Rodriguez's immediate superior is a staunchly partisan Democrat named Mark Tuohey IV, whom Starr has retained from the Fiske team in order to head off charges that the Starr probe is a Republican witch-hunt. Tuohey immediately begins reining Rodriguez in and preventing him from doing his job. Rodriguez is ordered early on to bring in a conclusion of suicide. He is prevented from bringing in outside experts to review inconsistencies and errors in the FBI's investigation. Evidence that the White House knew of Foster's death earlier than admitted is disallowed. Tuohey insists Clinton administration and park police witnesses be allowed to preview evidence before they testify, which Rodriguez fears would enable witnesses to alter and rehearse their testimony. Unwilling to participate in another Fiske-style cover-up, Rodriguez resigns in disgust.[11]

Despite these serious problems, Starr's grand jury probe does turn up some startling revelations. For example, paramedic George Gonzalez takes the stand and makes the shocking statement that *crime scene workers misrepresented the location of the body "for jurisdictional purposes."* What this may mean is that the site of the body was represented in such a way as to make sure that the park police—a less qualified police force, and one that is under the executive branch of the federal government—would have jurisdiction in the case. After Gonzalez and the other paramedics testify before the grand jury, the park police are brought in to testify. Starr sternly reminds them of the seriousness of perjury, then begins to question them. Incredibly, the park police officers refuse to answer, invoking their Fifth Amendment right against self-incrimination! Question: What could the Park Police officers have done in the course of investigating the Foster death that would expose them to criminal jeopardy?

We'll come back to that question in a moment.

The Dog Ate My Evidence

Remember the old school-days excuse, "The dog ate my homework"? Well, that same pooch has been chowing down on the evidence in the Vince Foster case. Let's review a list of some of the evidence that has mysteriously (and conveniently) vanished:

• *Foster's appointment book*—which could have provided clues to his whereabouts during the five missing hours when he died—has never been found.

• *The index of all of Foster's files*, maintained by his executive assistant, Deborah Gorham, was mysteriously missing after Bernard Nussbaum, Patsy Thomasson, and Maggie Williams went through Foster's papers. Without this index, there is no way investigators can know whether all the files from Foster's office have been properly produced or not.

• *The index of all data files* on Foster's computer on the day of his death was inexplicably erased.

• *The White House telephone logs* for the day of Vince Foster's death and Helen Dickey's frantic phone call are gone. After Larry Nichols broke the Helen Dickey story on my show, Ambrose Evans-Pritchard contacted the White House, asking for a copy of Helen Dickey's phone logs. He was told that there was a computer glitch that day and Dickey's phone logs—and only hers—were erased. Later, however, the story changed. Now the White House says that *all* the White House phone logs for that day were accidentally erased. Logs exist for every day prior and every day afterwards, but not for July 20, 1993.

• *The bullet* that supposedly killed Foster has never been found, despite numerous exhaustive searches of the area—and despite the fact that twelve bullets that do *not* match the Foster gun *were* found.

• *The 35mm photos* of the Fort Marcy Park crime scene were "underexposed" by the FBI lab. (They should have just taken the film to Kmart.) All the crucial photos showing the entire body, the surroundings, the landmarks—in short, every piece of photographic evidence that would conclusively show exactly where the body was located—were destroyed. Only thirteen Polaroid closeups of various parts of the body still exist. (Seven crime scene Polaroids taken by a park police officer have also been lost.) No photos have been officially released, though one Polaroid purporting to show the gun in Foster's hand, resting on a background of dense foliage, was leaked to ABC News. The crime scene photos would have resolved the mystery of exactly where Foster's body was found (see the next item).

• *The "first cannon"* has been removed. There were two cannons in Fort Marcy Park on July 20, 1993. According to Chris Ruddy, the "confidential witness" who first found the body, as well as emergency personnel and park employees who were on the scene, claim the body was located about fifty feet west of the so-called "first cannon," or south cannon. The Fiske report claims Foster's body was located immediately in front of the "second cannon," or north cannon. Witnesses, however, describe the site of Foster's body as being a densely foliated berm or hill; the site described in the Fiske report has long been a bare, shaded patch of ground, veined by exposed tree roots. For reasons that have never been explained, the "first cannon," where Foster was most likely found, was removed by the park service in late 1994, leaving only metal anchor fittings in the ground to mark the site.

• *The X-rays* of Foster's body, supposedly taken at the autopsy, are either lost or never were taken. The coroner in the case referred to X-ray evidence in his report, yet he now claims the X-ray machine was broken at the time.

• *Foster's briefcase* vanished from his car in the parking lot, where it was seen by four independent witnesses. Those witnesses were a passerby who was in the parking lot at about 4:30, the "confidential witness" (the driver of the white van) who first discovered the body, and emergency workers George Gonzalez and Todd Hall. Gonzalez not only saw but handled and opened the briefcase, finding it empty, when he was looking for the dead man's I.D. Four park police, however, claim there was no briefcase in the car. A few days later, that briefcase (or one *exactly* identical to it) showed up in Vince Foster's office with the infamous twenty-seven-piece note inside.

> • *Foster's fingerprints* are missing. That's right. The government claims it has no set of fingerprints for Vince Foster, even though he held a top-level security clearance and worked in the White House!

UNANSWERED QUESTIONS

Where Did Foster Die?

Let's return for a moment to the matter of Helen Dickey's phone call. Remember that troopers Perry and Patterson and former state police head Lynn Davis concur in pegging the time of the call at between 5:30 and 7:00 P.M., Washington time—long before the White House claims to have been notified. Larry Nichols broke the story on my show in early 1994, and for months afterward, he and I talked about it on the air while no one else would touch it. Even Ambrose Evans-Pritchard and Chris Ruddy, who had gone public with a lot of Larry's information in the past, thought Larry was out to lunch on the Helen Dickey story.

But after the troopers came forward and gave sworn affidavits in early 1995, first Ambrose, then Ruddy, began printing the Helen Dickey story. Sworn affidavits, of course, expose the person giving testimony to perjury charges if those claims are later shown to be false. And what do these affidavits contain besides a timeline that spells trouble for the White House? Perry's sworn affidavit, which has been publicly released by Larry Nichols, says that Helen Dickey advised him that Vince Foster "had gotten off work and had gone out to his car in the parking lot [of the White House] and had shot himself in the head."

Let me underscore that: Helen Dickey told Roger Perry that Foster had killed himself *in his car.* For months, that assertion went uncorroborated. And then came another bombshell: the release of a Secret Service memo, written the night of Foster's death. That memo was obtained during the Fiske probe, but the Fiske investigators totally ignored it. Then, in early 1995, the Senate Banking Committee released the memo, which contains the official version of how the White House was notified by the park police of Vince Foster's death. The memo does not say Foster was found dead near a cannon in the park. *It says that Vincent*

Foster was found dead in his car. The memo, dated 22:01 (10:01 P.M.) on July 20, 1993, read in part:

> On the evening of 7/20/93, unknown time, US Park Police discovered the body of Vincent Foster in his car. The car was parked in the Ft. Marcy area of VA near the GW Parkway. Mr. Foster apparently died of a self-inflicted gunshot wound to the head. A .38 cal. revolver was found in the car.

Notice that the memo doesn't say Foster was found dead in his car *in Fort Marcy Park*; it says he was found in *the Fort Marcy area* of Virginia, near the George Washington Parkway. This is an important point, especially in view of paramedic George Gonzalez's testimony before Kenneth Starr's grand jury that the position of Foster's body was misrepresented "for jurisdictional purposes." Remember, also, that the park police involved in the investigation of Foster's death then took the Fifth Amendment when questioned about the location of Foster's body!

Could it be that Foster's body was found near the location of historic Fort Marcy—but outside the actual grounds of Fort Marcy Park? And could it be that his body was actually found in a place that was outside the legal jurisdiction of the executive branch-controlled park police? And why would anyone want to move the body to a place that is under park police jurisdiction? To keep Virginia state police authorities out of the matter? To keep the FBI out? Did someone—say, someone at the White House—want to insure that the investigation was conducted by a police agency under White House influence and control rather than an independent police agency?

Another interesting fact that may shed light on this issue: During the Starr investigation, lead prosecutor Miquel Rodriguez believed the Helen Dickey call held the key to a possible cover-up in Foster's death, according to Chris Ruddy. By January 1995, Rodriguez had turned up evidence that officers of the park police's special forces (which Ruddy calls "an elite unit with close ties to White House security") was on the scene at Fort Marcy Park by 7:00 P.M.—*before* the Park Police claim Foster had been identified as a White House official. "Rodriguez apparently believed," Ruddy concludes, "the introduction of these elite officers to a crime scene seriously diminished Park Police claims that the death scene did not strike them as unusual, and that the White House was not notified until 8:30 P.M."

How Did Foster Die?

Did Foster die by his own hand—or the hand of another? On my radio show, I've always maintained that I felt Foster probably died by his own hand in his own car—as maintained in the Secret Service memo and in Helen Dickey's phone call. I have never said on the air that I believe Vince Foster was murdered, and I am not saying so now. Obviously, given the evidence, murder is one possibility, but it is not the theory I lean toward.

There is one bit of troubling evidence, however, that is difficult to integrate into a suicide scenario: the powder residue evidence. As Chris Ruddy reported in the *New York Post*, February 10, 1994, the park police have put forward two theories regarding the powder residue problem, and *neither* of these theories fits the evidence. The first theory was that Foster pressed the gun against the back of his mouth and pulled the trigger. The evidence shows it could not have happened that way. If Foster had shoved the gun to the back of his mouth and pulled the trigger, there should be thick deposits of gunpowder in and around the entrance wound, the wound should be seared and soot-rimmed, gunpowder deposits should be found on the tongue, there should be broken or damaged teeth, and there should be blood on the gun barrel. *None of these conditions existed.*

Confronted with this embarrassing information, the park police hastily amended their theory: Foster must have held the gun a few inches *outside* his mouth when he pulled the trigger. But if that was the case, there should be powder deposits and burn marks on Foster's face, particularly around his lips. *There were none.*

How, then, could Foster have received the kind of wound that was found inside his mouth—a small, clean hole, no powder residues or burns inside the mouth or outside, no damaged teeth, no blood on the gun? As Ruddy points out, there is only one way it could have happened: a *silencer.*

Many people think of silencers as fictional, James Bond gadgets that cause guns to go *fwip!* in the movies—but they are very real. In fact they are often used by gun enthusiasts on shooting ranges so they can plink away at targets without losing their hearing. A silencer fits onto a threaded gun barrel, suppressing sound like a car muffler, channeling the hot expanding gases from the fired bullet through a series of baffles that slow and muffle the sound waves. A silencer doesn't literally silence a gun, but it does quiet it down a bit—*and it absorbs recoil and powder residue!* If the wound in Foster's head was made by a gun with a silencer, that would account for everything—the lack of powder residue, the undamaged teeth, the lack of blood on the gun.

The gun found in Foster's hand was not threaded for a silencer. Most important of all, no silencer was found at Fort Marcy Park, and Foster could hardly shoot himself in the head, then dispose of the silencer before dying! One scenario that fits the silencer theory is that Foster was shot in the mouth with a silenced gun *after* he was already dead—a different gun, not the "drop gun" police found in his hand. The "drop gun" would then have been held in Foster's dead hands and discharged *away* from Foster in order to produce the powder burns on his fingers. Since the bullet that passed through Foster's head was never found, there is no evidence that the .38 revolver in his hand actually fired the bullet that entered and exited Foster's head. We have only the *assumption* that the gun in Foster's hand fired the fatal shot, based solely on the fact that it was found in Foster's hand. The lack of powder residues in Foster's mouth and on his face would seem to be conclusive evidence that the .38 revolver was *not* the gun that shot him in the mouth.

Why Did Foster Die?

Taking everything we know about the death of Vince Foster, here are a few possible scenarios to explain why he died. Remember, these are speculations, not certainties:

Theory No. 1: Travelgate and the mean old **Wall Street Journal.** This is one of the official White House versions. According to this scenario, Foster was depressed because of a number of *Wall Street Journal* editorials that criticized his handling of the White House travel office. This theory is bolstered by the concluding lines in the twenty-seven-piece so-called "suicide note" found in Foster's briefcase: "The WSJ editors lie without consequence. I was not meant for the job or the spotlight of public life in Washington. Here ruining people is considered a sport." This theory is seriously undermined, however, by logic (would a highly successful attorney really kill himself over a few newspaper editorials?) and by the fact that a panel of independent experts now find the "suicide note" to be a forgery.

Theory No. 2: Whitewater and conscience. According to this scenario, Foster—who was deeply involved in sorting through and making nonincriminating sense out of the Clinton's Whitewater mess—found himself in a tragic unresolvable conflict of near-Shakespearean proportions. Being a perfectionist with high ethical principles (according to some), he was caught between wanting to do what is ethically, morally and legally right and wanting to remain loyal to his longtime friends, Bill and Hillary Clinton. Through their Whitewater dealings, they had put him in a position where he could not be loyal and ethical at the same time—so he resolved the dilemma with a bullet.

Theory No. 3: Vince knew too much. Some would say it's a case of "Dead men tell no tales." Vince Foster was involved in every document regarding Whitewater and the tangled mess of the Clintons' personal finances. And there is also a mysterious connection between Vince Foster and the National Security Agency (NSA). In closed-door deposition proceedings on June 26, 1995, Foster's executive assistant, Deborah Gorham, made the startling disclosure that NSA binders were kept in Vince Foster's safe. One question I have asked repeatedly on my show is, "What was Vince Foster doing with NSA material in his safe?"

So far, there is no answer to the question, but Larry Nichols broke a story on my show that adds one more tantalizing piece to the puzzle. In July 1993, about a week after Vince Foster died, Larry received a call from a senior vice president for Systematics, a bank data processing company based in Little Rock. "Could Vince Foster have been killed because of what we've been working on?" the man asked.

"Depends on what you've been working on," said Larry. "Let's talk."

The Systematics exec arrived later, along with an attorney from the Rose Law Firm. They told the following story, and Larry has in his possession their sworn affidavits that confirm this story:

Several months earlier, Vince Foster and Web Hubbell came to this senior vice president at Systematics and asked him to run printouts on two foreign bank accounts. "I can't do that," the v.p. said. "That's against the law." At that point, Foster and Hubbell pulled out two I.D.s, showing that they worked for the National Security Agency. Foster said, "It's okay, we're working with the NSA and we're conducting a test." The questions raised by this story include: Why were Foster and Hubbell asking Systematics to run foreign bank accounts? Why were they flashing NSA badges? What does Web Hubbell know that he's not saying?

Foster's intelligence-community connections provide intriguing hints of potential motives for either suicide or murder—but only hints. So far, this theory is built less on answers than on questions. I have little doubt, however, that these are the *right* questions to ask if we want to get to the bottom of the Foster matter.

Theory No. 4: The Hillary affair. According to this scenario, Foster learned just an hour before leaving the White House that the *Washington Times* was planning to run a major story on his rumored long-standing affair with First Lady Hillary Rodham Clinton. According to this theory, he became despondent and either went to Fort Marcy Park and killed himself (a theory that clearly does not fit the evidence) or killed himself at another location (such as the "safe house" near the park) and was moved there. In either case, his death pushed the Hillary story off the *Times* agenda, and the paper never ran the story. An account of an affair between Foster and Mrs. Clinton was carried, however, in a January 1994 *American Spectator* piece by David Brock. The source of the story: Two Arkansas state troopers on the security detail at the governor's mansion in Little Rock, Larry Patterson and Roger Perry. "It was common knowledge around the mansion that Hillary and Vince were having an affair," Patterson told Brock.

Theory No. 5: Remorse over Waco. Foster's wife, Lisa, is quoted in FBI documents as saying that he felt responsible for the deaths at the Branch Davidian compound. Foster's role in that debacle, however, seems to have been indirect. This theory sounds like a stretch of the imagination.

Theory No. 6: Vince Foster was a spy. James R. Norman was fired from his position as senior editor of *Forbes* for his pursuit of a Foster story that *Forbes* refused to print. After the story was spiked by *Forbes*,

Norman published his piece, "Fostergate," in *Media Bypass,* with a follow-up called "Fostergate II."

According to Norman, Vince Foster discovered shortly before his death that he was under investigation by the CIA for espionage. Foster supposedly had a number of secret Swiss bank accounts, where money was deposited by the State of Israel in exchange for U.S. state secrets. Inquiring into one of those accounts, located at the Banca Della Svizzera Italiana in Chiasso, Switzerland, Foster was dismayed to find that someone had used his secret authorization code to withdraw the entire $2.73 million he had on deposit. Ominously, the money was moved to (surprise!) the U.S. Treasury. According to Norman, secrets Foster sold to Israel may even include "the top-level codes by which the president identifies himself when ordering military action, including the use of nuclear weapons."

The Norman scenario is a sprawling web of intrigue regarding a spy-master computer program called PROMIS, developed in the 1980s by the INSLAW corporation; international intrigue involving the CIA and the NSA; and money laundering through an Arkansas bank data processing firm called Systematics. Many facets of the Norman scenario intersect, more or less, with well-established facts, such as Ambrose Evans-Pritchard's discovery that Foster made a number of overnight round trips to Switzerland without his wife's knowledge during the last year of his life; the revelation by Foster's secretary that Foster possessed top-secret NSA files; the 1980s arms- and drug-running through the Mena airport; and Larry Nichols's story about Foster and Hubbell flashing NSA badges at Systematics.

But I'm convinced the story is bogus. I believe James Norman is well-intentioned—he believes every word of his story—but I think he's been sold a bill of goods.

For one thing, the bulk of Norman's scenario is based on information from a character who is regarded by knowledgeable people as a yarn-spinning, woman-chasing CIA-wannabe who tells incredible stories in order to make a big impression. Ambrose Evans-Pritchard calls the espionage suggestion "far-fetched" and "not consistent" with what he knows of Foster's character. Christopher Ruddy dismisses Norman's account on the basis that it would be the FBI, not the CIA, that would investigate a U.S. government official. And while the Systematics connection in Norman's story superficially seems to connect with Larry Nichols's story about Foster and Hubbell, there is actually a glaring contradiction: If Foster had been integrally connected with money laundering and other covert operations at Systematics since the 1960s, as Norman claims, why did he have to flash I.D. to a senior v.p. at Systematics, and why was this senior v.p. completely unaware of Systematics' ties to the NSA? It doesn't add up.

Larry Nichols says that, while he respects Norman's good intentions, the whole tale is reminiscent of tactics Clinton's people have used in the past. "When I was in the Clinton camp in Arkansas, we used to do it to keep the heat off of Bill," Nichols recalls. "If a reporter started getting too close to Bill's womanizing or campaign contributions or drugs or whatever, we'd dummy up a fantastic story, throw in just enough truth to make it sound plausible, feed it to the reporter and get him to bite on it—then *bam*! Gotcha! We'd easily prove the story was a pack of lies and we'd have the reporter completely discredited before he knew what happened to him. That's why all this crazy, wild stuff about espionage works against those of us who are uncovering the real story and corroborating it with documents, witnesses, affidavits, and depositions."

Nichols, who has produced several videos detailing the case against Bill Clinton & Co., says people keep asking him when he's going to do another tape. "I'm not going to do that anymore," he says, "because there's nothing left to say. There is enough documented proof on the record right now to topple Clinton and all his cronies. The question is: Will Kenneth Starr and Alphonse D'Amato and Jim Leach and the dominant media in this country ever take this proof and do what needs to be done?

"Even after all the evidence that proves Bill Clinton is the most corrupt president in American history, the media and the Congress seem to ignore it. A lot of people are frustrated by that. They want action, and some of them think the answer is to pile on more information. People are starting to fabricate incredible stories, and it's all working against us now. The clear, factual truth—the Secret Service memo, the Helen Dickey timeline, all the contradictions in the evidence at Fort Marcy Park—can end up buried under a pile of fantasies and disinformation. We have to stick to what can be documented. Otherwise Larry Nichols, Mike Reagan, Ambrose, Ruddy, and all the others who have worked so hard to expose the truth will end up whisked to the side with all the conspiracy kooks and nut cases—and Bill Clinton will have won."

Will We Ever Know?

Prior to November 1994, a lot of Republicans wanted to use the Whitewater scandal and the death of Vince Foster as a crowbar to pry Bill Clinton out of office. After the Republican landslide in that month, the party leadership lost its sense of urgency in pursuing the scandal and possible cover-up. Suddenly, the Republicans were confident that the White House could be retaken without using a scandal to blow Clinton out of office. In fact, there seems to have been a cynical strategy among Republican higher-ups to leave a weakened, impotent Clinton in office in order to have an easy election in '96. That strategy is not only immoral—if Bill Clinton is corrupt, we should get to the bottom of it, politics or no politics—it may also prove to be very dumb. He could get reelected; they don't call him "Slick Willy" and "the Comeback Kid" for nothing.

But I think another reason the Republicans have not pursued the Clinton scandals as vigorously as they might have is because these scandals are almost as scary to Republicans as they are to Democrats. Many Republicans are afraid that if you start digging into Whitewater and Vince Foster, you start digging up Republicans as well as Democrats. Here's why.

When you move into the stratospheric realm of political payoffs and deal-making, the distinctions between Republicans and Democrats begin to blur. Money flows like water through political campaigns and government operations. You are dealing with transactions in the millions and billions of dollars. That is why today you see Arkansas financier Jackson T. Stephens—a longtime friend of Jimmy Carter, a prominent client of the Rose Law firm, a longtime friend and supporter of Bill Clinton—taking a position as co-chair of Bob Dole's finance committee. Money moves where the power is, and it will leapfrog party lines and ideological lines to get there.

One Clinton scandal that scares the pants off of Republicans is Mena, Arkansas. As part of the secret Iran-Contra operation during my father's administration, the Mena airport in rural southwestern Arkansas served as a repair and refueling site for planes running arms to the anticommunist Contra rebels in Nicaragua. The planes didn't come back empty; they came loaded with cocaine destined for American streets—and they came in under the cover of a national security clearance, so there was no customs check. There is evidence that Bill Clinton knew all about it—and benefitted from it.

Terry Reed is a pilot who trained Contra rebel pilots in Arkansas during the 1980s, and who brought forward many of the charges of drug-running through Mena. He has been a guest on my show and has written a book about Mena called *Compromised*. In a civil lawsuit filed in federal court in Arkansas, Reed charges that Buddy Young, an Arkansas state trooper on then governor Clinton's security detail, conspired to frame him for a crime in order to discredit his accusations of drug-running and money-laundering in Arkansas. One of the star witnesses on Reed's behalf is trooper Larry Patterson—the same Arkansas state trooper who helped confirm the timeline of Helen Dickey's call to trooper Roger Perry. In sworn testimony, under penalty of perjury, trooper Patterson has testified unequivocally that he and then governor Clinton were present during discussions of massive shipments of drugs, money, and guns moving through the Mena airport (when rumors about Mena surfaced briefly during the 1992 presidential campaign, candidate Clinton brushed them off as "bull").[12]

There's no question in my mind that Mena was a checkpoint for billions of dollars' worth of drugs, money, and guns in the 1980s. The question is, were the drugs brought in by rogue pilots, or was the operation sanctioned by the Republican administration and the Democratic governor with, say, a wink and a nod. If it was sanctioned, whose wink and whose nod was it? How high and how deep does the scandal reach?

These are not questions, frankly, that trouble me personally. If anyone in the Reagan administration knowingly allowed government planes to be used to move drugs into America, he should get whatever's coming to him. As for my father, I know Ronald Reagan's character, and I know he would not and could not have given even a tacit go-ahead to such an operation. If any Reagan White House officials were involved in the drug trade through Mena, they did an end-run around the president of the United States—and they should pay.

I don't view the whole Whitewater-Vince Foster scandal the way many of my fellow Republicans do. I don't see it as a way of removing this president or that first lady from the White House. I simply believe the American people are entitled to know the truth. Lies, manipulations, and hidden agendas are the techniques used by Clinton and others to steal the government away from the people. The truth will set us free. We should pursue the truth in the Vince Foster case so that we can know who is truly running our government, how they are running it, and why. We should pursue the truth in order to put politicians on notice that the United States of America will not tolerate high crimes as a way of doing America's political business. We should pursue the truth for the sake of justice, because a man is dead, and his memory deserves a better accounting than the phony White House version of when, where, how, and why he died.

Are the Whitewater and Vince Foster matters really that important? Should we just forget all this sordid scandal-mongering and let the president do his job? Some perspective is in order. I think it's one of those cosmic coincidences that Oliver Stone's *Nixon* was released against a backdrop of all this emerging Whitewater-Foster information. If nothing else, it reminds us of both the similarities and the contrasts between the two scandals. Richard Nixon was forced to resign in disgrace from the highest office in the land over a bungled break-in of which he had no knowledge or participation, in which nothing was taken (the room was messed up a little), and in which the burglars were all caught. Nixon's personal involvement was in the cover-up, not the initial break-in.

According to Whitewater allegations, the Clintons are personally, intimately involved in the whole mess from the get-go. Numerous documents and witnesses suggest a wide-ranging pattern of criminal activity that would have personally involved the Clintons, including drug use, shielding and abetting drug trade, questionable commodities investments (which may have been a way of "laundering" a bribe), major campaign finance irregularities, questionable stock investments, misuse of state funds, the plundering of a taxpayer-insured savings and loan for personal and political gain, Hillary's conflict of interest in legally representing Madison Guaranty—and that's just Arkansas!

Then there is the Paula Jones case. Jones alleges that Clinton exposed himself, made unwanted sexual advances, and made veiled threats of retaliation through her employer if she didn't submit to his advances.

These allegations constitute sexual assault and sexual harassment, and normally carry both criminal and civil penalties. That's serious stuff.

Then the Clintons moved to Washington, where we have Travelgate and the misuse of the FBI; we have a man who died under (at best) mysterious and (at worst) criminal circumstances; we know that crucial documents were removed from the dead man's office, that files are missing to this day, that files were shredded, [13] that a crime scene was interfered with—and to any reasonable person, this is obstruction of justice, open and shut. Compared to all of this, Nixon, Haldeman, and Ehrlichman were choirboys. After all, who died at the Watergate Hotel?

So do I think these matters should be investigated, even after the Clintons leave Washington? Absolutely! Don't you?

The American press has been particularly reluctant to delve into the various Clinton scandals—and the reasons for that reluctance may be more sad than sinister. At the *Washington Post*—the paper most journalists revere as the arbiter of what is newsworthy—publisher Katherine Graham and editorial head Ben Bradlee have both expressed regrets over their role in the "regicide" that toppled Richard Nixon. "Neither," observes Ambrose Evans-Pritchard, "want to see the same thing happen again in their lifetime." Unfortunately, in the effort to salve their consciences, they are propping up a potentially criminal presidency. Is that what the founding fathers gave us the First Amendment for—to place it as a fig-leaf over the naked corruption of our government? I don't think so.

During an appearance on my show, Larry Nichols said, "I've talked to reporters in the press almost every day for months. They admit that something is very screwy about the Vince Foster case, but they are just not interested in talking about it. Just this morning, I said to a reporter, 'But what about this evidence and that evidence?' I could practically hear the guy shrug over the phone. He said, 'Look, everybody knows Foster didn't die in the park, but nobody knows *where* he died and nobody knows *how* he died and nobody knows *why* he died, so let's just go on from here. Nobody's interested in Vince Foster.' Now, that's scary, because the press privately admits that somebody moved the body, and if somebody moved the body, somebody broke the law. A top White House official and close friend of the president and first lady dies, and crimes were committed, and the press doesn't care and is not even interested. What's wrong with this picture?"

Everyone should care what happened to Vince Foster. The press should care. The president and first lady should care. Every decent American should care. If a top White House official like Vince Foster can die without anyone demanding and seeking justice on his behalf, if the system doesn't work even for him, none of us is safe. America has ceased to be America.

As always, if you want to hear the latest breaking news on this story, you'll hear it on my program. Also, check my website on a regular basis, because the Reagan Information Interchange is the exclusive Internet site for the latest news from investigative reporter Christopher Ruddy. Even though Foster's own friends don't seem to care how or why he died, we will continue to seek justice for Vince Foster.

PART 2

THE GOOD OLD U.S. OF A.:

◆

Things That Matter to "We the People"

CHAPTER 7

A Close Call for the Constitution

WHEW! THAT was close!

If you were one of the thousands of *The Michael Reagan Talk Show* listeners who picked up the phone, cranked up the fax machine, dashed off a letter, or personally trekked to your statehouse, then my hat is off to you—

Because *you* safeguarded our freedom. *You* protected the Constitution from one of the greatest threats it has faced in the past 200-plus years.

Most of us just take it for granted that the U.S. Constitution has always been there and always will be. Few people realize that the Constitution was up for grabs in 1995—and virtually the only people who knew about it were my listeners. The government didn't tell you about the danger. The dominant media didn't tell you. Not even the other national radio talk show hosts would tell you, because odds are, they didn't know either. But if you were listening to my show, you not only knew about it, you took action. You *saved* the Constitution of the United States of America from being revised and rewritten—

And destroyed.

If you don't know what I'm talking about, let me clue you in.

THE "CON-CON" CON

In the spring of 1994, Utah Governor Mike Leavitt, a Republican, joined up with Nebraska Governor Ben Nelson, a Democrat, to set in motion a plan to make fundamental changes in our government. They called this plan the "Conference of States." It all began, I believe, with the best of intentions—but to paraphrase the old saying, "the superhighway to hell is paved with good intentions." Here's what happened:

Like so many governors across this great and wonderful land we call the good old U.S. of A., Governors Leavitt and Nelson were frustrated with the dictatorial, high-handed, and blatantly unconstitutional way our federal government has been operating for decades. They were justifiably upset over perpetually unbalanced federal budgets, over federal trampling of states' rights, and especially over so-called "unfunded mandates," whereby Washington, D.C., forced states to pay for federally-decreed programs and benefits. For much too long, the state-federal relationship has been out of balance, and federal power and intrusiveness has been excessive and totally in violation of the Tenth Amendment to the Constitution.

So, in cooperation with the Council of State Governments, the National Governors' Association, and the U.S. Advisory Commission on Intergovernmental Relations, Leavitt and Nelson masterminded and force-fed a revolutionary attempt to reinvent American government. They proposed a "Conference of States," which would draft major changes in the U.S. Constitution—changes that (they hoped!) would limit the power and intrusiveness of the federal government. According to the Leavitt-Nelson plan, the Conference of States would:

- Be a deliberative body made up of appointed delegates (seven from each state, appointed by the state legislatures), authorized by formal resolutions of a simple majority of the fifty states (twenty-six states would comprise a quorum).
- Elect its own officers, form committees, make its own rules, and set its own agenda.
- Adopt amendments to the Constitution by super-majority (thirty-four out of fifty states).
- Convene in late 1995, preferably in an historic city such as Philadelphia.

In other words, the Conference of States would be a *constitutional convention.* In his early speeches and pronouncements on the Conference of States, Mike Leavitt referred to it as exactly that, a "con-con" or a "constitutional convention." Soon, he began to catch heat for his ideas. As one Utah state representative put it, "Mike got all wild and weird on us. . . . When he talked about that constitutional convention stuff, he made a lot of [people] really angry."[1] Recognizing he had made a tactical and public relations blunder by using the term "constitutional convention," Leavitt quickly back-pedaled on his "con-con" language—but he continued full-speed ahead with the "con-con" concept.

There are two ways of changing the U.S. Constitution, according to the provisions of Article V: An amendment may be proposed (1) by a two-thirds vote of both houses of Congress, or (2) by a constitutional convention called by Congress on the application of the legislatures of two-thirds of the states. Proposed amendments become part of the Constitution when ratified by three-fourths of the state legislatures. Since the addition of the Bill of Rights, our Constitution has been amended seventeen times. The last time it was amended was on May 7, 1992, when the Twenty-seventh Amendment—an amendment first proposed in 1789 by James Madison!—became law, imposing a ban on midterm congressional pay raises. Every time we have changed our Constitution, we have chosen the first path—the slow, deliberative, reflective process whereby an amendment is first proposed by a super-majority in both houses of Congress, then ratified by an ultra-super-majority in the state legislatures.

For more than two centuries, citizens and legislators have wisely resisted the temptation to take the second, more dangerous path—calling a constitutional convention. They have properly understood the danger: Once you call a constitutional convention, literally *anything* can happen. The entire Constitution is up for grabs. No one can limit or control the process. No one can keep special interest groups or liberal insurgents from moving against portions of the Constitution they don't like.

I know there are people in America who, perhaps with the best of intentions, would like to change the Constitution. They think that if they held a constitutional convention and didn't tell anybody about it, only the "good guys" would show up. That's a fantasy, not reality. Once you open that door and the "bad guys" start mobbing your convention, there's no way to bar the door and keep them out. You are in for a free-for-all.

Remember, each state would send only seven delegates to the convention—and where would those delegates come from? Would they be appointed by the governors of the states? By the leader of the state legislature? Would these delegates be selected from among special interest organizations such as NOW, the ACLU, the NEA, big labor, the Rainbow Coalition, People for the American Way, liberal think tanks, or the Hollywood left?

There might be delegates who think it's time do away with gun ownership in America. There might be delegates who think it's a good idea for the government to be able to search our homes and listen to our phone conversations and monitor computer traffic on the Internet. There might be delegates who would like to insert special rights for certain groups, certain forms of behavior, and certain sexual orientations. There might be delegates who would like to insert freedom *from* religion into the First Amendment in place of freedom *of* religion. There might even be delegates who think radio talk-show hosts (and all their "right-wing wacko" callers) have too much freedom of speech!

What Governors Mike Leavitt and Ben Nelson have done is challenge more than two centuries of constitutional wisdom. Perhaps with the best of intentions—but with the worst possible constitutional judgment—they set in motion a process that could have resulted in the altering or even the outright repeal of many of our most basic freedoms—our First Amendment freedom of speech, our Second Amendment freedom to keep and bear arms, and our Fourth Amendment protection against unreasonable searches and seizures. Many political and social forces in our nation today would love nothing better than to strip these freedoms out of our Constitution.

What made the Conference of States movement especially dangerous was that no one in the various states was aware that these resolutions were being proposed and passed at the state level! *It was all a big secret!* To me, anything that has to be put over on the country by stealth and secrecy—no matter how well-intentioned—is a con job, pure and simple. I don't like to be conned, and I bet you don't either. Yet, for many months, the Conference of States movement proceeded quietly through statehouse after statehouse—and you didn't know, I didn't know, nobody knew that a "con-con" movement was rumbling through the system like a steamroller.

In February 1995, my friends Karen Mazzarella and Gary Stewart of the grassroots organization Speak Out America faxed me the detailed game plan of the Conference of States. Karen and Gary had sent me a lot of quality information over the years, usually in the form of brisk, focused, one- or two-page faxes. This fax was twenty-five pages long. I read every page, highlighting the scariest parts with my yellow marker. I saw what the conference planners were up to—including changes to the Fifth, Tenth, and Fourteenth Amendments—and I was stunned. There was no public debate, no media scrutiny. All this was going on secretly and clandestinely, right under all our noses.

When I began talking about the Conference of States on my radio show, it had already been passed in eleven states and was being considered in dozens more. Not a single state had yet said no to the Conference of States. I went state by state, resolution by resolution, and I gave out the bill numbers, phone numbers, and fax numbers so that people could call their legislators. I had both Governor Leavitt and Governor Nelson on the show to explain their side of the issue—and we had a cordial, informative dialogue. Soon a lot of people were talking about it—and doing something about it. Suddenly, the roaring, "unstoppable" engine of the Conference of States began to sputter, cough, and die. After we began shining a spotlight on the Conference of States, only three more states passed the resolution—and *twenty-eight states* defeated it (fifteen by vote, thirteen by adjournment)!

As it became clear that the Conference of States drive was faltering, proponents of the movement—including Governor Leavitt himself!—began to panic. They blamed militias, patriot movements, and assorted "right-wing nuts" for the defeat. The dominant media—which claims to be the chief defender of the First Amendment in this country—jumped on board to defend this elitist raid on the Constitution and to attack the opponents of the Conference of States. One *Wall Street Journal* headline was typical: "States Postpone Meeting Opposed by Militia Network." (This was, of course, after the Oklahoma City bombing, so it was fashionable and politically correct to blame the militias for anything and everything that was supposedly going wrong in America.)

But as one of my callers, Debbie from Portland, Oregon, said on my show, "These people owe me an apology. I am not a member of any militia, and when I was down at the statehouse in Salem, opposing the

Conference of States measure, most of the people with me were business owners, attorneys—even a judge. The opponents of the Conference of States are average, rational, concerned citizens—not gun nuts or extremists." And Debbie is exactly right. The people who phoned and faxed and showed up at legislative hearings were not, by and large, people from the fringes. They were mainstream Americans who cared about their country and their Constitution. They were grandmothers and grandfathers, parents and teachers, veterans and students, employers and employees. These were not people in camouflage gear you'd meet out in the woods someplace. The collective wisdom of mainstream America stopped the Conference of States.

THE 600-POUND GORILLA

If you compare the Conference of States movement of 1995 with the original Constitutional Convention of 1787 (which gave us our Constitution), you'll find some very interesting parallels—and one big contrast. First the contrast: The two "con-con" movements originated in completely opposite problems. Today, the federal government is intrusive, excessive, intimidating, and totally in the face of every state and every taxpayer. Washington, D.C., arrogantly tramples the rights so clearly given to the states and to the people in the Tenth Amendment. The federal government is like the 600-pound gorilla of the old joke: It does whatever it wants, wherever it wants to.

The situation that gave rise to the "con-con" of 1787 was the opposite extreme. In those days, America was loosely bound together by a weak document called the Articles of Confederation, which gave the states so much individual power that there was hardly any central government at all! The country had no national chief executive, no national judiciary—and to amend the Articles of Confederation, you had to have the unanimous approval of all the states. As a result, the country was on the brink of anarchy and disunity.

Looking at the history of the original Constitutional Convention of 1787, I discovered that the catalyst for the first "con-con" was a dispute between two states, Virginia and Maryland, over commerce on the Potomac River. There were other problems in America owing to a lack of central government—economic problems caused by a lack of common currency, radical political uprisings such as Shay's Rebellion, and so forth. But the actual trigger event for the Constitutional Convention was the Potomac River issue.

In an effort to resolve the matter, delegates from Virginia and Maryland met together and drafted a compact regarding navigation on—and jurisdiction over—the Potomac. Many of the provisions of that compact are still in force today. The delegates took this agreement back to their separate states for ratification. But in order for the compact to be effective under the Articles of Confederation, all the states had to agree. So the delegates from Virginia and Maryland tried to call a meeting of the states—but only five states showed up. The delegates looked at each other and said, "This isn't going to work—we don't have a quorum." So they set a date for another meeting, and they worked hard to get every state to send delegates to the Annapolis Convention. This led to another meeting with an expanded agenda—a meeting that convened on May 25, 1787, at the Pennsylvania State House in Philadelphia. This time, they had enough delegates on hand to proceed with the organization of a convention. George Washington was elected presiding officer, and it was agreed that the sessions would be—you got it!—*conducted in secret.* Sound familiar?

The delegates of the states met from May to September. In the process, they completely scrapped the original Articles of Confederation and produced a brand-new United States Constitution—undeniably the finest instrument of government ever brought forth on the face of this planet. And it all happened because a "con-con" was called to write a minor revision into the Articles of Confederation to settle a river dispute between two states. The result was good—but the way the process worked should be sobering to us all. No one expected that the existing constitutional document would end up in the trash can when the meeting began—the process just sort of got out of hand!

Could the same thing happen again in the 1990s? You bet! Our Constitution could easily end up like a jump ball at a basketball game— the object of fierce contention between competing special interests. What would emerge from a modern-day "con-con" is anybody's guess, but there is a good likelihood we could see many of our most important freedoms in the trash can, alongside the old Articles of Confederation. We got lucky back in 1787—or I should say, God blessed us back then.

It is amazing that such a rambunctious, out-of-control process actually produced a form of government that is so nearly perfect, yet flexible enough to change and grow with the changing times. If we tried it again today, I doubt we would be so lucky or so blessed.

Now, back to 1787. After the Constitutional Convention had done its job in secret, the American people and the Continental Congress expected the Convention to report its modest revisions to the Articles of Confederation. Instead, it reported to the Continental Congress *a totally new Constitution*. Furthermore, the Convention had done a complete end run around the established procedure for changing the government. While the Articles of Confederation specified that no amendments should be effective until unanimously approved by all thirteen state legislatures, the Philadelphia convention demanded that the new Constitution be adopted by a supermajority formula: Once it was ratified by just nine states, the new Constitution would become the law of the land in *all* the states.

The delegates of the Constitutional Convention knew they were in for a fight from Congress, so they sent a special delegation consisting of congressmen James Madison, Nathaniel Gorham, and Rufus King to New York to placate the expected congressional opposition. The Continental Congress debated the new Constitution and, seeing its authority and influence waning, submitted the new document to the states for action on September 28. It made no recommendation to the states either for or against adoption of the new Constitution. As a result, a great debate raged between those who were for the new Constitution and those who were against. The writings of those who favored the new Constitution— men like Alexander Hamilton, James Madison, and John Jay—were widely published and disseminated, and are known today as the Federalist Papers. The Federalists won the debate, and on December 7, 1787, Delaware became the first state to ratify the Constitution; by September 13, 1788, nine of the thirteen states (a three-fourths supermajority) had ratified it, and the Continental Congress proclaimed the document to be the recognized Constitution of the United States. On May 29, 1790, Rhode Island became the last state to ratify, making it unanimous.

The parallels between the 1787 Constitutional Convention and the Conference of States are troubling. Both operated in secret. Both are designed to reconsider and restructure the balance of power between the states and the federal government. Both are deliberative bodies comprised of delegates appointed by the states. Both are authorized by formal resolutions enacted by a simple majority of the states. Both elect officers and function as distinct quasi governmental entities. Both produce proposals that are ratified by a supermajority of the states. Both ignore and exceed the amendment process clearly spelled out in existing constitutional documents. And here's the rub: Both start out with the potential to completely reinvent government in new and unpredictable ways.

THE AWESOME RISK

The Leavitt-Nelson proposal for a Conference of States does not follow the plan for a constitutional convention as laid out in Article V of the U.S. Constitution. While the Constitution requires that two-thirds of the states apply for a convention, the Leavitt-Nelson plan only requires a 50-plus percent majority. You might think that this means that the Conference of States would have no standing to alter the Constitution, since it does not conform to Article V. *Wrong!* The first Constitutional Convention of 1787 established precedent by completely *ignoring* the rules established for a "con-con" by the Articles of Confederation. Despite the fact that the Articles required a unanimous vote of all states to pass any amendments, the first "con-con" of 1787 completely remolded the government with a simple quorum of 50-plus percent!

The preamble to the Constitution spells out the rationale for ignoring the Articles—a rationale that no doubt would have been cited by the Conference of States as the basis for its own revamping or rewriting of the Constitution: "We the People of the United States, in Order to form a more perfect Union . . . " In other words, we the people are sovereign, and we have the sovereign right to consolidate our power through our state governments in order to reform and reinvent our government! We don't have to follow the dictates of the Constitution; we have the right to come together and make a *brand-new constitution* while disregarding the requirements of the old one! It happened once, in 1787—and it could happen again.

Once the Conference of States was in session it could petition the Congress to confer upon it the status of a constitutional convention—and if the Conference had the backing of a large number of states, the Congress might, as Colorado State Senator Charles Duke said in an interview in *The Michael Reagan Monthly Monitor,* "almost feel obligated to empower a convention" under the terms of Article V. But even if the Congress did not act to empower the Conference of States, there is still a great danger that the Conference could arrogate "con-con" status to itself! As Don Fotheringham observes in the *New American,* "The Conference of the States meets every requirement for a constitutional convention even though it has not been called pursuant to Article V of the Constitution. It would have the legal force of a free people if its proposals were adopted. It would make no difference whether Congress approved or not, since the whole people are superior to all institutions of government and have authority over them."[2]

In case you think this analysis is off-base, you should know that the Congress reaffirmed this principle in a 1935 joint resolution: "The government of the United States is not a concession to the people from someone higher up. It is the creation and the creature of the people themselves as absolute sovereigns." The Constitution itself recognizes that the sovereignty of the people is supreme and absolute, and the government of the United States of America is subordinate in every way to the God-given powers and rights of "We the People." As Senator Weldon Heyburn of Idaho observed on the floor of the Senate in 1911, "When the people of the United States meet in a constitutional convention there is no power to limit their action. They are greater than the Constitution, and they can repeal the provision that limits the right of amendment. They can repeal every section of it because they are the peers of the people who made it."[3]

That is the awesome power—and the awesome risk—inherent in a constitutional convention such as the Conference of States.

TILTED POWER

The irony of this whole situation is that a Conference of States is not only ill-advised, it is totally unnecessary. Yes, the balance of power between the federal government and the states is completely out of whack. Yes, federal intrusion into the business of the states is outrageous and excessive. Yes, the monster that is Washington, D.C., needs to be reined in, chained up, and maybe even horse-whipped. But that doesn't mean we have to change the Constitution. The Constitution is fine just as it is. All we have to do is start abiding by what it already says and the balance will be instantly restored!

When the founding fathers met in 1787 to write a stronger Constitution, giving more power to the federal government, they were very careful to retain *most* governmental power in the states! As James Madison wrote in *The Federalist Papers No. 45,* "The powers delegated by the proposed Constitution to the federal government are few and defined. Those which are to remain in the State governments are numerous and indefinite." And the Tenth Amendment to the Constitution affirmed and officially sealed Madison's viewpoint into the constitutional framework: "The powers not delegated to the United States by the Constitution, nor prohibited by it to the States, are reserved to the States respectively, or to the people." Clearly, the framers of the Constitution did not intend federal and state powers to be balanced, but to be heavily *tilted* in favor of the states and the people!

Thanks to the rogue actions of autocratic presidents, run-amok Congresses, and activist, revisionist Supreme Courts, federal power has gradually, steadily expanded over the years to a point that is far in excess of what the founding fathers envisioned or what the Constitution allows. The Constitution is absolutely, unmistakably clear in the precise number and kinds of powers it grants to the federal government: The Congress has twenty-six sharply defined powers; the president has six; the Supreme Court has three. That's it! Everything else, all other rights and powers, are granted to the states and to the people by the Tenth Amendment!

Let's keep the Constitution we've got. Let's make it a living, breathing document once again. Let's take a united stand and force the federal government to obey the Constitution and to respect the powers of the states and the rights of the people. The states already have the power to say no to the federal government; it's written right there in black and white. All the states really need is the intestinal fortitude to confront the federal government and back it right to the wall. If all the state governors got together by phone or fax or in a conference room at a Holiday Inn, if they agreed together to stand firm and unified against federal intrusion, the federal government would have to back down. The states, the Constitution, and the American people would be the big winners.

And don't be misled into thinking that the only problem states have with Washington is "unfunded mandates." The problem is *mandates,* period. Except in those few clearly defined areas where the Constitution gives specific powers to the federal government, *funded* mandates are just as wrong, just as unconstitutional, as *unfunded* mandates—and they are potentially more insidious and dangerous. Governors and state legislators will generally fall all over themselves to grab any federal money, heedless of the strings that are attached. The result is that the states eagerly hand over their constitutional powers to Washington in exchange for dollars. Federal money becomes a drug, dulling the sensibilities of the states to the fact that their powers have been stolen by the feds while keeping the states in a predicament of addiction and dependency. In order to assume their full constitutional powers, the states will have to go cold turkey and kick the federal money habit.

When the federal government writes a check to the states and says, "By endorsing this check, your state accepts federal controls and guidelines over your welfare programs, the education of your children, your transportation policy, and on and on," the people and the states must say, "We don't want federal money with strings attached. Washington, get your own house in order, cut taxes, cut spending, balance the budget, and let us run our state as we see fit, as the Constitution says we should."

THE FIGHT GOES ON

It is frightening to think that the "con-con" con came so close to succeeding without the American people even knowing what was happening. Thank God, it was stopped in time. But please understand this: I didn't stop the Conference of States; I just talked about it on my show. It was stopped at the grassroots level, on a state-by-state, person-by-person basis. It was stopped because a lot of people cared enough about our constitutional form of government to stand up, speak out, and be counted. This is *your* victory. You came through once again.

But the fight isn't over yet.

The old Conference of States proponents are still at it. They've changed the name from "Conference of States" to "Federalism Summit," but it's the same old mangy dog—and that dog won't hunt. The Federalism Summiteers met at the Omni Netherlands Hotel in October 1995 to plan their strategy to push for a "con-con" in 1996 or 1997. If these raiders of our Constitution are ever successful in their attempt to fix what ain't broke, to revise and rewrite the document that was chiseled, sculpted, and buffed to perfection back in 1787, then count on this: Our founding fathers won't just roll over in their graves. They'll pick up their graves and move elsewhere!

So keep your powder dry and your fax machine warm and humming. Most of all, keep your radio tuned to *The Michael Reagan Talk Show* and your computer plugged in to *http://www.reagan.com.* You can bet there'll be more raids on our Constitution—

But when they come, we'll be ready for them.

CHAPTER 8

What a ONE-derful World It Will Be!

I T'S BEEN the dream of the world's leaders for thousands of years—Alexander the Great, Julius Caesar, Genghis Khan, Napoleon, Lenin, Hitler—and it remains a wonderful dream today: Unite the entire world under a single central authority, and we will usher in a golden age, a new world order, a utopia. Once there are no longer many nations but a single world, under a one-world government, we can end poverty and injustice. We can redistribute wealth from the rich parts of the planet to the poor parts, so that there is no "first world," no "third world," just *one world* in which everyone shares and no one is in need. And just think: If there are no more nations, there will be no more wars!

Remember the words of the old Coca-Cola jingle? "I'd like to teach the world to sing in perfect harmony . . . " Imagine! The whole world singing one song, stepping to one drumbeat, giving allegiance to one flag, working under one economic system, living under one political system, obeying one world leader! Talk about heaven on earth!

A one-world government would be much more efficient than the almost two hundred individual governments we have today. Once all authority is concentrated in a single entity, the United Nations, then it will be so much simpler for the deal makers and power brokers to accomplish whatever they choose, anywhere in the world. Of course, to bring this utopia about, some things will have to change.

THINK GLOBALLY

We can't have individual rights and national sovereignty in a global utopia. We can't have this or that nation thinking of itself as a superpower. The power of the world body must supersede everything else. The world body must be the only superpower on the planet. How can this be accomplished?

You have to start slowly, so that evil opponents of the new world order don't see it coming. You begin by shaping the dialogue and language in such a way that people learn to think globally. President Clinton and others in his administration have made a great start in this regard by using the term *the world body* again and again to refer to the U.N. By hammering that term into the public consciousness, we gradually infuse the assumption that the U.N. is not just a bureaucratic assemblage of squabbling nations, but a unified world order, a government above all governments, an authority above all authorities. In short, a *one-world* government.

Next, you use esoteric approaches like 20,000-page trade agreements (NAFTA and GATT)—documents so convoluted that even the people who ratify them don't know what's in them—to shift control of various aspects of the domestic economy over to international bodies. Gradually, you teach American businesses and private individuals to respect U.N. authority and obey U.N. mandates. You get people to "think globally." You talk about the "global economy" and the "global village." You gradually introduce the idea that we are all part of a seamless economic, political, and social system that encompasses the entire planet. Most of all, you demonize anyone who opposes world trade agreements and the World Trade Organization as a "protectionist," an "isolationist," or a "nativist."

Once the average citizen begins to "think globally," it becomes much easier to remove impediments to the one-world government—impediments such as the U.S. Constitution. Eventually, people will begin to see that the Constitution just gets in the way of much more important goals, such as world peace, world population control, and world environmental control. The idea that a national government should "provide for the common defense" is totally outmoded in a world where the United

Nations has imposed world peace. There will always be uppity conservatives—columnists, talk-show hosts, and ordinary citizens—who will stir up opposition to the new world order, so that bothersome First Amendment has to go.

The Second Amendment is even worse, so it has to go, too—we can't have private gun ownership in our peaceful utopia. And that's only the beginning of what's wrong with the Constitution. If we can just get the American people to move beyond this tired, worn-out document, we could fix everything with a constitutional convention. If we could move the right people into positions of control in a constitutional convention, it would be a simple matter to scrap the old, worn-out, obsolete Constitution and substitute something more progressive and global in its perspective—say, the U.N. charter.

WARM AND FUZZY

Another great way to get people used to having a global government in their lives is by starting with our children. Let me ask you this: How do we in America defend the rights of children? With a government agency, of course! That agency goes by different names in different jurisdictions, but it is often called "Child Protective Services" or CPS. How, then, do we defend the rights of children on a global scale? Why, with a *global* CPS, of course! And that's exactly what the 1989 U.N. Convention on the Rights of the Child gives us!

That document, which is promoted under the auspices of UNICEF, is designed to enable people to feel all warm and fuzzy about the U.N., to let American parents know that the reason the U.N. wants to take over their children is that the U.N. *cares.* Boutros-Ghali cares. President and Mrs. Clinton care, too. So does U.S. Ambassador to the U.N. Madeleine Albright. That's why all of these fine people have decided to take over the task of rearing our children—to make sure it's done *right,* by people who really *care!*

Here's some of the neat stuff from the U.N. Convention on the Rights of the Child:

- It recognizes children as citizens of the world and, thus, wards of the United Nations, and requires that every parent or guardian inform their children of their rights under the U.N. Convention. All parents should *want* the world body as a partner in raising their children. There's an old saying, "It takes a whole village to raise a child," and nowadays, it takes a *global* village!

- The U.N. Convention on the Rights of the Child allows government to intervene in families that are not properly raising their children, and it subordinates parental rights to the rights of the child. The state has a responsibility to intervene in situations where it can do a better job of child-rearing than the parents. Sure, the child who is torn from his or her family will experience some pain of separation and loss, but sometimes that's just the price you pay to get a "healthy outcome." And we're all for healthy outcomes, aren't we?

- The U.N. Convention on the Rights of the Child spells out "the rights of the child to access to information, privacy, confidentiality, respect, and informed consent." So if a child finds that his parents won't provide him with pornography, or respect his right to hide drugs in his room, or allow his girlfriend to sleep overnight, all the child has to do is pick up the phone, dial 911-UN, and a blue-helmeted U.N. social worker will be right on the spot to remove that child and place him in a decent home.

- The U.N. Convention on the Rights of the Child requires that healthcare—including confidential sexual counseling, contraception, and abortions—be provided to a child upon request, with or without a parent's knowledge and permission.

This wonderful document has been signed by U.S. Ambassador to the U.N. Madeleine Albright and only needs to be ratified by the U.S. Senate. The problem is that nasty old Senator Jesse Helms—that well-known enemy of world peace and hater of children—is keeping the treaty bottled up in the Foreign Relations Committee. If we can just keep liberals in control of the White House and return liberals to both houses of the Congress, we can finally get blue-helmeted social workers to go out around the globe and across the U.S.A., protecting our children from evil conservatives.

Even though the U.S. has not yet ratified the Convention, other countries, such as Great Britain, have done so—and the wonderful benefits of the Convention are already being demonstrated. A U.N.

report on British compliance with the Convention, issued in early 1995, scolded the Brits for failing to do enough to prevent children from being disciplined in schools and in their families. The report also orders that country to take such child-friendly steps as consulting children on how their schools should be run and raising the age of legal responsibility, so that minor-age murderers and rapists can't be tried as adults. Not only is this a great step forward in the rearing of children, but it also shows how a warm-fuzzy issue like child welfare can be used to make nations more receptive to the involvement of the world body in their internal business.

THE GENDER AGENDA

A companion piece to the U.N. Convention on the Rights of the Child is the U.N. Convention on the Rights of the Woman. At the U.N. Conference on Women in Beijing, China, September 1995, Bill Clinton's Health and Human Services Secretary Donna Shalala was asked, "Why hasn't the United States ratified the treaty on ending discrimination against women?" Her reply: "You just wait. It will be ratified January 26, 1997"—that is, immediately after a new Congress takes power and after President Clinton is inaugurated for a second term. Meanwhile, as the conference was proceeding in Beijing, Democratic congresswoman Lynn Woolsey of California was introducing legislation in the Congress to ratify the treaty.

Many of the points in that treaty are identical to those outlined in the 121-page draft "Platform for Action" on women's rights hammered out at the Beijing conference:

- The world's governments should recognize that the differences between men and women are not natural differences but are the result of cultural stereotyping.
- Governments and societies should recognize that all the social problems of women are caused by male dominance and power, and governments should seek to rectify those problems.
- Governments should enact 50/50 male/female quotas for all elected and appointed offices and positions.

- The structure of societies and institutions should be altered in order to erase all distinctions between the genders.
- Governments should recognize "sexual and reproductive rights" of all persons, including full legal endorsement of the homosexual lifestyle and the right to abortion on demand.
- Religions that do not endorse all of the above points (such as conservative Christianity) should be "reinterpreted."

Participants at the Beijing conference talked about the need for "gender diversity" and "reimagining gender," and they recognized not just two but *five* reimagined genders—although there was some disagreement over exactly what those five genders should be. Some reimagined them to be heterosexual women, heterosexual men, lesbians, gay men, and bisexuals. Others reimagined males, females, hermaphrodites, merms, and ferms (don't ask—it's complicated).

Here again, we have a wonderful warm and fuzzy issue—women's rights—that can be used to give the caring and benevolent world body a measure of control over the internal affairs of various nations, including the U.S. Soon we will have women installed in office, regardless of election results, in order to meet the 50/50 quotas set by the U.N. We will advance the cause of women in the military, enabling them to be drafted and to serve on the front lines, where they can garner glory, promotions, Purple Hearts, posthumous decorations, body bags, and other battlefield accessories.

The U.N. is making the world a wonderful place for women.

GLOBAL GUN CONTROL

Here's a story you didn't see on NBC, ABC, or CBS—and it's a good thing! If the major news media hadn't spiked the global gun control story, the howl from conservative gun nuts would have been deafening! The story comes from the U.N. Conference on Crime held in Cairo, Egypt, in 1995, where delegates from 124 countries considered ways to counter urban violence, terrorism, and organized crime. The majority viewpoint at this conference was that the only people who should have weapons are *government* people. The government is wise and right, and average citizens are incompetent and can't be trusted with the means to defend themselves. Accordingly, measures considered at the Cairo conference included:

- Adopt uniform, worldwide legislation regarding the purchase and possession of firearms.
- Adopt a strategy of reducing the number of firearms in private possession.
- Outlaw the possession of "military weapons" by private individuals.
- Control and register all shooting and hunting associations.
- Control the sale of firearms to private persons; ban the sale of automatic weapons and certain types of ammunition; limit the sale of semiautomatic weapons; and require a firearm permit for the purchase of ammunition—and only ammunition for that authorized weapon.
- Worldwide, centralized, computerized registration of all firearms.
- Require the automatic seizure of firearms if the owner no longer meets legal requirements or presents a risk of violence.
- Permanent amnesty for anyone turning in unauthorized weapons.

At last, the U.N. will realize the cherished dream of all liberals: the demise of the Second Amendment!

SAVE THE WORLD

In conference after conference, the wise one-world wonks of the United Nations are gathering to save your planet and decide your future. In 1992, they met in Rio, gateway to the Brazilian rainforest, to figure out how to save us all from ecological catastrophe. It was George Bush who approved U.S. participation in the Rio conference, and ever since then, the world body has continued to turn out study after study, declaration after declaration, all focused on shutting down the evil, polluting, smoke-belching economies of the industrialized world. We still have a long way to go before everyone on the planet is reduced to riding a bicycle and it becomes a felony to cut down a tree or mow your lawn—but someday we'll make that dream a reality!

We're also working on saving the world from overpopulation, thanks to the 1994 Cairo summit. As U.N. Secretary General Boutros-Ghali says, the U.N. is planning to create "a wholly new kind of mechanism for international action . . . Today the age-old problems of poverty, unemployment and social dislocation, once considered to be the exclusive business of national policy to solve, now have become problems of global scale requiring global attention. New forms of global conciliation and mutual progress are now necessary and possible."[1] In other words, get outta the way, national governments! The one-world government is coming through!

Peaceful Surrender to the New World Order

People like Army specialist Michael New will need to be reeducated when the new world order finally arrives. When President Clinton placed New's Army unit under U.N. command to serve as peacekeepers on the border between Macedonia and Serbia, he refused to wear the U.N. patch and blue beret! He claimed he had sworn an oath to uphold the U.S. Constitution, not the U.N. charter! I mean, doesn't this guy care about world peace, world population control, or world environmentalism?

No doubt, a lot of the problems in New's thinking can be traced to the fact that the twenty-two-year-old Texan is a devout, born-again Christian who was home-schooled by missionary parents who worked in places like the Philippines and New Guinea. A lot of Christians seem to have a problem understanding the importance of submitting America's national sovereignty to a world body. You just suggest to them how awesome it will be to have the entire world peacefully united under the U.N. banner, and they start spouting off about the Book of Revelation.

Fortunately, the Army made an example of New by court-martialing and discharging him—though a few years at hard labor would have been better. At least it'll give pause to the next Army grunt who takes it on himself to oppose the new world order! If your commander in chief orders you to surrender your nation's sovereignty to some general from Finland, then—you-betcha-by-golly-wow—you surrender your nation's sovereignty, no questions, no arguments!

President Clinton has attempted to bring the American military into the new world order by signing Presidential Directive 25, which places the United States military under the direction of the United Nations.

Unfortunately, conservative obstructionists in the Congress managed to overturn the president's directive, but we have their names and we have already reserved places for them in the new world order reeducation camps.

President Clinton has continued his policy of building up the military strength of other nations—sending billions to Russia and other peace-loving nations—while dismantling America's military and handing American troops over to U.N. generals. Regardless of opposition in the Congress, President Clinton is determined to stay the course and will not rest until every segment of the American military, economy, government, and society has been completely surrendered to the one-world governing body.

GLOBAL INCOME TAX

For years, the U.N. has been hobbled by a lack of funds, unable to carry out its mandate of interfering in the affairs of member nations. It's tough to carry on all these conferences, studies, and peacekeeping missions on a lousy $10.5 billion budget per year. Even worse, a lot of member states are refusing to pay their fair share. A new idea may solve that: a *global income tax*. A U.N. income tax would not only raise much-needed funds for the world body to operate on, but it would also further establish the fact that the U.N. is truly a *government*, and that people around the world owe their allegiance and mega-moolah to that world body.

What would the U.N. impose taxes on? To begin with, there are the so-called "Tobin taxes" named after Nobel Prize-winning economist James Tobin, who engineered the global tax concept. These taxes are projected to bring in $1.5 trillion a year, which should go a long way toward financing not only much-needed relief programs in Rwanda but also urgent international conferences at beachfront hotels in Rio. Likely Tobin taxes to be imposed include:

- A tax on international currency transactions.
- A tax on international stock transactions.

Tobin is partial to such taxes not only for the enormous amount of revenue they might create but also because they help to control (and tend to discourage) such greedy capitalist activities.

Another Tobin proposal: Give the U.N. the power to mint its own money. This proposal would lead to massive worldwide inflation, which would cause everything you own to multiply in price—your house, your car, that loaf of bread you just brought home from the store. Another benefit: Giving the U.N. its own printing presses to turn out Boutros-Boutros-bucks would help cement the idea that the United Nations is a real, honest-to-gosh government, by Ghali!

Another proposal—this one from the Independent Working Group on the Future of the United Nations—would give the U.N. "special drawing rights" over the International Money Fund, much like Dan Rostenkowski, David Bonior, and Barbara Boxer used to enjoy over at the House Bank. Need some cash? Just write a check! Hey, don't worry about it. It's on the House! Under this plan, the U.N. could simply tap into the International Money Fund whenever it feels like it.

Some other ideas for taxing the world come from James Gustav Speth, who is a founder of the National Resources Defense Council and was appointed by President Clinton to head the United Nations Development Program. Gus Speth is an absolute genius. He found a way to marry the radical environmentalism of the NRDC to the fund-raising needs of the U.N. His concept: Put a tax on pollution! He wants to place U.N. taxes on carbon emissions into the atmosphere and he wants to tax oil pumped from the ground. His idea is threefold: (1) to make it more expensive (and less desirable) to operate cars and smokestack industries; (2) to protect the forests, so there are more trees for us all to hug; and (3) to transfer wealth from industrialized countries to countries that don't have cars and smokestacks.

Speth also wants to impose a global income tax on all the rich people in the world, which he estimates would bring in about $20 billion a year. The great thing about this proposal is that it is so *inclusive*. Even the poorest people in America would have the privilege of filling out a UN-1040 form and sending a check for their fair share to Geneva. Why? Because practically everyone in America is rich! Speth's definition of "rich" is someone who makes more than $10,000 a year. Until now, you might not have realized how rich you are, but to someone in Somalia or Haiti, you are Donald Trump and Leona Helmsley all rolled into one!

Speth and his UNDP have also called for a number of global bureau-cratic agencies to help spend all these billions of global tax dollars:

- A World Ministry of Agriculture
- A World Ministry of Industry
- A World Ministry of Social Affairs
- A global police force

The UNDP also calls for the nations of the world to cut back military spending by 3 percent and to send a check for the resulting "peace dividend" (estimated to total $460 billion by the end of the century) to the United Nations. This money would then be sent to poorer nations. The Clinton administration supports *all* of Speth's initiatives.

GET READY FOR THE FUTURE

Now, there are people who would say that the U.N. has become a bankrupt, bloated, wasteful bureaucracy, plagued by corruption, incom-petence, greed, and fraud. Some of those charges even come from people who should know better, such as the former under-secretary general of the U.N., Sir Brian Urquhart of Great Britain. In a totally unjust and mean-spirited attack on all the good that is done by the world body, he called the U.N. "a rather ridiculous group of foreigners spending Ameri-can tax dollars." A reeducation camp is *definitely* in Sir Brian's future!

After all, the U.N. does very important work among its 185 member nations. It employs 51,000 bureaucrats and spends $10.5 billion a year— and every dollar is carefully spent on maintaining peace and raising the standard of living for people around the world! For example, just think of how the U.N. has raised the standard of living for Secretary General Boutros-Ghali! He is paid $344,200 a year; he receives an indeterminate but generous vacation time; and he lives rent-free in a three-story midtown Manhattan house with a garden, paintings on loan from New York museums, a view of the East River, servants, and security guards.

Has the U.N. raised anyone else's standard of living? You bet! For example, while the U.N. was conducting peacekeeping operations in Somalia, U.N. agencies spent a cool million bucks a day on air-conditioned villas in Mogadishu and Nairobi. No doubt *somebody's* standard of living was raised by all that money!

And efficient? Boy, is the U.N. ever efficient! The administrative overhead on humanitarian assistance to Somalia was *only around 60 percent.* That means that of every dollar spent in the assistance program, *a full forty cents* actually went to help a starving Somali! Now, that's efficient! Sure, there are private organizations—show-off operations like Save the Children and World Vision—that do the same job with only a 5 or 10 percent administrative overhead rate. But that's not a fair comparison! They don't have a big bureaucracy to support like the U.N. does—and I'll bet they don't even have air-conditioned villas!

Change is just around the corner. The Soviet Union may have collapsed, but not to worry! The world needs global socialism, and the U.N. is going to give it to us. The Clinton healthcare plan may have aborted in the Congress, but no problem. The U.N. is going to give us global healthcare. There may be wars and rumors of wars now, but all that will come to a screeching halt when soldiers from every country put on their blue helmets or berets.

If all goes according to plan, we will soon see industry and capitalism replaced by global environmentalism. No one will be any richer or poorer than anyone else. No nation will have any more wealth than any other nation. The United States of America and Botswana will be exactly the same in every way. We'll all be singing the same song, stepping to the same drumbeat, giving our allegiance to the same government, and living in the same kind of mud-brick housing. Utopia at last!

Doesn't it just send chills up and down your spine?

Serious Postscript: Okay, the tone of this chapter was a put-on—but all the facts are frighteningly real. I just wanted to write one chapter, putting myself into a liberal mind-set to see how it feels. Frankly, it makes my head hurt. I promise not to do it again.

I have been talking for several years on my radio show about the U.N.'s various attempts to impose a one-world government on us all. Not only has the dominant media ignored this story, but oddly, you don't even hear about it from many conservative talk-show hosts. One prominent host even administered a "National Kook Test" to his radio audience. Those who answered "yes" to any of ten questions on the test were advised that they were "kooks" and needed to seek help. The first question: "Do you believe there is an international conspiracy to impose a one-world government on us all?"

Well, I guess I'm a "kook." But at least I'm a kook who got it *right.* Yes, Virginia, there really *is* an international conspiracy to impose a one-world government on us all. I've just documented it. If you want to keep the one-world government away from our shores, you'd better get busy. Talk to your elected representatives and to the candidates. Make sure you send the right people to Washington, D.C.—

Or get ready to welcome the blue helmets into *your* neighborhood.

CHAPTER 9

A Trillion Here, a Trillion There— of Our Money!

THE LAST time the U.S. Congress balanced a budget, Richard Nixon was president, Neil Armstrong walked on the moon, the New York Mets won the World Series, Ohio State won the Rose Bowl, Joe Namath led the New York Jets to victory in Super Bowl III, and Michael Reagan took second in a boat race in Miami. I remember it well—Broadway Joe and I were on the front page of the sports section of the *Miami Herald* the same day. Does that seem as long ago to you as it does to me? Well, that's because this country has not had a balanced budget since 1969!

Year by year, from 1970 to the present, the United States of America has steadily been spending up to $290 billion a year more than it takes in. When you spend more than you take in, that's called *deficit spending*. The difference between the amount you take in and the amount you spend is the *deficit*. When you continue year after year to rack up deficit after deficit, you accumulate *debt*. As I write these words, the amount of national debt we have accumulated since the 1960s is about $5 trillion dollars. That's a five with twelve zeros after it. To pay it off, you'd need *five million* sacks of money, each sack filled with a million dollars—five million millions.

In the time it would take you to read this sentence aloud (about six seconds), the United States will go another $47,600 in debt. Our government goes into debt at a rate of about $476,389 every minute, about $28,583,333 every hour, about $686 million every day. Whether or not we are aware of it, government borrowing has a profoundly negative impact on our daily lives. Whenever you take out a loan or lease a car, take out a mortgage or "pass the plastic" at the department store, you are competing for dollars with the United States government. You are forced to pay higher interest rates from your lending institution because, while you are at the front desk, pleading for a few shekels from a loan officer, Uncle Sam is in back, scooping money out of the vault with a skip-loader and a dump truck!

As if that weren't bad enough, $5 trillion is only the *official* federal debt figure. Most people are unaware that there is an even scarier *unofficial* debt figure—an *additional $7 trillion* of "shadow debt" that no one ever talks about! You don't hear the president talking about it. You don't hear the speaker of the House talking about it. You don't hear the majority leader of the Senate talking about it. And you certainly never hear about it in the press. What is the "shadow debt?" It is in the form of government commitments (such as pension funds), direct government loans, and loan guarantees (such as SBA, VA, and FHA loans). It doesn't come due all at once, but the extent of government involvement in the economy is grossly understated without it.

But wait! It gets even worse! What about various unfunded government obligations like FDIC/FSLIC insurance and disaster contingency "funds"—which are not true funds at all, just legal liabilities? When the S&L crisis struck in the late 1980s, $500 billion was tacked onto the national debt without warning. What guarantee have we against future financial upheavals and bailouts? None! So, thanks to these unfunded federal obligations, we the taxpayers have secretly been placed on the hook for *an additional $10 trillion* or more above and beyond both the official debt and the shadow debt. I guess we should call this "stealth debt"—you won't know it's coming till it gets here!

Meanwhile, the federal debt will continue to grow—not only between now and 2002, but even *after* 2002, when the Republican plan finally produces a balanced budget, according to the Congressional Budget Office. The plan passed by Congress in June 1995 (and repeatedly vetoed by President Clinton, triggering a series of government shutdowns) allows the official federal debt to top $6 trillion by 2002. But even if we don't add another nickel of deficit spending to the debt, the interest meter will continue running on the existing debt, causing it to continue increasing and compounding. Moreover, the Republican budget plan places no curbs on *unofficial* debt. Uncle Sam will continue taking on hundreds of billions of dollars worth of new off-budget obligations each year. Even with a seven-year balanced budget plan, the U.S. government is far from being out of the woods—and so are U.S. taxpayers.

THE DEFICIT SPENDING "RELIGION"

How did we get into this mess? The number one cause:

1. Dishonesty

Our leaders have not been honest with us, because pandering gets more votes than the hard truth. The press has not been honest with us in explaining how the budget process and the economy work. Most of all, we have not been honest with ourselves as a people. We have not faced the simple fact that we can't keep electing politicians who "bring home the pork," because that pork has to come from *somewhere.*

When the voters of the state of Washington kept sending Tom Foley back to Congress because he brought federal dollars back to their districts, those voters didn't seem to care that, in order for a politician to bring home the federal bacon, that bacon has to be taken off someone else's table. It may come from taxpayers in other districts. Or it may simply be borrowed from the tables of future generations—from your children and mine. That's what we've been doing—going on a wild federal spending spree, running up a $5 or $6 trillion tab, then sending the bill to our kids!

So what have we stuck our kids with? A child born today is already *$19,000 in debt* even before the doctor slaps that baby on the fanny, even before that child draws a first breath. That's his or her share of the federal debt on the day he or she is born—19,000 buckaroos! And get this: A child born in 1995 will, over an average lifetime, be forced to pay *$187,000 in taxes* just to pay his share of the *interest* on the national debt (according to a 1995 report issued by the Joint Economic Committee of Congress). That's more than $3,500 per working year of that child's life! And mind you, that doesn't even put a dent in the *principle* of the debt. And it doesn't count any *additional* debt the government will acquire after 1995.

Another reason we got into the mess we're in is because of an economic philosophy called *Keynesian economics.*

2. Keynesian Economics

John Maynard Keynes (1883-1946) was an Eton- and Cambridge-educated English economist whose economic theories were largely formulated in response to the Great Depression of the 1930s. The crux of Keynes's theory is that there are times in a market economy when there is not enough demand for the goods produced, resulting in a cutback in production and employment; a severe cutback results in a depression, throwing millions of workers out of jobs and into poverty. Keynes's solution to the problem was twofold:

(1) During periods of high unemployment, increase the money supply, which will lower interest rates and stimulate investment and business activity. This is a sound policy, and it has been skillfully used by Alan Greenspan and the Federal Reserve to manage and stabilize the U.S. economy, even through the economic downturns that followed the disastrous tax increases of 1990 and 1993. No problem there. It's the *next* part of Keynes's "solution" that gets us into trouble.

(2) Keynes also advocated *an activist federal spending policy* in which the government creates public works and other spending programs, *deliberately generating deficits and unbalanced budgets* in order to increase the demand for goods and services. By directly employing federal workers and by spending money to stimulate private sector employment, the government spurs the economy while incurring increased debt.

Keynesian economics have dominated American fiscal policy during two great periods. The first ran from the mid-1930s to the end of World War II, when FDR initiated a host of public works and social welfare programs in an attempt to lift America out of its economic doldrums. FDR's alphabet soup of federal money-spending agencies only blunted the pain of the Great Depression; it took World War II to really pull the country out of the Depression. The War enabled FDR to put America back to work in a perfectly Keynesian way: The government spent billions on ships, planes, and tanks, financing the war effort with deficit spending.

Prior to FDR, American fiscal policy had been guided by the classical conservative economics of Adam Smith and Jean Baptiste Say. These originators of supply-side economics—what we now call Reaganomics—held that supply tends to create demand, that government deficit spending encourages inflation, and that heavy government regulation and taxation hinders economic growth. Ronald Reagan didn't invent these principles; the country had operated on these principles for about a century and a half prior to the Great Depression. The Depression was not a failure of supply-side economics but the result of a number of disastrous conditions emerging at the same time—an unstable world market combined with high tariffs, the loss of jobs owing to rapidly advancing mass production technology, simultaneous downturns in the agricultural and industrial sectors of the economy, the blowout of an overheated and unrealistically inflated stock market, mass loan defaults and mass bank failures following a massive expansion in credit, and so forth.

Following World War II, the country returned to conservative fiscal policies under Truman, Eisenhower, and Kennedy (yes, JFK was a fiscal conservative who, like Ronald Reagan, advocated *tax cuts* in order to stimulate economic growth). But JFK's successor, Lyndon Johnson, ushered in the second great Keynesian-dominated period of the American economy. In cahoots with a Democratic Congress, Lyndon Johnson did two things that sent federal spending through the roof: He dramatically expanded the Vietnam War, and he vastly increased social spending with his "War on Poverty." *Both* of Johnson's wars were big-time losers for the American people, sending the federal government on a decades-long binge of taxing, deficit spending, and spiraling debt that continued right into the '90s. (Ronald Reagan attempted to rein in the liberal spending binge, but faced with a Democrat-controlled Congress, plus the need to rebuild the long-neglected U.S. military, he was forced to sign Democrat-created budgets that swelled the national debt from $900 billion to more than $2 trillion during his eight years in office.)

In January 1995, the Republican-led 104th Congress was sworn in, elected in large part because of a balanced budget pledge in the Contract with America. To date, the new Republican majority has not even begun to reverse America's debtward course—it has only tapped the brakes a bit in an effort to slow down the runaway federal government. Even if we get a balanced budget by 2002, we are still headed for the guardrail at about ninety-three miles an hour.

Is there any validity to Keynesian economic theory? Sure there is—in an emergency. Keynesian deficit spending is kind of like taking a prescription narcotic. If you take it when you are sick, and stop taking it when you get well, it can help you. If you make a habit of taking prescription narcotics, you may become addicted. Like a street-corner drug pusher, Johnson doped America with his Keynesian spending on a failed war in Vietnam and a failed "Great Society." Once started, Keynesian spending programs develop constituencies and become impossible to kill.

Keynesian economics is not just an economic theory. It's the *economic religion of liberalism;* the central dogma of the Keynesian faith is *an unbalanced budget.* The economic doctrines of John Maynard Keynes have driven this country to the brink of bankruptcy by placing his "Good Housekeeping Seal of Approval" on the worst instincts of liberal Democrats: tax and spend. Keynesian liberals may talk about balanced budgets, but they don't believe in them and they don't produce them. Balanced budgets are for Reagan supply-siders. Whenever a liberal tells you he is in favor of a balanced budget, he is—well, let's just say he is being a bit disingenuous. In the Keynesian religion, balanced budgets are heresy, pure and simple.

Now it all begins to make sense: Now we see why candidate Bill Clinton (a liberal who masqueraded as a moderate) campaigned on a promise of balancing the budget in five years, yet once in office he never came within $200 billion of submitting a balanced budget. Now we understand why, when Bill Clinton introduced his so-called "welfare reform plan," it was a plan to make welfare *more* expensive, not less, by adding more programs and services to an already bloated welfare state. Now we understand why Bill Clinton's first official acts as president were to blow off his promised middle-class tax cut, to propose the largest tax increase in history, and to push for a budget-busting $16.2 billion "economic stimulus program"—pure, distilled Keynesian deficit spending! Bill Clinton, Leon Panetta, Dick Gephardt, and their fellow liberals may *talk* about balancing the budget, but when the Republican majority in the 104th Congress actually began *doing* something about it, the liberals fought it hammer and tongs. The last thing in the world liberals want is a balanced budget—it violates their religion!

Need more proof? How about HR1158? That was the Recisions Bill, which the Republicans in the 104th Congress put forward to rescind (cut) $16.4 billion of pork-barrel spending that had been approved for fiscal year 1995 by the Democrat-controlled 103rd. The Democrats obstructed, using every stalling, foot-dragging, time-wasting trick in the book. They stretched out the debate, piled on amendment after amendment, and fought cloture like mad. They knew the bill was going to pass, so why did they stall? To give federal agencies *time*. Time for what? Time to spend all the money in their budgets before the bill could be passed. When the bill was finally passed, it was largely a moot point, because the money had all been spent—in many cases, simply frittered away to spite the Republicans and the taxpayers.

So why do liberals *claim* they want to balance the budget? Because liberals know that *talking* about balancing the budget makes them sound responsible and helps them win votes. They know that voters are angry and want the government to get its own house in order. They know that every taxpayer has to balance his or her own checkbook every month—and that taxpayers want their government to operate the same way.

In late 1995, when push came to shove and the government was shut down for the longest time in U.S. history, who was just *talking* about balancing the budget—and who actually came up with a plan to do it? You got it! Bill Clinton postured, demagogued, and vetoed. It was the Republicans who truly rolled up their sleeves, did the grunt work, took the risks and the political hits, and tried to get the job done.

WHY IS IT IMPORTANT TO BALANCE THE BUDGET?

Does it *really* affect our daily lives and the lives of our children if the government does or does not have its fiscal house in order? Well, let me just lay a few facts on you—then you tell me.

In 1995, the National Center for Public Policy Research and the Small Business Survival Foundation did some research and crunched the numbers, comparing the status quo under the Clinton economic plan against the 1995 Republican plan. Under the Republican package of tax cuts and slower spending growth, total spending would climb at a sustainable rate, from $1.5 trillion in 1995 to less than $1.9 trillion in 2002—a 22 percent increase in seven years. Best of all, the Republican plan would yield a balanced budget by 2002, according to the Congressional Budget Office. Under the liberal status quo, spending would soar to $2.1 trillion in 2002—almost a 40 percent increase in seven years—and the deficit would continue to swell the national debt.

What are some of the benefits of a balanced budget (with tax cuts) by 2002? Here's a partial list:

Interest rates would fall. Deficit spending and government borrowing drive up interest rates. A balanced budget would drop interest rates by at least 2 percent across the board. This would mean a savings of $37,400 over the life of a thirty-year, $75,000 home mortgage. It would mean a savings of $900 on a $15,000 auto loan. It would mean similar savings on all other forms of borrowing, including credit card rates. We are not talking macroeconomics here; we are talking about a massive improvement of every family's lifestyle and purchasing power.

The gross national product (GNP) of the United States would grow by an extra $10.8 billion in 2002. Roger Brinner, chief economist with the forecasting firm DRI/McGraw-Hill, estimates that a balanced budget would raise America's economic output by 2.5 percent a year over the next ten years—and on average, that would mean an extra $1,000 a year of income for each American family.

Housing starts would increase. A balanced budget would yield 104,000 additional housing starts between 1995 and 2002.

Employment would rise. Economic growth produces jobs. The Joint Economic Committee of Congress issued a report in 1995 estimating that a balanced budget would generate 6.1 million additional jobs over the next ten years.

The retirement and healthcare programs of seniors would be protected. Many people have worked for decades, paying into the Medicare and Social Security systems, only to see those programs imperiled by political demagoguery and fiscal irresponsibility. Young people today dutifully pay taxes to support these programs, though they are convinced they will never get a nickel back when they retire. Meanwhile, Medicare—one of the few government programs that has consistently operated in the black—is due to run its first deficit in 1996, and accumulated reserves will be completely drained by 2002 if nothing is done.

The only way to protect Social Security and Medicare is to balance the federal budget. That way, when the resources are needed, they will be there. "If we continue to run federal deficits year after year," says Bob Myers, chief actuary of the Social Security Administration, "and if interest payments continue to rise at an alarming rate, we will face two dangerous possibilities. Either we will raid the trust funds to pay for our current profligacy, or we will print money, dishonestly inflating our way out of indebtedness. Both cases would devastate the real value of the Social Security trust funds."

Liberals, of course, have tried to demagogue the issue, trying to Medi-scare the elderly to death with charges that the Republicans plan to "cut" Medicare protection. The fact is, there never were any cuts in the Republican plan. Instead, Medicare spending per beneficiary increases from $4,800 in 1995 to $7,100 in 2002. Even if you were educated in the Los Angeles public school system, you know that $7,100 is a bigger number than $4,800. Your L.A. education may not equip you to do the math and see that this is an increase of $2,300 or 48 percent—but you can easily see that what the liberals call a "cut" is not a cut at all!

As to liberal claims that the Republicans want to cut Medicare to "pay for" tax cuts: Medicare and tax cuts are completely separate issues. The tax cuts were going to happen no matter what; they're a key element of the Contract with America. And the slower growth (not "cuts"!) in Medicare were absolutely necessary to preserve and protect Medicare, regardless of anything that happens with the rest of the budget. Moreover, the Republican-sponsored Balanced Budget Act contains a protective guarantee that no Democrat-controlled Congress ever was willing to offer: a "lockbox" provision, which "locks up" Medicare funds, making it illegal for the government to spend Medicare funds for other purposes.

The government will be better able to address important needs. If we do nothing to balance the budget now, entitlements and interest on the debt will consume 100 percent of tax revenues by 2012. There will be no money for national defense, building and maintaining infrastructure, medical research, scientific research, or education. Instead of spending money paying the interest on a ballooning debt (much of which goes to foreign financiers), we could be funding needed programs and making America a better, happier, safer place in which to live. Or does that make too much sense?

Our standard of living would rise. The nonpartisan Concord Coalition has determined that if the economy was not carrying the drag of deficit spending and $5 trillion in debt, the average family income today would not be $35,000, but $50,000—a $15,000 a year difference! President Clinton's own 1995 budget estimated that the newborn generation in the cradle today faces *a lifetime tax rate of 82 percent* at all levels if the current trend continues in the federal debt. Clearly, we need to do more than merely balance the budget; we need to begin operating with *surplus budgets* so that we can eliminate this obscene level of debt.

The American Dream would be restored and secured. I envision an America in which every American, regardless of race or economic starting point, would be free and unhindered in pursuing his or her dream. The Declaration of Independence says that we are endowed by our Creator with "certain unalienable rights" including "life, liberty, and the pursuit of happiness." As Newt Gingrich says, that doesn't mean a happiness entitlement or happiness stamps—just the freedom to pursue happiness. That's the American dream—the freedom to pursue happiness however we define it. Yours may be a dream of financial success or financial security, a dream of great achievements for yourself and your society, a dream of service to your community and your world. But you can't achieve your dreams if you are held in economic bondage by your government.

From the early 1970s, when government spending first began to spiral out of control, until 1993, the income of Americans (in real dollars) has remained fairly static. American families neither gained much nor declined much on average in their lifestyle and spending power. In 1993, however—the first year of Clintonomics and the year the Democrat-controlled Congress passed the biggest tax hike in U.S. history—median family income declined by $709, according to the U.S. Census Bureau. If we balance the federal budget, we will see taxes, interest rates, and unemployment fall—and we will see income and prosperity rise. Then we will discover how amazingly limitless the American dream truly is!

THE POLITICS OF ENVY AND FEAR

You've heard the old rock and roll song by Alvin Lee and Ten Years After, the one called "I'd Love to Change the World." There's a line in that song that could well serve as the mantra of class-envy politics: "Tax the rich and feed the poor, until there are no rich no more." Notice that these refugees from a bad acid trip don't want to eliminate *poverty*! Oh, no—they want to eliminate *wealth*! Somehow it seems to me that class envy, spitefulness, and covetousness make a pretty miserable foundation for a society, a social philosophy—or a tax code. Wouldn't it make more sense to lift everyone up rather than pull some people down? Instead of wanting to spread *failure* around, shouldn't we be teaching everyone how to *succeed*?

That's the difference—or rather, one of many differences—between liberals and conservatives. Liberals believe you can't build up some people without tearing down others. Conservatives believe that "a rising tide lifts *all* boats." Liberals look at the economy as a pie to be carved up between the winners and the losers. Conservatives see the economy as a limitless horizon of opportunities in which, if everyone works and produces, *everyone wins.*

A good example of the liberal view of economics is the way estate taxes are structured in America. Why should dying be considered a taxable event by the IRS? The money being taxed was already taxed once when it was earned. The fact is, estate taxes are a prime example of liberal philosophy embodied in the tax laws. It's called "the redistribution of wealth." Liberals spend their lives making sure everyone ends up with exactly the same outcome and exactly the same income, whether one person works eighty hours a week, or forty hours a week, or not at all. It's not fair that one person lives in the penthouse while another lives in the outhouse—so we have to punish the achiever in the penthouse in order to make things fair. Whenever someone accumulates "too much" wealth, we have to take it away and redistribute it to those who don't have enough.

So what happens when people die? Well, if they worked hard, denied themselves, planned for the future, invested wisely, and saved, then they accumulated something to pass on to their descendants. And of course, liberals don't think that's fair (unless those descendants are named "Kennedy"). So the liberals created laws to rob the dead and give their worldly goods to Uncle Sam. Old Unc then redistributes it among the more deserving and noble among us—that is, among the constituent groups of liberal politicians.

And what is the result? When a business owner dies, his or her grieving survivors must scramble to sell off assets in order to pay punitive tax rates. These taxes kill family-owned businesses and family farms. When these small businesses die, jobs disappear. According to the Small Business Survival Committee, 60 percent of small, family-owned businesses do not survive to the second generation, and 90 percent do not survive to the third generation—in large part because of federal estate taxes. If these taxes are so destructive, why does the federal government collect them? It's not because they are such a great cash-cow for the treasury. In fact, estate and gift taxes are big money *losers*. In 1994, estate and gift taxes accounted for a mere 1.2 percent of total federal government receipts (about $15.2 billion), and the IRS estimates that up to 75 percent of collections are frittered away by compliance and litigation costs.

So why do it? One reason and one reason only: to satisfy skewed liberal notions of "fairness." In the warped world of liberalism, "rich" is synonymous with "evil," which justifies their "soak the rich" demagoguery. Liberals love to portray themselves as heroes in the Robin Hood tradition—taking from the rich and giving to the poor. The problem with that analogy is that the liberals don't know their Robin Hood!

As I recall, Robin Hood didn't rob the rich; he went after thieving politicians! The chief bad guy in the Robin Hood legend was King John—a false king who snatched the throne away from his brother, Richard, while he was out crusading in the Holy Lands. (I'm not sure, but I think John stole the throne by grabbing 43 percent of the vote.) King John's henchman was the Sheriff of Nottingham, who went out extorting outrageous taxes from middle-class serfs. Robin Hood would ambush the sheriff, snatch the saddlebags filled with ill-gotten tax money, and ride away, leaving the sheriff tied to a tree. Robin would then give the money back to the middle-class serfs from whom it was unfairly taken in the first place. So from where I'm sitting, if you want to use the

Robin Hood tale as an allegory for today, King John is Bill Clinton, the Sheriff of Nottingham is Dick Gephardt, and Robin Hood is a Republican freshman in the 104th Congress!

There's so much nonsense in all the liberal posturing at budget negotiating time. "The Republicans just want to give tax cuts to the rich!" Face it: Republicans want to give tax cuts to *everyone*. Liberals like to arbitrarily target one group for favorable treatment (the poor) while excluding and punishing another group (the rich) for being rich—and they call that "fairness." Conservatives think that true fairness means you treat everybody the same (what a concept!). So when you cut taxes, you cut them for everybody, not just this or that group. It seems like whenever you practice the liberal form of "targeted fairness," you don't end up soaking the rich, you end up soaking the middle class, because that's where most of the money is. But when you practice conservative fairness, cutting taxes evenly across the board, the middle class benefits the most.

As an example, take the $500 per child tax credit proposed as part of the 1995 Republican budget plan. Liberal Democrats like Gephardt claimed that this tax credit somehow constituted a "huge tax break for the rich"—an absolutely bizarre claim, even coming from a liberal. Does Gephardt think that only rich people have children? Hasn't he heard that 74 percent of the tax relief goes to families with incomes below $75,000, that families earning less than $25,000 will have their entire tax liability wiped out? That's 4.7 million American families who will pay no income tax at all! How is that a "huge tax break for the rich"? Somehow, we need to get these people in touch with reality!

The "tax break for the rich" charge is silly enough—but Clinton and Gephardt didn't stop there. They went from the silly to the outrageous, claiming that the 1995 Republican plan not only cut taxes for the wealthy but "raised taxes on the poor"! Without any factual support, they made this charge again and again—and the liberal media dutifully broadcast the liberal soundbites without questioning the absurdity of the claims. What in the world were Clinton and Gephardt thinking of when they accused Republicans of "raising taxes on the poor"?

Their claims were based on a twisted interpretation of something called the EITC—the Earned Income Tax Credit. The EITC is the fastest growing item in the federal budget. Though it's called a "tax credit," it is really a government giveaway program that primarily gives money to low-income people who pay little if any income tax. Before Bill Clinton came to Washington, it was a rarely used loophole for the lower classes in the tax code. But in his 1993 budget, Bill Clinton vastly expanded the eligibility criteria and the size of benefits for the EITC. Thanks to Bill, the EITC suddenly became a handsome cash prize to nontaxpayers, illegal aliens, and even tax cheats and wealthy taxpayers—a terrific vote-buying scheme for a president who's in a perpetual campaign mode.

But suddenly, in November 1994, the Republicans were elected to clean up the fiscal mess created by forty years of Democrat control—and the Republicans proceeded, as part of their 1995 budget plan, to reform abuses of the EITC. The Republican plan rolls back eligibility criteria to pre-Clinton levels, targets fraud and abuse of the EITC, which Clinton had made easy and inviting in 1993, and coordinates the EITC with the $500 per child tax credit to save costs. The Republican plan doesn't raise taxes on the poor; it reduces the amount of money the government pays out in direct transfer payments to those who don't pay taxes at all. Under the tortured logic of liberalism, a government check for people who don't pay taxes is called a "tax cut," and taking away that government check is called "raising taxes on the poor." Yet, under the Republican plan, eligible families earning less than $18,000 still receive their EITC payments, but illegal aliens, tax cheats, and affluent taxpayers are cut off. Also losing their EITC checks: childless taxpayers who were never eligible before 1993 anyway, and who won't get the $500 per child tax credit. There is not one person covered by the EITC whose taxes would be raised by the Republican budget plan.

THE POLITICS OF FEAR

Another strategy skillfully employed by liberals during the budget wars is fear-mongering. A prime example is *Medi-scare*. Clinton and his gang relentlessly hammered away at the charge that "Republicans want to cut benefits to the poor and needy" and "Republicans want to destroy Medicare and Medicaid." According to liberals, the Republicans are a bunch of sadistic monsters who would love nothing better than to toss children and old people into dumpsters and set them out for curbside pickup.

The fact is, Republicans were trying to *save* these healthcare programs, not destroy them. The Democrats did everything in their power to obstruct the process, proving they would rather see Medicare and Medicaid collapse than allow Republicans to get credit for preserving them. The 1995 report of the Medicare trustees predicted a $118 billion shortfall from 1996 through 2000. If the spiraling costs of Medicare were not brought under control, the program would completely collapse in the year 2002. The trustees who wrote the report are largely Clinton appointees, and three are Clinton White House cabinet officials, so these are not Republican projections we're talking about.

The Republicans, however, are the only ones with the courage to attack the problem. And they attacked it *not* by "cutting" the programs as Democrats claimed, but by *slowing the growth* of these programs. Medicare and Medicaid would both continue to grow and keep pace with growing healthcare needs—but they would grow at sustainable, controlled rates that would allow them to remain solvent and viable. During the seven years from 1989 through 1995, we spent $926 billion on Medicare. Under the Republican plan, Medicare would spend $1.684 trillion during the seven years from 1996 through 2002. Let's stack one number on top of the other, then you tell me: Which is more money? Is this an increase or a cut?

1996-2002	$ 1,684,000,000,000
1989-1995	$ 926,000,000,000

The fact is, the Republican plan *increases Medicare spending by 82 percent* over seven years! Yet, during a January 11, 1996, press conference, Bill Clinton repeatedly—eight times, in fact—claimed the Republican plan "cut Medicare."

And Medicaid? Let's stack the numbers again and you be the judge:

1996-2002	$ 839,000,000,000
1989-1995	$ 443,000,000,000

A no-brainer, right? I mean, are we all agreed that $839 billion is more than $443 billion? Yet Bill Clinton called the 1996-2002 Republican plan—*which happens to be an 89 percent increase*—"cutting Medicaid."

Find the Hidden Tax Breaks!

In December 1995, President Clinton claimed he couldn't sign the budget bill passed by the U.S. Congress because the Republicans had put in a "huge tax break for the wealthy." House Democrat leader Dick Gephardt claimed that the "huge tax break for the wealthiest 1 percent of Americans" was the reason for the so-called "train wreck"—the government shutdown that idled 800,000 federal workers in late 1995 and early 1996.

My staff at *The Michael Reagan Talk Show* and I were baffled. We had thoroughly examined the Republican budget plan, and we had never seen these huge tax breaks for the wealthy. So we called the White House three separate times and talked to three different White House staffers. We talked to Alice Rivlin's staff at the administration's Office of Management and Budget. No one at the White House could tell us where in the bill we could find the hidden "tax breaks for the wealthy."

So we called Congressman Dick Gephardt's office. Surely he would know. But we were disappointed. The congressman's office didn't have a clue—but they suggested we talk to the Democratic Policy Committee. We called them, but they didn't know either. So we started calling a number of Democratic congress members. We didn't ask any trick questions, and we didn't try to trip anybody up. We just wanted to know what Bill Clinton, Dick Gephardt, and their fellow Democrats were talking about. None of them could tell us where those elusive "tax breaks for the wealthy" were lurking.

One Democratic representative suggested we read the Republican Budget. So we read it again. We looked all through it. Had this "huge tax break for the wealthy" somehow been sneaked into the $500 per child tax credit? No, there is an income cap of $75,000 on that tax credit, limiting the benefits to the middle class. Was it smuggled into the capital gains tax cut? Not possible, since that was limited to individuals, not companies—and it, too, had a cap. So where was it?

We never found it. And no one in the White House or the Congress could tell us where it was. It's puzzling. I'm sure that if the liberal Democrats say there's a "huge tax break for the wealthiest 1 percent of Americans" in the Republican tax plan, then it must be there. I mean, making something up that isn't true would be a *lie*. And liberals wouldn't lie to the American people— would they?

Well, would they?

And you know what? Bill Clinton *knows* the Republican plan wasn't about Medicare and Medicaid "cuts." He knows because *his* budget plan does exactly the same thing to Medicare and Medicaid—it increases funding for both programs, but at a slower rate than previously projected. His budget plan operates the same way the Republican plan does, only with different numbers—numbers that fall $200 billion short of balancing. Yet when Bill Clinton talks about his reductions in growth, he calls them "dollar savings." When he talks about Republican reductions in growth, he calls them "cuts."

Bill Clinton and his fellow liberals have always maintained a double standard about budget-cutting. During his first year in office, President Clinton had this to say about his own 1993 budget plan: "So when you hear all this business about cuts, let me caution you that that is not what is going on. We are going to have increases in Medicare and Medicaid, and a reduction in the rate of growth."[1] But in 1995, the Clinton White House hired a private PR firm (at taxpayer expense) to blitz media markets nationwide with the message that Republicans are "cutting Medicare." Do I detect the aroma of liberal hypocrisy in all this?

HONEST AND DISHONEST NUMBERS

Soon after the Republicans took over the Congress in January 1995, Representative John Kasich of Ohio called my show. John chairs the House Budget Committee, so he's the point man on the House side in the congressional budget battles. During his call, he told the following story:

"A reporter called me off the House floor," he said, "and said to me, 'John, I hear that the new Republican majority plans to define budget terminology differently than previous Democrat majorities. So I'd like you to tell me how you would define such terms as *spending cuts* and *spending increases*.'

"I said, 'Okay, get out your pad and pencil, and I'll explain it to you: If we spend *more* in 1996 than we did in 1995, we're going to call that an *increase*. If we spend *less* in '96 than in '95, we're going to call that a *cut*. And if you spend the *same* in '96 as in '95, we're going to call that a *freeze*.' Now, that's radical, isn't it?"

Well, that really is radical for Washington, D.C. The wonks who run that town are so used to verbal trickery that simple, straightforward language (like calling a cut a cut) seems like a radical innovation! How did the thinking in our federal government get so screwed up that increases could be called "cuts" and spending cuts could be called "tax increases"? How did we get to a point where words lose their meaning and politicians lose all grasp of economic reality?

It all goes back to 1974, when Congress passed the Congressional Budget Impoundment Control Act. At the time, Congress was mad at President Richard Nixon, not just over Watergate, but because Nixon had blocked the spending of funds for certain programs that the Congress had enacted. Nixon's rationale was that the budget was unbalanced, there was no money to pay for these programs, and therefore the government should not be financing new programs. Congress didn't like having its will thwarted by the president, so in order to prevent Richard Nixon from impounding or withholding funds for these new programs, the Democrat-controlled Congress passed the Impoundment Control Act. This law created the budget process that remained in use from 1974 until the 104th Congress took office in 1995. As a result of this budget process, annual federal spending increased from $267 billion in 1974 to almost $1.5 trillion in 1994, as the Democratic-controlled Congress went on the biggest, most expensive spending spree in human history.

One of the central features of that budget process is something called "current services baseline budgeting," and it's one of the dirty little secrets of how our government does business.

CURRENT SERVICES BASELINE BUDGETING

Though it may sound technical, it's actually a very simple little gimmick, designed to fool the American people. Here's how it works:

Let's say you are a liberal congressperson and you have a particular program you want to fund. Let's call it the Bureau of Intrusive Government, Burdensome Rules, Outrageous Taxpayer Harassment, and Excessive Regulations (or BIGBROTHER for short). You want to make sure that BIGBROTHER keeps growing more powerful year after year, so every year you vote a 10 percent increase in BIGBROTHER's budget. Now you have established your "current services baseline." Every year, supposedly in order to maintain so-called "current services," you have to get that 10 percent increase. Sure, it's way more than the inflation rate, but gee-whiz, every year there are more burdensome rules to administer, more excessive regulations to enforce, and more taxpayers in need of harassment. So, of course, BIGBROTHER needs to grow faster than the inflation rate just to keep up with the fast-growing demands of the bureaucracy.

But then, all of a sudden, a big budget-cutting mood sweeps the country. You, being a smart politician, know you need to portray yourself as an ax-wielding budget cutter in order to get reelected. So instead of giving BIGBROTHER its usual 10 percent boost, you hold the increase down to mere 8 percent. BIGBROTHER's budget, which currently stands at $10 billion, was all set to be increased by an additional $1 billion (10 percent of $10 billion). But by cutting the increase from 10 percent to 8 percent, you have reduced the increase to only $800 million. Now you can go back to your constituents and say, "My fellow Americans, I am taking good care of your hard-earned tax dollars. Just look at what I've done: I've cut BIGBROTHER's budget and saved you, the taxpayers, $200 million dollars!"

You see what just happened here? You just *increased* BIGBROTHER's budget by $800 million—and you called it a "cut"! Your constituents hear the word *cut,* and, being normal, commonsense people who use language in normal, commonsense ways, they think you actually *reduced* BIGBROTHER's budget! You fooled 'em! And that's how current services baseline budgeting works. Slick, huh?

Now, you may recall that one of the first acts of the new Republican majority in the 104th Congress was to do away with current services baseline budgeting. Officially, Congress is supposed to follow John Kasich's example and call an increase an increase, and a cut a cut. Unfortunately, the liberals in the White House, the Congress, and the dominant media can't get this simple concept through their heads. They still think and speak in "current services baseline budgetese."

So, during the 1995 budget battles, when the Republicans proposed to slow the growth of various entitlement programs, the liberals (who had apparently just discovered the word *draconian* and wanted to work it into every sentence) kept shouting, "Draconian cuts! Mean, draconian Republicans just want to starve children and old people! Evil, draconian Republicans just want to rape the environment! Look out for the draconian Republicans and their mean-spirited draconianism!" The Republicans, meanwhile, were forced to go on all the talking-heads shows and shout, "There are no cuts! There are no cuts!"

Oh yes, there were a few places where actual, honest cuts were made in the budget. The Republicans reduced foreign aid, got rid of bureaucracy, cut farm subsidies, and closed down a few unneeded programs. But of all the programs that the Democrats hysterically claimed Republicans were cutting—school lunches, Medicare, Medicaid—*not a single program was cut; all were increased!* Personally, I think many of these entitlement programs should be cut, but the fact is, they weren't.

It's time we truly, finally, fully rid ourselves of the deceptive smoke and mirrors of "current services baseline budgeting" and start using honest math. It's time we all start comparing apples to apples, not apples to cowpies. Instead of asking the various agencies, "How much of an increase do you need this year?" we should be asking, "Why should your program be funded at all? How do you justify the existence of your agency?"

DEVOLVING GOVERNMENT

A lot of programs truly ought to be zeroed out. The process of cutting programs and making government smaller is called *devolving* government. The natural tendency of government is to *e*volve, not *de*volve. Those in the bureaucracy, the Keynesian pro-government-growth politicians, the unions, and the various piggish corporations and interest groups that gorge themselves at the federal feeding trough will fight the devolvers of government tooth and nail. They will lie, slander, destroy reputations, and do whatever it takes to maintain their power and their flow of taxpayer money. So while devolving government is a *simple* thing to do—you just kill old, worn-out programs and don't start any new ones—it is not an *easy* thing to do, because the opposition is powerful, pervasive, and well-financed (usually at public expense).

Where should we begin to reduce the size and cost of government? We should start with cabinet departments:

- *The Department of Commerce*—a government giveaway program that selectively benefits certain corporations. There have been times when an effective Commerce Department could have been helpful in defending the interests of the entire business community, as when the Clinton White House proposed a sweeping healthcare initiative that would have ruined and bankrupted many American businesses while placing one-seventh of the private sector economy under federal control. Unfortunately, when business needed an advocate in the White House, Commerce Secretary Ron Brown was silent—in fact, he was coconspirator with Bill and Hillary *against* the business community. Fact is, if we have a pro-business White House, we don't need a Department of Commerce—and if we have an anti-business White House like the Clinton administration, a Department of Commerce is worse than useless. So why have it?

- *The Department of Energy*—a Carter-era holdover, the complete uselessness and corruption of which has been demonstrated by the Hazel O'Leary scandals in the Clinton Administration. The responsibilities of this department are 100 percent domestic, involving such matters as the national energy labs and the storage of strategic oil reserves—yet Secretary O'Leary took sixteen foreign junkets during her first three years in office, spending 130 days overseas—50 percent more days overseas than Secretary of State Warren Christopher.

  One of those trips was a ten-day flying cocktail-party to South Africa aboard rock star Madonna's luxury jet, replete with 109 staffers and invited guests plus a video crew and photographers to record the festivities. Cost to the taxpayers: more than half a million bucks. O'Leary claims these trips drum up business for U.S. corporations—but that is a duplication of what Ron Brown is doing at Commerce (a useless function even when Brown does it).

O'Leary obviously can't keep herself busy here in the States, doing Department of Energy business—so the logical question arises: What do we need the DoE for, anyway? The logical answer: We don't. Time to pull the plug on Energy.

- *The Department of Education.* To assure a quality education for our kids, control should be vested in local school boards and the states, which are accountable to parents and taxpayers—not a bureaucratic agency in Washington, D.C., which is beholden to unions.
- *The Department of Housing and Urban Development*
- *The Department of Labor*

Next, we should eliminate, downsize, restructure, and/or dramatically limit the powers of intrusive, oppressive regulating agencies such as:

- *The Internal Revenue Service (IRS)*
- *The Occupational Safety and Health Administration (OSHA)*
- *The Bureau of Alcohol, Tobacco, and Firearms (BATF)*
- *The Environmental Protection Agency (EPA)*
- *The Bureau of Land Management (BLM)*

Finally, we should eliminate programs or agencies that promote the liberal agenda or subsidize special interests at taxpayer expense:

- *The National Endowment for the Arts (NEA).* We have separation of church and state—why not separation of art and state? You can't have true artistic freedom when the arts community is sponsored by the government. NEA dollars are dispensed by a group of elitists to a select clique of approved, politically correct artists. The result has been an outpouring of "art" calculated to offend and belittle the values of those who are forced to pay the bills—the American taxpayers. The NEA is bad for the arts and bad for taxpayers.
- *The National Endowment for the Humanities (NEH).* Uncle Sam just doesn't belong in the "patron of the arts and humanities" business.
- *The Corporation of Public Broadcasting.* If you really want to "soak the rich," have Big Bird, Kermit, and Barney the purple dinosaur cough up to save PBS. Those fuzzy little guys could buy and sell Ted Turner!

- *The Equal Employment Opportunity Commission.* Just another in-your-face government agency that has outlived its usefulness.
- *The Market Promotion Program.* This corporate welfare program subsidizes overseas marketing costs for American companies such as Pillsbury, McDonalds, and the Gallo Winery. Nix it.
- *Farm subsidies.* ABC newsman Sam Donaldson is just one among thousands of multimillionaires receiving huge farm subsidy checks from the federal government. In 1993 and 1994, he received $97,000 in wool and mohair subsidies to raise sheep and goats on his New Mexico ranch, and $3,500 to install livestock watering equipment. I don't particularly care to see my hard-earned tax dollars going to pay Sam Donaldson's welfare checks. There may have been a time when farm subsidies could be defended as a way to stabilize ag production by guaranteeing return, but in these days of ag insurance and futures markets, farm subsidies should go away—or at least be means-tested to weed out network anchors and other rich guys.
- *Electric car development subsidies*

How do we know whether a given government program should be cut or not? Here's a simple test: We should go through the entire roster of government agencies and programs, from top to bottom, A to Z. With each agency, we should ask ourselves, "If we weren't already doing this program, would we *start* such a program today?" If the answer is no, then the program should be ruthlessly cut.

APPLES AND ICBMS

Ironically, the one federal department that should *not* be cut is the *only* department of the government that has shrunk under the Clinton administration: the Department of Defense.

In January 1996, Bill Clinton claimed that, as president, he had cut the federal workforce by 200,000. The fact is, there were 770,000 federal civilian employees when Bill Clinton took office in January 1993, and there were 800,000 federal civilian employees—30,000 more!—three years later when he made that claim. So how does he figure he reduced the workforce by 200,000? He arrives at that number by counting our men and women in uniform as if they are civil service employees! Bill Clinton wants the American people to think he is cutting the bureaucracy, when in fact it has expanded under his administration. *All* the personnel cuts Bill Clinton has made have come from the *military*. If nothing else, this fact proves Bill Clinton meant what he said in his 1969 draft-dodging letter: He truly does "loathe the military." Under his dubious stewardship, the effectiveness, readiness, and morale of our military have fallen to even lower levels than under the disastrous policies of Jimmy Carter. A few facts:

In December 1995, Bill Clinton shipped troops to Bosnia to enforce a brittle, externally imposed "peace" that neither side in the conflict seemed to want or respect. At the same time troops were landing in Bosnia, Bill Clinton was wielding his veto pen against the Defense Authorization Bill, thus denying the entire U.S. military force (including the troops in Bosnia) the 2.4 percent pay raise they were due. Also vetoed in that same defense bill were such items as:

- Servicemen's life insurance increases for troops in Bosnia, Haiti, and other high-risk deployments.
- Enlistment and reenlistment bonuses (to attract the best quality people to the shrinking defense force).
- Much-needed, long overdue repairs and maintenance to existing military living quarters. As Senator Dan Coats (R-Indiana) said on the Senate floor, December 19, 1995, many base housing units are "over 30 years old [and] in a state of disrepair. In fact, by Department of Defense standards, over 80 percent of the existing military housing is inadequate. . . . I have personally visited the family quarters and the bachelor quarters on a number of bases throughout this country and some overseas. I would not put my family in some of these living situations. . . . Roofs are caving in, ceilings are caving in, water is running down the walls, broken plumbing, exterior windows cracked, cold air rushing through the windows and the walls."
- Increased living quarters allowances (without which many military personnel forced to seek off-base housing would be driven below the poverty line).
- Hazardous and special duty pay.

- Authorization to recruit and train service chiefs and technicians to operate high-tech equipment (the level of these personnel has become dangerously low, leading to a serious problem with equipment operation and maintenance).

All of these genuine issues of support for our men and women in uniform and their families were vetoed by Bill Clinton—and then he had the gall to demand that the Congress "support our troops" by endorsing his dangerous policy in the Balkans!

The erosion of defense spending has gradually placed our nation at greater and greater risk. The defense budget has declined every year from 1985 through 1996. The Clinton administration's budget projection for defense in fiscal year 1996 (in constant dollars) equals the dangerously low 1975 spending level. The 1997 projection trims defense even further, to the 1955 level. Since 1985, we have cut active duty personnel by 32 percent, to the lowest level in sixty years. In that time, Army divisions have been reduced by 45 percent, Navy battle force ships have been reduced by 37 percent, and the number of Air Force attack and fighter aircraft has shrunk by 40 percent.

Defense procurement has declined 71 percent in the decade between 1985 and 1995. Funds for technological research, development, and testing have been cut 57 percent in the same ten-year period. If current trends continue through 1999, defense spending will have declined to 2.8 percent of the gross national product—the lowest rate since just before the sneak attack on Pearl Harbor in 1941!

While we have been drawing down our forces, we have been increasing the deployment of those forces—which means we have increased the strain on our troops and we have spread our defensive resources more and more thinly with each passing year. While reducing our forces in Europe from 314,000 during the Cold War to just over 100,000 under Bill Clinton, we have sent those forces on more missions in the last five years than in all the previous forty-five years combined. A soldier can now expect to spend 138 days a year away from home on long-duration, short-notice deployments, not to mention time spent away from home on training missions. Air Force deployments have quadrupled over the past seven years, though the overall strength of the Air Force has been slashed by a third.

Even before Bill Clinton took office, the gap between military missions and military funding was gradually widening—and under Clinton, that gap has blown wide open. Our men and women in uniform are doing an absolutely amazing job despite growing problems with obsolete facilities and equipment, spare parts shortages, and procurement slowdowns. We have already reached the point where we could no longer mount another Desert Shield/Desert Storm operation. How long can this decline continue before our readiness and our ability to defend ourselves tempts some dictator with Saddam-size delusions to stir up more trouble than we can handle? How long before our own nation is in peril?

While defense spending has declined 35 percent from 1985 and 1995, what has happened to the rest of the budget? Domestic discretionary spending increased 12 percent. And spending on so-called "entitlements"—welfare and other mandatory social spending? It soared by 38 percent![2] The ballooning costs of nondefense programs is choking our ability to meet our number one priority as a nation: to defend the United States of America.

You cannot put defense spending on the same chopping block with the rest of the budget. You cannot equate the security and survival of the United States of America with such transitory and ephemeral interests as the National Endowment for the Arts or the Department of Commerce. It's not just a case of comparing apples and oranges, but of comparing apples and ICBMs.

REAL MONEY

When the government becomes too big and too expensive, you have to cut it back and spend less on it. If it does too much, you have to make it do less. No matter how noble and worthwhile this or that new program might be, you have to "just say no" to it, because adding new programs makes government bigger and more expensive. Only *cutting programs* makes government smaller.

To paraphrase and update that famous quote by Everett Dirkson (the conservative leader of the Senate Republicans during the 1960s), "A trillion here, a trillion there, pretty soon we're talking about real money." Are we talking about real money here? You bet: $5 trillion of national debt, scheduled to hit $8 trillion by 2010 if nothing is done about it. But we're also talking about the standard of living, the hopes and dreams, and the checkbook and wallet of every American family—because that's "real money" too. And the future of every American is at risk so long as this obscene and unsustainable debt is hanging over our heads.

Never before have we had such an opportunity to make a lasting difference in the future of America. With the new Republican majority, we finally have a chance to turn this nation back from the brink of collapse and toward a future of promise and hope. America is balanced on a razor's edge of great opportunity—and great danger. The danger we face is the danger of retreat and failed resolve. What we have accomplished so far, compared with the record of the last forty years of Democrat rule, is astonishing and revolutionary. But compare those accomplishments with the task ahead of us—the job of producing surplus budgets and paying down a multi-trillion-dollar national debt—and it's clear that we have scarcely even begun.

The spending cuts and program restructuring called for by the Republican majority in Congress have been painless and modest—a few cuts, but mostly just slower growth in a number of programs. The Republican plan still allows the national debt to swell by an additional trillion dollars by 2002. We are still sliding swiftly into a black hole of debt, even as we reach for a balanced budget. Despite the desperation of America's fiscal crisis, despite the absolute painlessness of the Republican plan, liberal Democrats in the White House and Congress have howled, fought, kicked, scratched, clawed, lied, and demonized the Republicans as a bunch of Nazis and thugs. What will the liberal mob do if we ever start making the *really* hard choices that are needed to save this nation from bankruptcy, and our children and grandchildren from economic slavery?

We have to continue moving forward. We have to keep electing people who understand the danger of uncontrolled deficits and mounting debt. Those who obstruct the effort to rescue America, those who put their own political fortunes above America's future, must be replaced with people of courage, integrity, and vision. We have a narrow window of opportunity over the next few years to preserve the American dream for our children and our grandchildren.

If we fail to seize *this* moment, we will *never* get another chance.

CHAPTER 10

What's So Progressive About the Progressive Tax?

THE UNITED States of America began with a tax revolt.

The Declaration of Independence in 1776 was a response to a series of taxes imposed by England's King George III upon the American colonies—the American Revenue Act (or the Sugar Act) of 1764, the Quartering Act and Stamp Act of 1765, the Townsend Act of 1767, the Tea Act of 1772, and the Coercive Acts of 1774. In addition to imposing taxes without the consent of the taxpayers, these acts allowed English bureaucrats to interfere with and override American legislative and governing bodies (shades of today's unfunded mandates and states' rights issues), to deprive citizens of trial by jury, and to establish a legal presumption of guilt until proven innocent (much like the IRS's authority today). The Declaration of Independence also cited the fact that the king had "erected a multitude of new offices and sent hither swarms of officers to harass our people, and eat out their substance"—exactly what Washington, D.C., is doing today through such agencies as the BATF, the IRS, OSHA, the EPA, the FDA, the BLM, and many other regulatory and enforcement agencies.

And get this: The taxes that inspired the tax revolt of 1776 were a *tiny fraction* of the taxes we pay today! In those days, there was no income tax, no capital gains tax, no estate tax. The tax burden that so enraged the American colonists were largely taxes on imports (textiles, rum, wine, hides, raw materials, tea), on printed matter (newspapers, almanacs, legal documents, insurance policies), and on selected domestic commodities (lead, glass, paints, paper, and so forth). For the average American colonist, such taxes would not add up to more than 5 percent of his income—by today's standards scarcely an annoyance, much less a hardship. Today, we pay up to 40 percent of our annual income to the IRS alone—*plus* state taxes, county taxes, local taxes, and host of additional federal taxes on gasoline, tires, lodging, airline tickets, and other goods and services.

Why did such comparatively modest taxation propel a bunch of early "angry white males" into an honest-to-gosh shooting war back in 1776— a war in which people died and a country was founded? Sure, they were furious about being taxed by an elite group of politicians in England, but aren't we just as furious over being taxed by that elitist bunch in Washington? You might say, "Well, there were a lot of other government abuses in the 1770s, not just taxes." Okay, but there are plenty of other government abuses today.

The federal government has ignored the Tenth Amendment and usurped the power of the states and the people. The Justice Department has intimidated its citizens by filing multi-million-dollar lawsuits against those who legally, constitutionally petition their government not to place drug- and crime-attracting federal housing projects in their neighborhoods. The government has sent unelected IRS bureaucrats to confiscate the property of Americans without due process. It has even *killed* innocent American citizens—men, women, and children—at places like Waco and Ruby Ridge. On top of all these unconstitutional abuses, the average American taxpayer works from January 1 to July 9—more than half the year!—just to support the government in the lavish style to which it has become accustomed.

The average American family pays more in taxes than it spends on food, clothing, and shelter combined. As a nation, we devote 5.4 billion hours a year to federal tax-related paperwork—about 3.6 billion hours for businesses and about 1.8 billion hours for individuals and families. The average family spends about twenty-seven hours a year keeping records and preparing its Form 1040 and additional schedules. Does that sound like freedom to you? It doesn't to me. We are *enslaved* by the IRS and by the tax-and-spend politicians in Washington. It's insanity, and it's got to stop.

Why has there not been another Boston Tea Party, another Declaration of Independence, another American Revolution in the 1990s?

In a way, there has. It took place at the voting booths in November 1994, when the Republicans were swept to power in both houses of Congress for the first time in forty years. But why has it taken so long—and why is the conservative revolution under such intense attack from so many quarters?

WHY SUCH RESISTANCE TO CHANGE?

I see several reasons for our lack of fervor for change. *First, there are many people and institutions in America that profit from high taxation.* Despite today's outrageous tax rates, a lot of people make out like bandits, thanks to government largesse. I don't just mean welfare recipients, with their government checks, their food stamps, their Medicaid, and their rent subsidies. There are others in the government office with their hands out, including wealthy companies receiving corporate welfare and wealthy farmers collecting farm subsidy checks. There are a lot more people living off government welfare (in all its forms) than we ever imagined. They vote, they lobby, and they don't want a bunch of conservative tax revolutionaries coming in and killing the federal goose that lays their golden eggs.

A second reason America has been slow to rebel against outrageous taxes is that we have such a high degree of prosperity in America today. We have conveniences and entertainment choices unparalleled in the history of the human race. We fail to realize that much of that prosperity is *borrowed* prosperity—borrowed not only on our personal credit cards, but borrowed by the government from our children and our grandchildren in the form of trillions of dollars of national debt. Because we have nice cars, nice homes, VCRs, movies, stereos, and a vast choice of restaurants to enjoy, we are dulled to the fact that we and future generations are being fiscally raped by our government. We fail to understand that our present prosperity is a house of cards, destined to collapse, if we don't bring our national spending habits under control.

A third reason America has been slow to rebel against outrageous taxes is that payroll withholding dulls us to the pain. Employers and self-employed individuals know what taxes are all about, because they see how much they earn and how much of what they earn gets taken by the government—and they experience the pain of writing a check to Uncle Sam every quarter. Employees whose taxes are withheld, however, become used to thinking of their income as so-and-so much "after taxes." The amount withheld from your check by your employer is money you never see, so you never miss it.

And when you get your refund check back from the IRS—why, you're actually *grateful,* as if kind-hearted Uncle Sam is giving you a gift! Folks, that refund check is *your* money that the government took from you and kept for months without paying a penny of interest. And if you underestimate and underwithhold, and end up writing a check to the IRS on April 15? Why, "kind-hearted Uncle Sam" turns right around and wrings not only interest but penalties out of your hide!

WHAT'S "PROGRESSIVE" ABOUT IT?

Why does our government tax its citizens? The obvious answer: The government needs money to operate. The first income tax in 1861 was imposed to finance the Civil War (the tax was repealed ten years later). The income tax made a comeback in 1913, when the Sixteenth Amendment to the Constitution was adopted. But over the years, the income tax has been structured to do much more than simply raise operating capital for the government. Particularly since World War II, tax policy in America has been used to further social, political, and economic goals.

Uncle Sam used to be a great old guy. He always looked so classy with his white goatee, his stars-and-stripes tux, and his top hat. But lately, old Unc has turned into a nasty, cantankerous, tax-happy old coot! I mean, he taxes everything! He taxes the production of wealth, the receipt of income, the ownership and transfer of wealth, the interest on savings, the gain on investment, the sale of commodities, the use of services, the sale of property—and as a final insult, he even taxes you when you die! Doesn't he know what all this outrageously excessive taxation does to the country that bears his initials? As Stephen Moore, director of fiscal policy studies at the libertarian CATO Institute has pointed out, the American tax system

Taxes: Then and Now

Year	1914	1994
*Taxes paid	$6.7 billion	$683 billion
*Per capita taxes	$69	$2,622
Individual filers	360,000	113,829,000
Percentage of population filing	0.5 percent	45 percent
*IRS budget	$110 million	$7.1 billion
IRS employees	4,000	110,000
Pages of tax law	14	9,400
Pages of IRS forms	4	4,000
Top tax rate	7 percent	40 percent
Median family tax rate	0 percent	28 percent

*Measured in constant 1994 dollars.

Source: Citizens for an Alternative Tax System.

- "reduces economic growth through punitive tax rates on savings and investment";
- "imposes large costs on American business and workers" because of the incredible complexity of the tax code; and
- violates the Constitution by its "tremendous and growing intrusiveness." The IRS treats taxpayers as guilty until they prove themselves innocent. One's property—bank accounts, homes, farms, businesses, and tangible assets—can be, and are being, confiscated without the government having to prove its charges.

One of the fundamental concepts in American tax policy since 1913 has been the so-called "progressive tax." Now, whoever came up with that term was a PR genius! The word *progressive* sounds like it refers to *progress,* suggesting that the "progressive tax" is a wonderful, forward-thinking, *enlightened* tax! What a sick joke! The fact is, the word *progressive* here pertains to a tax that advances steadily like a cancer, *progressively* spreading throughout the body and killing the patient. It refers to a tax rate that escalates, taking a higher and higher percentage of your earnings as your income rises. The so-called "progressive tax" actually stifles economic progress—but the beauty of a progressive income tax is that it is politically an easy sell, because it appeals to the "soak the rich" mentality pervading much of the country.

The progressive income tax that was first imposed in 1913 exempted the first $3,000 of income while taxing the remainder at escalating rates ranging from 1 percent for income up to $20,000 to 7 percent for income over $500,000. Because $3,000 a year was a very comfortable upper-middle-class income in those days, more than 99 percent of the population was exempt and paid no income tax whatsoever. The government was financed by the "rich" who earned $3,000 a year or more.

From 7 percent in 1913, the top rate soared to 77 percent by 1918 to help pay for World War I. The top rate slipped to 25 percent from 1925 to 1928—but by the mid-1930s it was again topping 77 percent. During World War II, the top tax rate had reached a confiscatory 94 percent. (It was also during WWII that payroll withholding first began; prior to that time, all taxpayers were required to write a check to the government.) The top tax rate remained above 90 percent until it was dropped to 70 percent by the Tax Act of 1964. The '64 tax cut was conceived by JFK as a way to get the sluggish economy moving again. (By the standards of today's liberalism, Kennedy was a Reagan-style supply-sider.) After Kennedy's death in '63, the Tax Act was signed into law by LBJ. In 1981, under Ronald Reagan, the top rate was cut to 50 percent. The Reagan Tax Reform Act of 1986 went even further, closing loopholes on a wholesale basis and replacing 14 brackets (ranging from 11 to 50 percent) with just two brackets—a mere 15 and 28 percent!

When you look at some of those top marginal rates in the history of American taxation—50, 70, 90 percent and more—you wonder why anyone would bother creating and amassing wealth, only to have it confiscated. But you are very much mistaken if you believe that the rich ever really paid such punishing tax rates. That's what tax loopholes are all about—to enable the rich to keep their riches while the politicians make a big show of "soaking the rich" with 90-plus percent tax rates. The "progressive tax" has always been riddled with loopholes for the rich, and as a result, the middle class has always paid most of Uncle Sam's bills. The richest Americans can usually structure their finances in such a way that they never pay a dime in taxes. After all, the rich are the ones who play golf and break bread with the guys who write the tax code, so do you really think they're going to end up paying 90-plus percent rates?

The rationale for the "progressive tax" is the same rationale that underlies socialism and communism: The rich don't deserve to be rich, and the wealth they have accumulated must be stripped from them and redistributed in order to make things "fair." You find that concept explicitly stated in *The Communist Manifesto* of Karl Marx; you cannot find it stated anywhere in the Constitution or the writings of the founding fathers. But for most of this century, our tax policy has been derived from the same basis as the government of the now-defunct and discredited U.S.S.R.: "Soak the rich." (Even though our tax code really soaks the middle class, who see themselves as far from rich.)

It's time we return to the founding principles of this country: life, liberty, and the pursuit of happiness. That means the unbridled pursuit of our dreams—even dreams of riches and success, if that's what we want. As long as this is truly America, no one has the right to put a ceiling on what you can achieve, on what you can earn or acquire. Instead of penalizing success with punitive tax rates and rewarding failure with government handouts, we should be teaching those who fail how to become successful!

I could sit back every day and complain, "Rush Limbaugh made $25 million last year! I worked as hard as or harder than he did! We both have three-hour talk shows! My accuracy rating is even higher than his; after all, Rush supported NAFTA and GATT! It's not fair that I didn't make the same amount of money! Nobody has a right to be as rich as Rush Limbaugh! I want the U.S. government to equalize the outcome between Rush and me! I want the government to take a bunch of that wealth away from Rush and give it to me so it will be fair!" Maybe that's what a whiny liberal talk-show host would say, but not me. To me, Rush Limbaugh is not a target to shoot *at* but a target to shoot *for*. I have a goal to aim for. I see what he's done, and I think, "I'll just keep working harder."

And that's what we need to teach the envying, covetous, spiteful people in this country who begrudge the rich their riches: Don't rob from the rich. *Learn* from the rich. Don't try to pull others down. Lift yourself up. Don't look to the government to "soak the rich." Demand that the government unshackle the economy so that you can become rich too.

THE GREAT TAX DEBATE

Fortunately, the days of the "progressive tax" are numbered. What sort of tax system will replace the current system? As I write, all that can be said for sure is that the new Republican majority is determined to reform the system from top to bottom. Here are some of the options on the table in the great tax debate:

A *consumption tax* is a tax imposed on spending for goods or services and may or may not be imposed at the point of retail sale. One form of consumption tax is the *VAT (value added tax),* which is common in Europe. The problem with VATs is that they are often imposed at each stage in the manufacturing and distribution process, inflating the price of goods and services with hidden taxes that consumers are not even aware of. These taxes also compound at each stage, so that the consumer ends up paying a tax on a tax. Congressman Bill Archer (R-Texas) is a leading proponent of a consumption tax.

A *sales tax* is similar to a consumption tax but is imposed only at the point of sale to the consumer. In a real sales tax, there are no hidden taxes to compound and inflate the price of goods and services. The amount of tax paid is clear to the consumer. While sales taxes are commonly used by states and localities, a *national sales tax* is a new idea that is gaining momentum. Leading proponents of a national sales tax include Senator Richard Lugar (R-Indiana) and Citizens for an Alternative Tax.

One advantage of replacing the income tax with a national sales tax is that it slams the door in the face of the snoopy, intrusive IRS. A good argument can be made that it's really nobody's business (including Uncle Sam's) how much money you make or how you make it. Imagine a world in which you do not have to fill out tax forms, a world without withholding, a world in which there are no more IRS audits to worry about. Imagine a world in which April 15 has lost all power to strike fear in the hearts of decent taxpaying Americans, and has become just another sunny spring day.

But!

Sales and consumption taxes have a serious downside. While Senator Lugar proposes a 17 percent national sales tax rate, economist Bruce Bartlett has crunched the numbers and concludes that the sales tax rate would have to be set at 13.3 percent to replace the income tax, *plus* an additional 13.6 percent to replace the Social Security tax, *plus* another 3.3 percent to replace the corporate income tax—and that adds up to a 30.2 percent tax! How would you like to have to pay a 30.2 percent sales tax on a $25,000 car? Or worse (and more likely), Congress would just hide a lot of those taxes in the hidden layers of a VAT so that taxpayers wouldn't know how much they are paying in taxes.

Even if we only had a 17 percent national sales tax, as Senator Lugar proposes, legitimate manufacturers and merchants would be hurt by the massive "sticker shock" this tax would cause. Human nature being what it is, black marketeering would run rampant as buyers seek ways to evade the massive federal sales tax. There would be an exploding underground economy like nothing we've ever seen before. Proponents of a national sales tax admit that the "sticker shock" effect would decrease consumption, at least initially, but they point out that it would likely steer more Americans toward savings and investment (the savings rate of U.S. citizens is the lowest of any industrialized nation). Personally, I don't think the American people ought to be steered in this direction or that direction like a herd of cattle; I think they should be *liberated* and *trusted* to spend or invest their money in any way they choose.

I've already had a glimpse of how a national sales tax would affect the economy—and I think it's a scary prospect. I was in the boating industry for many years. I raced and sold boats, and I was pretty good at that business and it was good to me. The boat business paid for the house and cars I have to this day. So I knew exactly what the result would be, a few years ago, when the Democrat-controlled Congress passed a 10 percent surtax on "luxury yachts." The liberal Democrats thought they were going to stick it to the greedy, self-indulgent rich people in the yacht set. They thought the rich would keep buying "luxury yachts," same as always, and the surtax would take money away from the rich and give it to the politicians in Washington, D.C., to spend. But it didn't work that way.

Boat buyers walked into the showroom and took a look at the inflated stickers on all those shiny new boats. Then they turned right around, walked out of the showroom, and bought their boats in the Bahamas! Who got burned by the "soak the rich" luxury yacht surtax? The middle-class, as usual. About 20,000 working-class people lost their jobs in the boat business—and these were people with mortgages to pay and kids to raise. That's the way it has always been, that's the way it will always be: If you inflate prices with sales taxes, you only succeed in driving buyers offshore or into the underground economy.

The national sales tax is often touted as a way finally to dismantle the hated IRS—but would it really work that way? Which government agency has the responsibility for making sure sales taxes get paid? Which agency will be given the responsibility of investigating sales tax fraud and black marketeering? The IRS will always be with us, even if the income tax goes away.

And what about the "regressivity" problem? Regressivity is the perceived unfairness to the poor who would be required to pay the same tax rate as the rich on everything they buy, including the necessities of life. A uniform national sales tax or consumption tax would take a larger percentage of a poor person's income than a rich person's income. To solve this problem and make it "fair," the proponents of sales and consumption taxes have suggested various complex formulas for exempting certain purchases and reimbursing the poor for taxes on necessities. With a sales or consumption tax, we are back to a complex system with thousands of pages of tax law to cover all the exemptions.

Do you think a national sales tax would do away with lobbyists and special interests? Hoo-boy! Not long ago in my home state of California, we saw the kind of silliness that sales taxes often produce. The California legislature passed a special "snack tax" to raise additional revenue—and instantly, lobbyists were swarming over Sacramento, yammering at legislators: "You can't call potato chips a snack!" "Our chocolate-covered granola bar isn't a snack—it's a health food!" "What if we move the Slim Jims and beef jerky from the checkout stand to the deli section— they wouldn't be snacks, they'd be meat!" "Okay, maybe Cheddar Puffs are a snack in a 1.3-ounce bag, but in the big 11.9-ounce bag, they're a grocery item!" Get the picture? Now multiply that by about a zillion times, and you'd get some idea of the chaos that would descend on Washington, D.C., if a national sales tax was signed into law. You'd see

Highway 495—the beltway encircling Washington, D.C.—become one big traffic jam filled with screaming lobbyists!

But there is an even more dangerous risk in a national sales tax. My friend Grover Norquist, president of Americans for Tax Reform, stated it well in the November 1995 issue of *The Michael Reagan Monthly Monitor:*

> Advocating a sales tax to replace the income tax could well lead to the imposition of a sales tax/VAT *in addition to the present income taxes.* Every nation in Europe that has a VAT also has a personal income tax and a corporate income tax as well as wage taxes like Social Security.[1]

Remember, there's always the possibility that liberals will retake the Congress—and you know how those people love taxes! If you have a sales tax or VAT in place when they get there, they're liable to revive the income tax *alongside* the existing sales or consumption tax—and then where will we be? Imagine being eaten alive by two different tax systems at the same time!

How do you keep the old, "progressive," oppressive, complicated, wasteful income tax from being revived sometime in the future? By replacing it with *another kind of income tax*—one that is simple and fair. Politicians could easily impose several different kinds of taxes at the same time—and they frequently do. But a politician can't impose more than one kind of income tax at a time! When you replace the old "progressive" income tax with another form of income tax, you can be reasonably sure that the old income tax is truly dead and not likely to rise again.

So how do you make income taxes simple and fair? Easy. You throw out the old system and replace it with a flat tax.

THE FLAT TAX POSTCARD TO UNCLE SAM

The *flat tax* is a tax on gross income. Also called a "proportional tax" (in contrast to a "progressive tax"), a flat tax collects one flat percentage rate from *all* income levels, and eliminates or severely restricts deductions. The most popular version of the flat tax is the Armey-Shelby Flat Tax, named after its two primary sponsors, Congressman Dick Armey (R-Texas) and Senator Richard Shelby (R-Alabama). The beauty of a flat tax is its simplicity. You don't clutter it up with 9,400 pages of regulations. Instead of filling out pages and pages of tax forms and schedules, you fill out a postcard and send it to the IRS.

One feature of the Armey-Shelby Flat Tax that is widely misunderstood is how it would impact lower- and middle-class wage-earners. Many people mistakenly assume that eliminating the "progressive tax" in favor of a flat tax would sharply raise taxes on lower-income wage-earners while drastically reducing taxes on the wealthy. In fact, the Armey-Shelby Flat Tax is far friendlier to the poor and middle-class than the so-called "progressive tax." Here's how it would work:

Under the Armey-Shelby plan, all taxpayers are assessed a flat rate of 17 percent on gross income—*but* the plan also provides a per-child deduction of $5,300, plus a generous personal allowance of $13,100 for an individual, $17,200 for a single head of household, and $26,200 for a married couple. That's how much of your income is tax-free under the Armey-Shelby plan. Only what you make over and above those allowances is taxed at the 17 percent flat tax. Given these allowances, it is easy to compute what your *effective tax rate* would be—that is, the percentage of your entire income that is paid to the government in taxes. Just look at the scoreboard below, find the example closest to your own situation, and compare what you would be paying under Armey-Shelby versus what you have been paying under the "progressive" status quo. Which plan leaves you better off?

Status	Income	Effective Rate	Taxes Paid
Single	$13,100/yr.	0.00 percent	*nothing, zilch!*
Single	$20,000/yr.	5.87 percent	$1,173
Single	$40,000/yr.	11.43 percent	$4,573
Single	$50,000/yr.	12.55 percent	$6,273
Single	$100,000/yr.	14.77 percent	$14,773
Single	$250,000/yr.	16.11 percent	$40,275
Married	$20,000/yr.	0.00 percent	*zero, nada!*
Married	$40,000/yr.	5.87 percent	$2,346
Married	$50,000/yr.	8.09 percent	$4,046
Married	$100,000/yr.	12.55 percent	$12,546
Married	$250,000/yr.	15.22 percent	$38,046

Note: All of the above calculations are for *childless* individuals and couples. Add the $5,300 per-child deduction to this equation and these effective rates and the amount of tax owed shrink even further. The calculations are incredibly simple. For example, a couple earning $40,000 a year with one child would take that $40,000 figure, subtract the $26,200 personal allowance, which leaves $13,800; then subtract the $5,300 allowance for one child, which leaves $8,500 of taxable income; 17 percent of $8,500 is $1,445, which is the entire tax the family would pay on $40,000 income. The effective rate this family would pay on its $40,000 income after these few simple deductions is a mere 3.61 percent! Add a second child and the tax owed drops to $544, or 1.4 percent! Is that cool, or what?

Best of all, the flat tax is so simple, it's tamper-proof! The math is simple. The form is simple. And the concept is so simple and elegant that politicians, accountants, lawyers, and lobbyists can't tinker with it. They won't be able to hide loopholes and tax dodges and dirty little tricks in 9,400 pages of tax laws, because the entire tax code will fit into a pamphlet that anyone can read and understand. There are no inheritance taxes, no depreciation schedules, no more planning your entire life around the vagaries and complexities of the tax code. The simplicity of the flat tax makes it harder for future Congresses to raise the rate. Since everyone pays the same rate, any attempt to increase the rate would be opposed by *all* taxpayers, not just one group or another—a built-in safeguard against tax rate tampering.

"The beauty of the flat tax," says Grover Norquist, "is that it taxes all income, *just once,* visibly, with no intermediary between government and taxpayer. . . . [It] is also perfectly neutral with respect to all economic decisions. There is no penalty against saving, to be sure, and no double or triple taxation of corporate income. But on the other hand, there is no bias against saving either. You can save or consume, spend now or spend later, invest your money wisely or waste it if you will. . . . There is no way a government planner can encourage you to spend money one way or the other with differential taxation. Your purchasing decisions just don't matter. The tax in all cases is exactly the same."[2]

UNLEASH THE ENGINE OF PROSPERITY

The flat tax is not the be-all and end-all in fixing the way government conducts its financial business. Simplifying the tax code and reducing the tax burden on Americans is just one step toward the overall goal of reducing the size, power, and reach of the federal government. To complete the job, we must:

Cut the capital gains tax. The capital gains tax is currently a loser for the U.S. government, bringing in a tiny trickle of revenue. It exists in its current form not to generate money for the government but to punish the rich. It is a tax on the creation of wealth, and it is unjust and counterproductive.

Capital gains are not currently covered under proposed flat tax legislation—but could easily be married to the flat tax. Why not tie the capital gains rate to the income tax rate? If we cut capital gains taxes from their current 28 percent tax rate to only 17 percent, experts predict it would bring more, not less, money into the federal treasury. How is that possible? Because at present, people are sitting on their investments, refusing to sell because of a confiscatory tax rate. Cut the rate to a modest, reasonable level, and you would unleash an avalanche of economic activity. Investments, properties, and assets would be sold, taxes would be paid, and the U.S. treasury would be awash in cash!

The capital gains tax should also be indexed for inflation. Here's why: Suppose you invested $100,000 in 1980. Maybe you bought shares of stock or real estate or a truckload of baseball cards; it doesn't matter. You held those assets for twelve years, selling them in 1992 for $200,000. According to Uncle Sam, you made a cool $100,000 on your investment, so he takes 28 percent of your capital gain, or $28,000. But wait! According to the government's own consumer price index, inflation rose at a 4.5 percent annual rate during those twelve years—which inflated your investment a total of 70.4 percent by the time you sold it. That means that while your "nominal gain" on your investment was $100,000, your actual gain, adjusted for inflation, was only $29,600. A full 70.4 percent, or $70,400, of your $100,000 "gain" came from inflation. So if you are being taxed $28,000 on a $29,600 actual gain, your effective tax rate is a whopping *94.6 percent*!

If we would index capital gains for inflation and only tax the real, adjusted-for-inflation gain at the same rate as the flat tax rate, the capital gains tax would be fair—and it would free the economy. A rational capital gains policy, indexed for inflation, would encourage (instead of punishing) savings and investment, and would take investments off the shelf and put them into circulation in the economy.

Would a capital gains cut benefit the rich? Of course it would—but so what? The middle-class would benefit even more! Remember, you are subject to capital gains taxes whenever you sell a home or cash in a retirement investment. The fact is, 70 percent of those who would benefit from a capital gains cut earn $50,000 or less. Cut capital gains taxes, and everyone—the rich, the poor, and even cash-strapped Uncle Sam—will be better off.

Dramatically cut spending. The government is not just a few hundred billion dollars oversized. It is *orders of magnitude* larger than it ought to be. The modest cutbacks and reductions in growth rate that were included in the Republican budget plan of 1995 are like a 1,000-pound man standing before a full-length mirror and saying, "You know, I could stand to lose a few pounds. I'd better cut back—instead of fifteen hot fudge sundaes a day, I'll just have fourteen." The 1,000-pound man needs radical reduction—and so does the U.S. government. It's long past time to get serious—not just about "trimming the fat" here and there, but about wholesale dismantling and devolving of entire departments and programs of the government.

Does this mean you hold off on tax cuts until after you cut spending? No way! You have to cut taxes and spending *at the same time.* Why? For one thing, you cut taxes to bring in more money. The Kennedy-Johnson tax cut in 1964 and the Reagan tax cuts of the 1980s have proven that lower tax rates stimulate economic activity, bringing more money into the treasury. Ronald Reagan cut top marginal rates from 70 percent to 50 percent in 1981, and from 50 percent to 28 percent in 1986—yet overall tax revenues rose in every year but one throughout the 1980s. Even with all those tax cuts, the take at the U.S. Treasury swelled from $599 billion in 1981 to almost a trillion buckaroos in 1990!

Did the government continue to run deficits during the Reagan 1980s? You betcha! Those are the "Reagan deficits" the liberals love to remind us of. Of course, they conveniently fail to mention that all of Ronald Reagan's budgets were pronounced "dead on arrival" by liberal Democrats in the Congress. The deficits rung up in the '80s are liberal deficits, composed primarily of uncontrolled social spending that Ronald Reagan opposed for eight years. The tax cuts that Ronald Reagan shoved down the unwilling throats of the Democrats dramatically swelled federal tax revenues—but the deficits continued to grow because no matter how much money gets shoveled into the treasury, spend-crazy liberals shovel it out even faster. That has to change. We have to cut taxes, but we also have to change our ways and slash spending—radically, relentlessly, determinedly.

Liberals always try to balance the books by raising taxes instead of cutting spending—and sometimes Republicans (like George "Read-My-Lips" Bush in 1990) fall for that kind of thinking too. Balancing the budget by raising taxes never, ever works. Remember what preceded the 1990 tax hike that destroyed the Bush presidency? Bush had a chance to grab a $490 billion Republican deficit reduction package without tax increases—but he had bound himself to a deficit reduction target of $500 billion. He could have taken the Republican plan and kept his "no new taxes" pledge, but because the Republican plan was $10 billion short of that magical $500 billion mark, he balked. He ended up signing onto a 1990 Democrat tax hike scheme designed by Leon Panetta, the same guy who crafted the 1993 Clinton tax increase and the Great Train Wreck federal shutdown of 1995.

According to Bush and his Democrat "friends" in Congress, the 1990 tax hike was suppose to give us a balanced budget in five years. Now, I ask you: Did the budget look balanced to you in 1995? But that's what happens when you try to balance the budget by gouging taxpayers. And what did George Bush get by going along with the Democrats? Why, the Democrats turned right around and used it against him, making a campaign issue of his broken no-tax pledge!

The point is, the 1990 tax increase didn't cut the deficit or balance the budget. Neither did the 1993 Clinton tax increase (like George Bush before him, Clinton promised the 1993 deal would "balance the budget in five years"—as Yogi Berra would say, it's deja vu all over again!). For a sound, well-managed, responsible government, you have to cut taxes and cut spending, period.

Give the president the line-item veto. I don't care whether the president is a Republican, a Democrat, a Libertarian, or a Green Party Socialist, I would give him (or her) the power to cross out spending provisions in any bill the Congress sends up. Now, I would *not* give the president the power to line out a tax cut—that would be like poison in the pen of a liberal chief executive. But any president should have the same ability that forty-three out of fifty state governors already have— the ability to eliminate waste and pork from spending bills. Forty years of Democrat-party rule have shown that it is dangerous and oppressive to have one set of rules for one party and another set of rules for the other party. We must give the line item veto *not* to this or that occupant of the Oval Office but to the *office of the presidency.*

I am continually amazed at how well our economy performs, year after year, even with the drag of outrageous tax rates and spending policies, even with the dead weight of millions of nonproducers taking from producers, even with a massive federal debt and unconscionable federal borrowing that continually threaten to sink us. Just think of what this economy could do if the government would stop this insane taxing of its people and the wasteful squandering of America's substance. Just imagine the prosperity that would result if we would just remove the weights and chains from our economic engine. Think of the money that would be freed up for genuine social needs, for those who are unable to take care of themselves, for scientific research, cancer research, heart disease research, AIDS research, muscular dystrophy and multiple sclerosis research. Imagine the utopia we could create—a land of prosperity and opportunity for all Americans, beyond our wildest dreams.

But we can't wait until the next century rolls around. We have to start right now. We have to sacrifice. We have to make hard choices in our spending programs. Those of us who receive from the government will have to be willing to accept changes and maybe even a little pain, so that all of us, and especially our children and grandchildren, can gain. We have to be patient; it took us forty years to get into this mess, and it will take more than a year or two to get out. And we have to have a vision for the future: A 17 percent flat tax is a good start, but it still takes too big a bite out of our wallets. A balanced budget is a good start, but we need to begin running *surplus* budgets in order to shrink the national debt. As we hack away at the debt, as we slash away at the size of government, we can gradually move toward a goal that now seems visionary but is really only reasonable: a government that operates in the black, year after year, and that imposes no more than a 10 percent flat tax on its people.

"A 10 percent flat tax!" you say. "Michael, have you lost your mind?"

No, America was out of its mind when it was imposing 50, 70, 90 percent tax rates on its people. Only recently have we come to our senses. A 10 percent flat tax should be our goal. After all, back in Bible times, the people of Israel paid a "tithe"—that is, a 10 percent flat tax—to God. If God Himself only demands a tithe, who does Uncle Sam think he is, demanding more?

CHAPTER 11

Why Not Promote the GENERAL Welfare?

M Y FATHER'S father, Jack Reagan, was one of the few Democrats in the mostly Republican town of Dixon, Illinois. After FDR's inauguration in 1933, Jack was appointed to oversee some of the new federal relief programs that were intended to alleviate the suffering of the Great Depression. Jack Reagan's experience with these government programs had an enormous influence in shaping Ronald Reagan's views on such issues as government bureaucracy and the welfare state.

In his autobiography, *An American Life,* Ronald Reagan recalls dropping by his father's office after his classes at nearby Eureka College so that he and Jack could go home together. "I was shocked," my dad wrote, "to see the fathers of many of my schoolmates waiting in line for handouts—men I had known most of my life, who had jobs I'd thought were as permanent as the city itself." He saw the despair and the shame in those faces; the Depression had robbed them of their dignity and their manhood. They had become dependents of the state—and not one of them was proud of it.

Jack Reagan saw what government handouts were doing to the spirit of these men, so on his own time, totally apart from his duties with the government unemployment program, Jack traveled around the county, asking if any temporary jobs were available, and even jawboning a farmer or a shopkeeper to take on an extra man or two. Then Jack would go back to his office and start handing out these jobs to those who had been out of work the longest. My dad, who was in his early twenties at the time, was impressed by the look he saw on the faces of these men who had just found work—even temporary work—in the midst of the Depression. "I swear the men were standing a little taller," my dad recalled. "They wanted *work,* not handouts."

Soon, however, when Jack would bring his list of jobs into the unemployment office, he found there were no takers. He'd announce that this or that job was available and the men would just shuffle their feet and look at the floor. Finally, one of the men broke the silence. "Jack," he said, "the last time you got me some work, the people at the relief office took my family off welfare; they said I had a job and even though it was temporary, I wasn't eligible for relief anymore. I just can't afford to take another job."

Later on, Jack was put in charge of the Works Progress Administration (WPA) office in Dixon. The WPA put people to work building roads and bridges—the kind of government program that could not exist today because the unions would never allow it. It was an early experiment with what we now call "workfare"—welfare that gets important work done, allowing people the satisfaction of knowing they *earned* that government check. Everything was humming along nicely until Jack noticed that the number of people applying for work was steadily dwindling. He knew that the Depression was still in full swing, so there should still be plenty of unemployment going around.

So Jack began asking questions. He found out that, down at the welfare office, federal workers were advising able-bodied men not to take the WPA jobs. These bureaucrats were saying, "The welfare office is taking care of you now. You don't need a WPA job." So—in the very depths of the Great Depression, when there were not enough private-sector jobs to be had—Jack Reagan had lots of public works jobs to offer and hardly any takers! From that example, Ronald Reagan learned a valuable lesson that, decades later, he would take with him into the White House: "The first rule of a bureaucracy is to protect the bureaucracy. If the people running the welfare program had let their clientele find other ways of making a living, that would have reduced their importance and their budget."[1]

The sins of the welfare state are many. Its destructive effects on individual lives and on society include:

- Rewarding idleness and punishing work;
- Killing individual initiative;
- Sapping our economy and diminishing our productivity;
- Forcing middle-class taxpayers to support those who refuse to support themselves and their families;
- Rewarding immorality and unwed childbearing (welfare benefits increase when additional children are born);
- Rewarding irresponsibility of unwed fathers;
- Encouraging families to split up (benefits are terminated if the father stays in the home);
- Rewarding and even subsidizing drug abuse and alcoholism;
- Subsidizing crime (gang members sometimes live with welfare-dependent girlfriends, using the young women's government checks to support a hangin', gang-bangin' lifestyle).

ROADBLOCKS TO CHANGE

Welfare is kind of like the weather: Everybody talks about it but nobody does anything about it. Even people with the power to do something about it don't do anything about it. Bill Clinton ran for president on a promise to "end welfare as we know it." Once in office, he showed us what his promise meant: In typical liberal fashion, he was going to make welfare bigger and more expensive! He actually claimed that it was impossible to reform welfare without spending *more* money on it!

The Clinton "welfare reform" plan called for $9.3 billion in *new, additional* spending on education and job training programs, employment placement assistance, and childcare. Certainly, not everything about the Clinton plan was bad: It did call for limits on how long individuals could remain on welfare, encourage welfare recipients to find employment, and increase efforts to collect child-support payments from deadbeat parents. But even the best proposals in the Clinton "reform" plan were like a turtle crawling down a freeway on-ramp, plodding more or less in the right direction, but a long way from the fast lane. On the whole, however, the Clinton "reform" plan was driving head-on into a thicket of WRONG WAY signs. The problem with welfare is not that it underspends by $9.3 billion a year but that it overspends by $300 billion a year.

The Clinton "solution" to welfare is typical Washington wonkthink: Let's just create yet another layer of bureaucracy! Well, we just can't afford any more Washington-style "solutions" to the welfare crisis. It's too far out of hand, it's too big a drag on our national economy and our federal budget, it's too big a burden on the taxpayer, and it has destroyed too many families and individual's lives. We can no longer continue treating welfare as just another government program to be tinkered with. It's a drastic crisis, calling for drastic solutions.

But there are a number of very big roadblocks in the way of a lasting solution to the welfare crisis:

Roadblock No. 1: The assumption that government belongs in the charity business. A lot of people—liberals, moderates, and even some conservatives—automatically assume that one of the functions of government is taking care of people who can't take care of themselves. A careful look at the Constitution shows this was never the intent of the founding fathers. In writing the Constitution, they created a government that was very limited in scope and function. Here's the purpose of government, as stated in the Preamble to the Constitution:

> We the People of the United States, in Order to form a more perfect Union, establish Justice, insure domestic Tranquility, provide for the common defence, promote the general Welfare, and secure the Blessings of Liberty to ourselves and our Posterity, do ordain and establish this Constitution for the United States of America.

Note that term *general welfare.* That means "the common good," the well-being of *everyone* in the country. What we now call "welfare" in this country actually destroys the *general* welfare, the common good and well-being of our society at large. Welfare robs the average taxpayer, deepens the national debt, reduces national productivity, kills the human spirit, divides families, and enslaves the poor. The best thing we could possibly do to "promote the general Welfare, and secure the Blessings of Liberty to ourselves and our Posterity" would be to *end* so-called "welfare," once and for all.

From the founding fathers until FDR, the primary role of government was limited to two basic functions: (1) national defense, and (2) protecting rights and freedom. In other words, government existed to prevent harm, not to do good at taxpayer expense. James Madison used to worry (with good reason, as it turned out) that politicians might someday twist the meaning of that phrase, "promote the general Welfare," into a mandate for expensive do-gooder government. And so did other important figures in our history. In 1759, the great economist Adam Smith warned, "Benefi-cence [charity] is always free, it cannot be extorted by force" (and "force," incidentally, includes jack-booted IRS agents). Smith's warning was echoed in the early 1800s by Congressman Davy Crockett, who said, "We have the right, as individuals, to give away as much of our own money as we please in charity; but as members of Congress we have no right so to appropriate a dollar of the public money."

These days, you hear a lot of people blaming FDR for starting the entire welfare mess—and it's all true. But what few people realize is that, had he lived to complete his final term, Roosevelt might well have shut down many of the Depression-era welfare programs he started. As Ronald Reagan observes in *An American Life,*

> I think that many people forget Roosevelt ran for president on a platform dedicated to reducing waste and fat in government. He called for cutting federal spending by twenty-five percent, eliminating useless boards and commissions and returning to states and communities powers that had been wrongfully seized by the federal government. If he had not been distracted by war, I think he would have resisted the relentless expansion of the federal government that followed him. One of his sons, Franklin Roosevelt, Jr., often told me that his father had said many times his welfare and relief programs during the Depression were meant only as emergency, stopgap measures to cope with a crisis, not the seeds of what others later tried to turn into a permanent welfare state. Government giveaway programs, FDR said, "destroy the human spirit," and he was right. As smart as he was, though, I suspect even FDR didn't realize that once you created a bureaucracy, it took on a life of its own. It was almost impossible to close down a bureaucracy once it had been created.[2]

Compassion is a wonderful thing, and history has shown America to be the most compassionate, charitable nation in the history of the world.

But compassion is a personal act, not an institutional program. You can't legislate compassion. You can't tax and spend compassion. You can't dispense compassion through a government office.

If you really want to experience genuine compassion, where would you go? Would you stand in line to talk to a government bureaucrat? Or would you go to a church or a private charitable agency? There's no contest. Compassion belongs in the hands of religious institutions and private charities. Government should get out of the charity business. The welfare state has got to go.

Roadblock No. 2: The assumption that everyone has a "right" to a decent standard of living.
No such "right" exists. You won't find it in the Constitution. You won't find it in the writings of the founding fathers. You won't even find it in our Judeo-Christian heritage. The Bible says, "If anyone will not work, neither shall he eat" (2 Thes. 3:10).

Government exists, according to the Preamble to the Constitution, to "secure the Blessings of Liberty to ourselves and our Posterity." Note: government exists to maintain our *liberty*—not our *prosperity*. Liberty entails the freedom to succeed. In fact, our liberty enables us to prosper; that's one of the "Blessings of Liberty" mentioned in the Constitution. But liberty also entails the freedom to fail. If you want to spend your days sitting under a shade tree with a straw in your mouth, that is your right under the Constitution—but the Constitution doesn't say I have to subsidize your life of leisure. Nowhere in the Constitution is there any suggestion that you have the right to stand in line to receive money that the government has forcibly taken from my pocket. The welfare state is fundamentally wrong, and it's fundamentally un-American.

If you want to live well in the good old U.S. of A., then you have to get out of that line in the government office and learn how to access the unlimited opportunities of this country. The American dream is the free and unfettered ability to work as hard as you want, to be as productive as you can be, and to enjoy the fruit of your labor. *That's* where a decent standard of living truly comes from: ingenuity, work, and productivity. Everything we have in America comes from work and productivity. All the wealth and goods and services we enjoy are a direct result of the fact that a lot of people in America get up and go to work for eight or twelve or sixteen hours a day.

Roadblock No. 3: The myth that poverty programs alleviate poverty. In 1964, Lyndon B. Johnson introduced what he called "the Great Society," which he kicked off with a massive increase in government spending on antipoverty programs. From 1964 to the present, spending has increased from $50 billion to over $300 billion a year. In total, since the beginning of Johnson's "Great Society," we have spent *more than $5 trillion dollars* trying to end poverty! It was, said LBJ, a "war on poverty." So did we win the war? It's an interesting coincidence that the pricetag for the welfare state exactly equals the present level of the national debt: $5 trillion! Clearly, the war on poverty is a war we couldn't afford.

What, exactly, have we gotten for our $5 trillion? Go to the center of any large American city and you can see for yourself.

Go to the federal housing projects, where people live without hope and without a future. Go to the inner-city schools where kids can't read. Go to the needle parks where people convert their government checks into smack and speed and crack and crank. Go to the inner-city maternity wards and look at the writhing crack babies and AIDS babies. Look at the hopelessness and anger in the faces of the inner city. Look at the neglected, fatherless children.

Take a good look. *That* is your "Great Society."

How do you like it?

Roadblock No. 4: Welfare is big business. Welfare in America is a multibillion-dollar industry supporting millions of people across the country. The poverty industry has created many millionaires and billionaires with taxpayer money. It provides job security for thousands of bureaucrats. Powerful, well-organized interests seek to perpetuate and grow the welfare monster—and the obscene amounts of money that flow like water through the welfare system make it a very difficult monster to kill.

Who benefits from welfare? The recipients themselves? The honest answer may surprise you. Richard Benedetto, in the Gannett's *People and Politics* column, June 24, 1994, cited a study of 2,300 unwed welfare mothers. Beginning in 1989, these women received (in addition to their

regular welfare benefits) job training, education, intensive family planning, and counseling services. Two years later, *82 percent* were still
jobless and on welfare—*and 57 percent had become pregnant again!* A
control group that did not receive any such additional services actually
did slightly *better* than the test group! Did the women in this program
benefit from their added services? Obviously not. If anything, they were
worse off than before.

But *somebody* benefited! Who? The contractors and government employees, the administrators and service providers of the programs! They
benefited plenty—but they produced nothing. They had no positive
impact on the lives of the people they "helped." That's the problem with
welfare: The welfare recipients themselves don't benefit! Only the
special interest groups, the government employees, and the private
contractors benefit—and that's why these groups lobby so fiercely to
keep welfare programs expanding.

The poverty industry is unbelievably huge—bigger than the total
combined revenues of Exxon, Ford, GM, Chrysler, IBM, and General
Electric! At the federal level, the welfare budget includes Health and
Human Services ($258 billion), Housing and Urban Development ($24.5
billion), the Food Stamp program in the Department of Agriculture ($23
billion), and a certainly large but unquantified portion of the Social
Security budget ($281.5 billion). In all, we spend more than $300 billion
a year transferring wealth from those who work to those who don't.

As a business, welfare is wasteful beyond belief. Did you know that
of every tax dollar that goes to the welfare budget, *only 24 cents* actually
gets to the welfare recipient in the form of cash transfers and other
services? The other 76 cents goes to administrative overhead. That's
right! Put it another way: For every welfare dollar the bureaucracy puts
in the hand of a welfare recipient, the bureaucracy spends three dollars
on itself! What is compassionate about a "charity" that keeps three times
more than it gives away?

It won't be easy to defeat the powerful political establishment and
wealthy special interests that profit from keeping millions of Americans
dependent on government checks. These forces know how the game is
played in Washington, D.C., and they've got plenty of cash with which
to play it—our cash, taxpayers' cash. They're playing to win, and if they
win, you and I and millions of taxpayers and welfare recipients lose.

Roadblock No. 5: The assumption that everyone on welfare is "poor." Five trillion dollars is a lot of money. That's five followed by twelve zeros, or a thousand billions. What on earth did we spend all that money on? A large part of it, of course, went to direct cash transfers—that is, welfare checks. Some went to housing relief and urban development, nutrition assistance and family planning, education and job training. With all that government assistance, we must have lifted an awful lot of people out of poverty. Surely, there must have been *some* decrease in the level of poverty in America—wasn't there?

No, there wasn't. Though the poverty rate was declining in America prior to 1964, it has steadily *grown* ever since we started throwing bales of money at the problem—from 14.6 percent of the U.S. population in 1964 to 15.1 percent in 1995. In part, this is because handouts and programs can't help people who are unwilling to help themselves, and the more money and benefits we give away to poor people, the greater their incentive to remain eligible for those benefits—that is, to remain "poor." As soon as they start to lift themselves out of poverty, their benefits are cut off—so why bother?

But another reason poverty has grown is that the definition of "poor" is so slippery. Every few years, the government redefines "poverty" so that those in the poverty industry can maintain their power and profits. When you increase the number of people eligible for government benefits, you enlarge the poverty industry and generate full employment for bureaucrats.

Today, many of those considered "poor" by the government would have been called "middle class" just a few decades ago. Nowadays, it is commonplace to think of people as being above or below the "poverty line." Prior to 1963, however, there was no federally ordained "poverty line." In that year, the government first established the poverty line at $3,128—including *all* sources of income. In 1995, the official poverty line was set at about $14,000—*but measured only cash income.* While cash assistance accounts for only 25 percent of total welfare spending, the value of other welfare benefits—such as food stamps, healthcare, childcare, job training, educational benefits, and subsidized housing—is not even counted in the equation. Because of all these noncash benefits that welfare recipients enjoy on top of their cash benefits, the "welfare poor" in America are not in such bad economic shape as a group.

According to a 1991 American Housing Survey, nearly 40 percent of those below the official poverty line own their own homes! Similarly, the officially designated "poor" are likely to enjoy a generally middle-class lifestyle: housing with one room per person, a complete bathroom, air conditioning, central heat, telephone service, a dishwasher, and a clothes dryer, according to a 1990 study conducted by Christopher Jencks of Northwestern University and Susan Mayer of the University of Chicago. And a study by Kathryn Edin of Northwestern University found that *virtually all* welfare recipients interviewed had some source of income that was concealed from social workers.

It's hardly surprising, then, that income reported by welfare recipients is strangely out of balance with their spending power. In 1988-89, the bottom tenth of all households with children reported a mean income of $5,588. However, Jencks and Mayer found that the government's own data shows that a household reporting a mean income of $5,588 *spends an average of nearly $14,000!* During the Reagan administration, the poorest households with children reported that while their income declined, their consumption level *increased* 13 percent—from $12,022 in 1980 to $13,558 in 1989.

A study by the CATO Institute, concluded in early 1996, compared the welfare benefits in all fifty states to the average earnings for various jobs in those same states. The study, entitled *The Work Versus Welfare Trade-Off: A 50 State Analysis of the Real Level of Welfare Benefits*, combined both cash transfers and noncash benefits, and found government spending to be so high that:

- In 47 states, welfare pays more than a janitorial job.
- In 40 states, welfare pays more than an $8 per hour job.
- In 17 states, welfare pays more than a $10 an hour job.
- In Hawaii, Alaska, Connecticut, New York, Rhode Island, and Washington, D.C., welfare pays more than a $12 an hour job—over two and a half times the minimum wage.
- In 9 states, welfare pays more than the average entry level salary for a computer programmer.
- In 6 states, welfare pays more than the average first-year salary for a teacher.

- In 29 states, welfare pays more than the average starting salary for a secretary.

Consider the irony: The welfare worker enjoys a higher standard of living than the secretary, yet the government makes the secretary pay to support the welfare recipient! What a country! No wonder so many people choose welfare over work.

Roadblock No. 6: The assumption that ending welfare is politically impossible. When, on November 8, 1994, the Republican party swept into power, it was called a "Republican revolution," but that's a misnomer. In a true revolution, the old system is overthrown and a whole new system is installed. When the Republicans came to power, they didn't overthrow the welfare system; they just offered to revise it. The Republican plan, called the Personal Responsibility Act, is a good start, though it hardly goes far enough. As my friend Errol Smith pointed out in the January 1995 issue of *Michael Reagan's Monthly Monitor,* "The good news is that welfare reform is finally on the front burner in both the Democratic and Republican camps. . . . The bad news is that if you take all the current proposals for welfare reform being trumpeted by both Democrats and Republicans, combine them, and implement them in their entirety, 70 percent of our welfare problem would still exist."

Reform and revision don't go far enough. The problem with government programs is that you can't trim them back, you can't reform them, you can't fix them—because government programs won't *stay* trimmed, reformed, and fixed. They invariably grow back and become larger, more bureaucratic, and more powerful. The only way to make sure a government program doesn't grow back is to kill it, period.

That's right, I said, *"Kill it."*

Granted, a phase-out period is needed to enable people—on both sides of the counter in the welfare office—to adjust to life without welfare. But the phase-out of welfare should be certain and firm and should take place within a limited period of time.

I can already hear the objections—and I bet, so can you:

"Objection! What about compassion and caring? What kind of a cruel, heartless society do you want us all to live in?"

The fact is, it is neither compassionate nor caring to perpetuate the welfare state. Conservatives envision an America that is light-years beyond the faded dream of a government-sponsored "Great Society." We have a vision of an *opportunity society* in which men and women are set free from addictive government handouts and oppressive federal taxes—free to pursue a better, more productive, and happier life, free from poverty, drugs, and violence. That kind of freedom doesn't come from a government check. It comes when people learn that they alone have the responsibility for their lives and their choices.

"Objection! What about the truly needy? How can we refuse to take care of people who can't take care of themselves or are down on their luck?"

We are not talking about doing away with charity in America; we are talking about *privatizing* charity. Seventy years ago, virtually everything that the welfare state does for people today was done—more compassionately, more effectively, less expensively, and with much less fraud and abuse—by private and religious charities. Given what we now know about what government welfare does to individuals and to a society, moving backwards seventy years can only be called *progress*. The welfare system can and must be devolved—not just to the states and other lower levels of government but completely to the private and religious sector, where it belongs. Only by killing the welfare state do you allow true compassion and generosity to be displayed.

I recently heard a story that tore my heart out. A little boy, a fourth-grader named Ahmad, was hauled off his elementary school playground for fighting. He had knocked down another boy and kicked him repeatedly in the head. You might think, "What a rotten kid!"—yet the fact is, this boy had never been in trouble before. Fortunately, the other boy wasn't seriously hurt.

When questioned by the principal, Ahmad said that the reason for the attack was that the other boy had made a disparaging remark about Ahmad's mother. Questioning Ahmad further, the principal learned that Ahmad's mother was home in bed, dying of AIDS. There was no other adult in the house. All by himself, Ahmad prepared meals and did all the housecleaning for his mother, himself, and his seven-year-old half-sister, Raschel, and he got himself and Raschel to school every morning. He was the man of his family, and he was scared to death of what would happen to him and his half-sister when his mother finally died. All of this pent-up fear caused Ahmad to lash out when another boy insulted his mother.

Liberals would say, "And you evil conservatives want to cut these children and their dying mother off! You want to throw them out in the streets to starve!" No. I want them to be adequately cared for by people who really care about them—not just a case worker from the government. I'm not saying case workers are all a bunch of heartless bureaucrats or that they are all incompetent. But the odds are much greater of finding caring, compassionate, competent people in private and religious charities than in government agencies. If we privatize the compassion industry, and unleash the economy so that more funding will flow to charities, then people like Ahmad and his mother will get the quality, compassionate help they need.

"Objection! Private and religious charities are already overburdened! They can't absorb $300 billion a year in added human need!"

Wrong on two counts. First, the fact that the government spends that much doesn't mean there's that much need. Remember, three-fourths of that $300 billion pricetag goes to administrative overhead—and more goes to fraud, waste, and abuse. Private and religious charities operate on much less administrative overhead and are much better at weeding out cheats and con artists so they can better serve the deserving and the needy.

Second, ending welfare will free up enormous, undreamed-of, never-before-tapped resources for private and religious charities. When you kill the welfare state, you can cut taxes—drastically! And what happens when you cut taxes? People feel more economically secure, and when they feel economically secure, they are free to be more generous. They give to charities, and those charities then have greater ability to help people in need. This principle works; it has already been proven.

People often call the 1980s the "Me Decade" or the "Decade of Greed," but the facts prove that the 1980s were actually the "Decade of Caring." What happened in the 1980s? Ronald Reagan cut taxes. The economy boomed. People and corporations had more money to spend—and more money to give to good causes. Charitable giving soared in the 1980s compared with previous decades. According to a study by Richard B. McKenzie of the Graduate School of Management at the University of California, Irvine, the annual rate of growth in total giving throughout the Reagan '80s was nearly 55 percent higher than in the entire preceding quarter century. Predictably, those rates flattened considerably after the Bush-signed tax deal of 1990 and the Clinton tax hike of 1993.

"Objection! If you take all those people off welfare, how will the economy absorb them? There won't be enough jobs for them all!"

Ending welfare and drastically cutting taxes will unleash an economic boom in America, leading to a surge in productivity, economic activity, hiring, and consumerism, accompanied by a massive reduction in poverty—and in the need for poverty programs. The people who now get rich in the poverty industry won't like that—but taxpayers and the people who have been emancipated from slavery to a government check will ultimately be much happier.

Even after welfare has been killed, the temptation will be to retain some vestiges of the welfare state in the postwelfare society. Some will say, "We need job training and job placement programs for all the people who are leaving the welfare rolls." Fine—if they are run by the private sector, not the government. Programs that teach basic typing skills, computer skills, job interviewing skills, communication, remedial reading, and the like can be helpful in making people more marketable to potential employers—but there is no reason why such programs have to be run by a government bureaucracy.

Most of the poverty in America is self-inflicted—and self-curable. If we stop rewarding the behavior that leads to poverty—behavior such as idleness, drug abuse, alcoholism, broken families, teenage sex—then the poverty problem will begin to correct itself as people start taking responsibility for their own lives. America is a paradise of opportunity, but we have to start teaching people that you don't find those opportunities while waiting in line at the welfare office.

CHAPTER 12

Within Reach: Dr. King's Dream

"I STILL HAVE a dream," he said, his voice rolling in rich, round waves across the crowd of 200,000 who had gathered in the shadow of the Lincoln Memorial. It was a hot, humid Washington day—August 28, 1963—but this peaceful, multiracial crowd didn't seem to notice. They were all swept up in the bright, cool vision of Dr. Martin Luther King's dream. "It is a dream," he continued, "deeply rooted in the American dream. . . . I have a dream that my four little children will one day live in a nation where they will not be judged by the color of their skin, but by the content of their character. . . .

"With this faith we will be able to transform the jangling discords of our nation into a beautiful symphony of brotherhood. With this faith we will be able to work together, to pray together, to struggle together, to go to jail together, to stand up for freedom together, knowing that we will be free one day. This will be the day when all of God's children will be able to sing with new meaning, 'My country 'tis of thee, sweet land of liberty, of thee I sing. Land where my father died, land of the pilgrim's pride, from every mountainside, let freedom ring.'

"When we let freedom ring, when we let it ring from every village and every hamlet, from every state and every city, we will be able to speed up that day when all of God's children, black men and white men, Jews and Gentiles, Protestants and Catholics, will be able to join hands and sing in the words of the old Negro spiritual, 'Free at last! Free at last! Thank God Almighty, we are free at last!'"

209

That is a beautiful dream. It's a dream of a truly unified, color-blind society. It's a dream of true social and economic freedom. It's a dream that, tragically, America has retreated from for more than three decades. It is a dream that has been gradually eaten up by fear, division, and mistrust. Today, the beautiful dream of Dr. Martin Luther King, Jr., is imperiled by the very programs and policies that were inspired by the great speech he gave back in 1963—the programs and policies that are known collectively as *affirmative action.*

A RACIAL MELTDOWN

Let me state it strongly and bluntly: Affirmative action frightens me more than any other policy adopted by the liberal political establishment over the last thirty years. You might wonder what could be so frightening about a policy intended to produce racial justice, harmony, and equality. The answer is simple: Affirmative action produces none of those things. In fact, affirmative action actually drives a wedge between the races. Instead of speeding the day when all of God's children, regardless of color and race, can join hands and be free at last, affirmative action speeds the day when America collapses, Bosnia-like, into racial warfare and chaos. Having abandoned our once-proud American identity as a racial melting pot, we are fast approaching the flashpoint of a horrible, violent racial meltdown.

But a racial armageddon is not inevitable. We are poised at a historic moment of both danger and opportunity in America. The danger is real, as the L.A. riots and the black-white division over the O.J. Simpson verdict have clearly demonstrated. But the opportunity is equally real. The conservative mainstream in America has never been stronger, more involved, or more informed than it is today. Dr. King's dream of a society where all people of all races would "not be judged by the color of their skin, but by the content of their character" could come about—if you and I care enough to make it happen.

THE SINS OF AFFIRMATIVE ACTION

Liberals try to frame the debate over affirmative action as a struggle between tolerance and racism. Those who want to end affirmative action, they say, are really just a bunch of angry white guys who resent minorities for "stealing" white jobs. That's not it at all. This isn't about being mad at minorities. It's about doing what's right and best for *all* people, minorities included. If I truly thought that affirmative action was a positive force for lifting minority people out of poverty and injustice, I would be for it. But I know better.

Affirmative action is a destructive force in our society and in individual lives. It hurts not only whites but the very minority people it was intended to help. Here are a few of the sins of affirmative action:

Affirmative action is racist.

What, after all, is the definition of a racist? "A person who thinks it is justifiable to treat people differently simply because of their race." Affirmative action is really just a reinvention of nineteenth-century racial paternalism. The "progressives" of that era talked about a so-called "white man's burden," the responsibility of the white elite to "civilize" and care for the "uncivilized" people they had subjugated and to indoctrinate them in the values and beliefs of "progressive" white culture.

Today, the liberal "white man's burden" is affirmative action, which keeps minorities subjugated and beholden to liberal government policies. Affirmative action also indoctrinates minorities into the liberal belief system. It says to minorities, "You are victims. You are inferior. You can't make it in life without liberals and big government." As my friend Errol Smith said, addressing a University of California Regents meeting, July 20, 1995, "I refuse to accept a system that takes as its foundation the premise that I am inferior because I happen to have been born black."

Some people think that those who want to end affirmative action simply want to bring back discrimination. Absolutely wrong. If we completely ended all affirmative action programs and laws today, discrimination would still be completely illegal tomorrow. There are hundreds of antidiscrimination laws on the books, plus the equal protection clause of the Fourteenth Amendment. These laws prohibit racial and gender discrimination, and they have nothing to do with affirmative action.

Affirmative action isn't about fairness; it's about preference. Affirmative action does not end discrimination. It *is* discrimination. It is a racist policy.

Affirmative action undermines achievement.

It does so in (at least!) three ways:

(1) It tells people from certain groups that they don't have to work as hard as those in other groups to get what they want. In many cases, people discover they can get jobs, promotions, raises, and other benefits without earning them. All they have to do is threaten to file a discrimination complaint, and they get everything they want through legal blackmail.

(2) It insults and degrades minority individuals who achieve on their own merits. If a minority person rises to a position of responsibility and prominence, his or her accomplishments will always bear the taint of affirmative action: Is this person really qualified—or did this person just happen to meet some racial or gender quota?

(3) It undermines self-esteem and teaches minority individuals to think of themselves as inferior, incompetent, handicapped, or victimized. People cannot truly achieve unless they feel confident and empowered to achieve. I am convinced that affirmative action has had a dampening effect on the aspirations and dreams of minority individuals—and statistics bear me out. In 1970, the median income of black families was 61 percent of the white family median income. Then came affirmative action, which was supposed to lift blacks and other minorities out of poverty and raise them to a level of parity with whites. How did it work? Not as predicted, that's for sure! By 1992, black family median income had *fallen* to 54 percent of white family median income! Why? I believe it's because affirmative action teaches people to invest their hope for the future in the government rather than in themselves—and that is a surefire prescription for failure.

Affirmative action is unwanted by our society.

Polls show that over 70 percent of all Americans oppose race-based preferences, and a recent *Newsweek* poll showed that support for such programs has been waning even in the black community. The question was asked, "Because of past discrimination, should qualified blacks receive preference over equally qualified whites in such matters as getting into college or getting a job?" Only 40 percent of black respondents said yes, and more than 50 percent said no!

Affirmative action is capricious, arbitrary, and unfair.

Case in point: In 1995, Bill Clinton's race czar, Assistant Attorney General for Civil Rights Deval Patrick, decided he didn't like the hiring percentages in the Orange County, California, community of Fullerton. The city's racial composition is about 37 percent nonwhite; less than 2 percent of the population is black. But Deval Patrick decreed that it wasn't good enough for the city to set hiring quotas that only *matched* the racial makeup of the community. In his infinite wisdom, Mr. Patrick decided that Fullerton should maintain a "minority hiring pool" of 44 percent and should set aside 9 percent of its jobs for blacks—about five times the percentage of blacks in the community. He ordered the city to spend huge amounts of taxpayer money on: (1) aggressive recruitment in minority areas and minority print and broadcast media; (2) aggressive hiring of all minority applicants who were previously turned down for police and fire positions, regardless of qualifications; and (3) to compensate those applicants with up to ten years' worth of back pay and benefits. If there is fairness and logic in that formula, I can't see it.

Affirmative action is an intrusive and unwarranted violation of constitutional rights.

It is also an expensive drag on our economy, and results in lost business, lost earnings, and lost jobs. Compliance costs to businesses in the private sector total an astonishing $20 billion a year. Affirmative action is the "bureaucrat's full employment act." All employers with more than fifteen employees (that's 86 percent of the private-sector workforce, folks!) come under the affirmative action guidelines of the Equal Employment Opportunity Commission. And if you, as an employer, are foolish enough to do business with the federal government, you'd better cultivate a taste for heavy reading, because the government's manual of hiring mandates for government contractors is *700 pages long*!

Thousands of cases illustrate the absurdity of hiring quotas. One of the absolute silliest examples came to light in November 1995 when the Equal Employment Opportunity Commission (EEOC) ordered the Hooters restaurant chain to hire male waiters to work alongside its presently all-female force of "Hooters Girls." The fast-growing burger-

and-chicken-wings chain (with 170 outlets nationwide) built its reputation on food service by perky waitresses in skimpy uniforms. If the EEOC gets its way, however, Hooters customers will find themselves being served by guys in orange hot pants and white tank tops.

Now, I'm not endorsing or defending the use of blatant sex appeal to sell burgers. But I have to ask the EEOC: "Don't you people have anything more important to do than *this*? How will you make America a better place by putting hundreds of waitresses out of work?" If the EEOC wins, half the female workforce at Hooters loses—and the Hooters Girls know it. Immediately after the EEOC edict was announced, waitresses sported orange pins that read "Save Our Jobs." And that's exactly what's on the line: the livelihood of thousands of female employees (including many single mothers) who would be muscled out of their jobs by an arbitrary government quota.

Another question naturally arises: If an all-female workforce of Hooters Girls constitutes discrimination, why doesn't the EEOC go after even more blatant examples of discrimination? What about businesses that not only discriminate but *exploit* on the basis of sex? Shouldn't the EEOC start proceedings against Playboy clubs and force them to suit up a bunch of hunky studs in bunny ears and cottontails? Shouldn't *Playboy, Penthouse,* and similar magazines be required to hire male models as well as females to appear in their pages? Shouldn't Vegas showgirls be integrated into a 50/50 workforce of male/female "Vegas showpersons"? Shouldn't the EEOC take its brand of "equal opportunity" into topless bars and stripjoints around the country?

But the EEOC won't do that. Why? Because the bureaucracy, in its infinitely cockeyed wisdom, has decided that *it's okay to discriminate as long as you are selling sex!* David Larson, described in an AP wire story as "a former professor-in-residence" at the EEOC, explained the government's "logic" this way: "The distinction is that there was never any question that *Playboy* was selling sex, not in the sense of prostitution, but the image of the club had a very heavy sexual aspect to it. I don't think Hooters is doing the same thing. They've made it clear publicly that they're selling food." In other words, the government rewards sex-peddlers with exemptions that are denied to businesses like Hooters. If you're selling smut—no problem! If you're selling burgers, we'll put you out of business!

This whole situation looks like a case of EEOC bureaucrats with too much time on their hands. The lesson of it all is clear: Quotas don't produce fairness. They just produce bureaucratic stupidity.

Affirmative action generates distrust, anger, resentment, and competitiveness between the races.

Far from uniting all Americans as a single people, affirmative action divides America into competing, warring tribes. Those who receive the so-called "benefits" of affirmative action are taught to resent and distrust other races for supposedly holding them down; the core doctrine of affirmative action is that America is a fundamentally racist society and that only the federal bureaucracy can defend minorities from oppression by a racist majority.

Meanwhile, affirmative action breeds resentment and backlash among those who feel unfairly barred from jobs, educational opportunities, and other benefits because they happen to belong to the "wrong" group. The bitterness that affirmative action produces on all sides is a major factor in the racial tension that seems to be worsening, not healing, in our country. Only when we adopt a truly color-blind race policy in America will our long national nightmare of racial injustice and racial violence come to an end. Only when we remove the "race" box from our paperwork and our minds will we finally become "one nation under God, indivisible, with liberty and justice for all."

KINDER AND GENTLER?

Upon taking office, Ronald Reagan said, "We must not allow the noble concept of equal opportunity to be distorted into federal guidelines or quotas which require race, ethnicity, or sex—rather than ability and qualification—to be the principal factor in hiring or education." Bucking a Democrat-controlled Congress and a liberal Supreme Court, the Reagan administration rolled back many affirmative action policies during the 1980s.

In a cynical power play, the Democrats passed a bill they called "The Civil Rights Restoration Act." The bill and its title were a complete joke for two reasons: (1) The title suggested that civil rights had been lost under the Reagan Administration and needed to be "restored" by Congress; and

(2) the title falsely advertised that the bill had something to do with civil rights. In fact, it was nothing more than a bunch of expensive pork programs for a few liberal pet causes. Ronald Reagan took a lot of heat and was called a "racist" for vetoing that bill, and Congress overrode the veto.

President Bush thought he could win votes and influence Congress with his kinder and gentler "can't-we-all-get-along?" approach to governing. As a result, he signed into law an absolutely abysmal piece of legislation, the falsely named Civil Rights Act of 1991, which significantly broadened a number of affirmative action programs and policies.

When Bill Clinton was elected, he vowed to appoint a cabinet that "looks like America." In other words, he was going to give us an affirmative-action White House, with quotas and racial preferences. And what a stellar group of appointees he came up with! We have a HUD secretary who is under investigation for lying about paying hush money to his mistress. We have a high-flying, jet-set energy secretary who thinks she's Madonna. We have a commerce secretary under investigation for high-stakes influence peddling. We have an ag secretary who resigned under pressure for renting his influence to Don Tyson, the Arkansas chicken king. We have an attorney general whose solution to child abuse is to send tanks and tear gas into buildings where the children are. We've had a whole chorus-line of Clinton nominees who "forgot" to pay taxes on their nannies. We had one Clinton surgeon general appointee who preached masturbation and "wear your rubbers" to children, and another who couldn't remember if he did six abortions or a hundred. To top it off, we have a dangerous assortment of extreme-left-wing ideologues in key administration positions.

If the Clinton cabinet proves one thing, it is this: We need to choose people for our government according to "the content of their character," as Dr. King said, not the color of their skin or the circumstances of their gender.

A SICK JOKE

In 1978, the National Association for the Advancement of Colored People (NAACP) filed suit in federal court on behalf of black students in the San Francisco Unified School District. Faced with a wrenching, expensive court battle, the district agreed to a consent decree. That decree, drafted by a federal judge, went into effect in 1983 and—get this!—appointed the NAACP as the *sole representative* of the *entire* student body. That consent decree remains in effect to this day. The NAACP continues to oversee the district's racial balancing policies to this day. While 86 percent of San Francisco's students are of minority descent, *only 18 percent* are black—yet *all* of the students are represented by a black civil rights group, the NAACP.

From 1983 to 1995, the district spent more than $250 million on special desegregation projects. Much of that money was used to upgrade schools in predominantly black areas. But here's the kicker: Because of the district's racial balancing rules, many of the black students these policies were supposed to help were put on buses and driven right past their newly upgraded campuses and forced to attend schools in largely Asian and Hispanic neighborhoods! One black community leader said that, given a choice, most black parents would "bring back neighborhood schools overnight."

But wait! It gets even crazier! Feeling the heat from angry parents, the school district, the federal judge, and the NAACP came up with a wonderfully screwball solution: If you don't like the school your child goes to, just change your race! Here's how it works. Let's say you are black, but your nice, newly updated neighborhood school is "capped out" with African-Americans, thanks to affirmative action and racial quotas. The school district wants to send your child across town. What do you do? You simply have your child "re-labeled" as Hispanic or Asian! It's just a matter of checking a different box on the paperwork.

And it doesn't stop there! The San Francisco school district operates what is called a "magnet school" or "enriched school," with special courses and programs designed to challenge and inspire gifted students—yet affirmative action is used to deprive a minority group equal access! The "enriched school" admission program actually discriminates against American children of Chinese ancestry and makes it more difficult for them to enroll. What's the rationale? The liberal social engineers say that an even playing field would enable too many Chinese-American children to enroll in the school. So, to make things "fair" (according to the liberal definition of "fairness"), Chinese-Americans are required to get much higher test scores than whites, blacks, and Hispanics in order to qualify. To top it off, not only do whites, blacks, and Hispanics have lower admission standards, but a number of spots are held exclusively for black and Hispanic students *regardless* of test scores.

Do Asian-Americans have reason to gripe about the way affirmative action has discriminated against them? You bet they do. Though they receive no protection from affirmative action programs, Asian-Americans have suffered grievously from racism and discrimination over the years. In fact, there was a time when Asian immigrants in America were routinely subjected to the same kind of hate, violence, and discrimination that blacks have experienced in our history. In California's early history, a racist brotherhood called "The Native Sons of the Golden West" used to persecute and lynch Asians with the same ferocity that the Klan has practiced against blacks. Why, if affirmative action is intended to compensate for past discrimination, do liberals deny the "benefits" of affirmative action to people of Asian descent?

Liberal newspaper columnist Molly Ivins recounts a conversation she had regarding affirmative action and education: "An admissions officer at the University of California, Berkeley, who must remain nameless for obvious reasons, recently told me what would happen if affirmative action didn't exist at that school: 'We have 20,000 undergraduates: We'd end up with 19,000 very bright Asians and 1,000 very bright Jews.' Which is pretty funny, when you think about it."[1]

Funny, Molly? I don't think it's funny. I think it's racist. I think it's sick. And I think it's very scary that liberals would think that's funny. It's scary that there are people in key decision-making positions and positions of influence in our society who think it's "fair" to practice apartheid against Asians or Jews or any other segment of our society. I think it's a sick and distorted society that would say to a gifted, hopeful young person, "Yes, you did the work, you got terrific grades, and your test scores were terrific—but you can't come to school here because you're Chinese." Sorry, Molly, I can't see the humor in that. I guess I just don't get the joke.

TIME'S UP

It's not going to be easy to end race preferences and quotas in America. Affirmative action is big business, and people in the affirmative action industry make big bucks. Conservative economist and columnist Thomas Sowell calls them "race hustlers" and notes that many people have managed to become outrageously rich by hitching themselves to the affirmative action gravy train. He recalls,

> Some years ago, I had a private lunch with a well-known black civil rights leader in his hotel suite. The suite had an upstairs and a downstairs, with a spiral staircase connecting the two. I have never known any conservative, black or white, with a hotel suite like that. He is one of those whose annual income is more than twice Clarence Thomas' net worth.
>
> There should be no mystery as to why the real money in racial matters is on the liberal and militant end of the political spectrum. When you promote the creation and expansion of minority social programs . . . you may expect to run such programs, be a consultant to such programs or get grants from such programs. When you oppose these programs, there is no job, no grants, and no political mileage to get out of such opposition.[2]

Sowell adds that blacks such as himself, Walter Williams, Clarence Thomas, and others who don't go along with the liberal affirmative-action agenda are commonly accused of "selling out." The paradox of that accusation is that those who supposedly "sell out" by opposing affirmative action never make a dime from their outspokenness (more often than not, they actually pay a heavy economic price for opposing liberal programs). Liberals, however, enrich themselves at the affirmative action trough, making mega-loot as bureaucrats, activists, attorneys, consultants, seminar leaders, and educators in the civil rights and "diversity" fields. Why is it that the people who make a killing off of affirmative action are never accused of "selling out"?

Those who have gotten fat off of racial division and racial distrust are on notice: The gravy train is pulling away from the station—and it ain't coming back again. Time's up for affirmative action; in fact, it's an idea whose time should never have come. This fatally flawed concept violates the letter and spirit of the Constitution and of the Civil Rights Act of 1964. Worst of all, it has needlessly delayed the realization of Dr. King's beautiful, shining dream of a free and color-blind society.

I am committed to seeing that dream come true. When quotas, set-asides, preferences, and all the other trappings of affirmative action are just a memory, when the issue of race finally becomes a nonissue in America, then all of God's children, blacks and whites, Jews and Gentiles, Protestants and Catholics, will be able to join hands—and be free at last.

CHAPTER 13

In a Nuclear War, We're Sitting on Ground Zero

I N MY entire life, I have only seen my father defeated one time—in 1976, when he lost the Republican presidential nomination. The Reagan family was gathered together in the hotel suite the night the Republican convention nominated Gerald Ford. Afterwards, my dad looked at us and grinned in a bittersweet way. "You know what hurts the most about not getting the nomination?" he said. "It's that I really looked forward to representing the American people at the SALT talks."

The threat of nuclear war was a major concern of Ronald Reagan's, and he was especially concerned about the many one-sided concessions America had made to the Soviets in the Strategic Arms Limitation Talks, which had been going on since 1969. He gestured expansively as he spoke, and I could see that he pictured the scene in his mind's eye.

"I wanted to sit down at a big, round conference table with the Russian secretary general," he continued, "and I wanted him to tell me through his interpreter everything the United States would have to give up in order to get along with the Russians. I was going to listen to him very calmly, nodding and smiling. And then, when he had listed all his demands, I was going to get up from my chair, walk around that table, and whisper in his ear, 'Nyet.' I'm really sorry I won't get to say 'nyet' to the Soviets."

Ten years later, in Reykjavik, Iceland, he got his wish—though I'm not sure it was as satisfying an experience as he imagined in 1976. It was

October 1986, and it was the second summit meeting between Ronald Reagan and Soviet leader Mikhail Gorbachev. The two leaders had come very close to an agreement that would have dramatically reduced the nuclear arsenals of both nations, but the Soviets had one demand that Ronald Reagan had to say "nyet" to: a demand that the United States abandon the Strategic Defense Initiative (SDI). In the end, both leaders left Iceland without an agreement—and the photographs taken at the summit show that neither leader was happy with the result. But Ronald Reagan stood firmly behind SDI, and history has proven him right.

A $36 BILLION BARGAIN

In 1983, Ronald Reagan gave what came to be known as his "Star Wars" speech, announcing the Strategic Defense Initiative, a bold and innovative effort to use cutting-edge American technology to render the United States less vulnerable to nuclear missile attack. Liberal legislators and the liberal press fought Ronald Reagan every inch of the way. His opponents stuck the "Star Wars" label on the concept, hoping to brand SDI as a far-out fantasy straight out of Hollywood. After all, look at what SDI would be asked to do: target, intercept, and destroy a nuclear-tipped missile in flight—a monumental task since the Soviets had an arsenal of ten thousand nuclear weapons mounted on then unstoppable intercontinental ballistic missiles (ICBMs)!

The idea of defending against nuclear attack was not new, but in 1983, the only known antiballistic missile (ABM) technology involved firing interceptor missiles armed with nuclear weapons at the ICBMs. Even if you managed to stopped the incoming ICBMs, your own ABMs would create an unacceptable level of radiation and fallout. So Ronald Reagan's SDI plans called for a radical innovation: a *non*-nuclear missile defense. The research that resulted from SDI was enormously successful, resulting in rapid strides in "hit-to-kill" technology designed to knock out an incoming warhead without making a nuclear mess of its own.

The SDI concept consisted of a "layered defense," attacking the incoming missiles at various stages of their thirty-minute flight, from launch until just before they reached their targets. A system of surveillance satellites would detect the heat given off by the missiles' launch. Space- or ground-based high-energy lasers would strike at the missiles during the boost phase, before they could unleash their multiple warheads. X-ray and particle-beam weapons would strike at any surviving missiles as they arced through space. The entire system would be controlled by powerful, ultrafast supercomputers. The cost of the original plan was enormous: $100 billion or more—and this initial pricetag forced planners continually to seek cheaper alternatives. The Patriot missile program, which intercepted a substantial number of Iraqi Scud missiles during the 1991 Gulf War, was an outgrowth of one of those alternative avenues of research.

As of 1995, the United States government had spent a cool $36 billion on SDI. Yet, twelve years after Ronald Reagan first announced the Strategic Defense Initiative, America still has no SDI nuclear shield in place. We *could* have built it—but we didn't. So was all that money wasted? No. In fact, it was probably the wisest, most strategic investment this country has made in its entire 200-plus year history.

What did we get for our money? For one thing, we got the collapse of the Evil Empire—and without going to war or losing a single human life. At the time the Soviet Union fell apart in 1991, SDI was eight years old and the cost for the entire eight-year program stood at about $30 billion—*or about one-tenth of what we spend on welfare in just one year.* In my book, that's a real bargain.

The Soviets knew that America had the technological prowess to build a nuke-proof shield—and they couldn't compete. Just the threat of SDI put an enormous strain on the Soviet economic system. Soviet power in the world was based primarily on fear of its force of big, expensive nuclear missiles. The Soviets worried that SDI could render their entire nuclear force obsolete, and in a hopeless attempt to catch up with American technology, the Evil Empire spent its bankrupt economy and bankrupt society into oblivion. Meanwhile, the independence movement caught fire in Eastern Europe, and one after another, the U.S.S.R.'s satellite states tossed the Communist ideology onto the ash heap of history. Finally, withered by the winds of change and the heat of SDI, Russian Communism dried up and blew away.

Even an unbuilt, undeployed SDI was well worth $36 billion. But the question remains: Why didn't we build it? We could have at least had the first phases of a workable SDI in place during the Bush administration—but we didn't. The reason for that is not technical. It's political. People in the United States government—that's right, your government and mine—simply don't want it built.

DUMBING DOWN OUR DEFENSE

On February 25, 1991—at the height of the Gulf War—an Iraqi Scud missile raced toward U.S. forces stationed in Dhahran, Saudi Arabia. A U.S. Patriot missile was fired in an attempt to intercept the Scud. The Patriot failed. The Scud plunged into a U.S military barracks and exploded, dismembering, burning, and killing American servicemen and servicewomen. Twenty-seven soldiers died, and ninety-eight were wounded.

Needlessly. Shamefully.

Considering the difficult job the Patriot missile was called upon to perform—essentially shooting an oncoming bullet with another bullet— the entire system performed admirably and saved uncounted lives during the Gulf War, particularly in its defense of Israel. But the tragic fact is that we had the technology to make the Patriot even more effective—and we didn't use it. The Patriot defense system was deliberately hobbled by the restrictions imposed by the U.S. government bureaucracy.

Right now, today, we could build antimissile missiles capable of intercepting ICBMs in flight—but we won't build them. Government restrictions *specifically forbid* the building of an effective antiballistic missile system. The Patriot system is deliberately prevented from hitting incoming missiles until late in flight. It is forbidden to use tracking and positioning data from satellites, even though that data is easy to access with current technology. In short, the Patriot is deliberately designed *not* to hit an incoming missile until that missile is practically on top of Ground Zero. The result: Debris from the missile and even a live warhead will occasionally get to the target or close to the target. If *you* are sitting on Ground Zero, that's very bad news.

How in the world did we end up with a missile named "Patriot" that occasionally functions more like "Benedict Arnold"? And why, if we have missile defense technology just sitting on the shelf, don't we use it to protect the American people from attack? Because liberals in the government are opposed to building a system with space-based antimissile components. They don't want to annoy the Russians or go back to the bargaining table and renegotiate the outdated, lopsided, Cold War-era ABM Treaty of 1972. So instead of building the best system our scientific brains can build, we built a system that was deliberately designed to allow some Americans to get killed. And that's exactly what happened in Dhahran.

As missile defense expert and former senator Malcolm Wallop (R-Wyoming) said, "In plain English, we spent the taxpayers' money to 'dumb down' the American people's defensive weapons."[1] As a senator, Wallop was a member of the Armed Services and Intelligence Committee and has since formed a conservative think tank called Frontiers of Freedom—so he knows what he's talking about. He spent many years in the Senate, trying to change U.S. policy and unleash the enormous power of U.S. defense technology. Now, having retired from the Senate, he says there is a secret 120-page book of regulations governing SDI that is actually designed to *cripple* any attempt to mount an antiballistic missile shield over America. The fact that the regulations in that book could well cost millions of lives someday is a crime against the American people. In fact, given the fact that those regulations betray the constitutional requirement for government to "provide for the common defense," it is a crime against the U.S. Constitution. Given our tragic experience in Dhahran, we now know that the regulations in that book have already cost dozens of American lives and limbs.

Unless the restrictions on SDI technology are lifted, any future ABM technology this country develops—new sensing systems, new computers, new weapons, anything we can dream up and build—will end up being hobbled just like the Patriot missile. The next time Americans are subjected to a missile attack, the deaths may number in the millions instead of the dozens.

GOING BARE WITH BILL

In November 1992, something happened that placed American national security in severe jeopardy: Bill Clinton was elected president. One of the many love affairs of Bill Clinton's life is his love affair with the 1972 ABM Treaty. On several occasions, he has referred to this treaty as "the cornerstone of strategic stability" between the U.S. and

Russia. Even though this treaty was made between the United States and the Soviet Union—a nation that frequently cheated on the agreement, a nation that doesn't even exist anymore—Bill Clinton has committed the U.S. government to abiding by its terms. That treaty was the ratification of the old, discredited doctrine of "mutually assured destruction," or MAD.

Unlike Ronald Reagan, who believed that the American people deserved to be defended against nuclear blackmail and nuclear attack, Bill Clinton is dedicated to the proposition that it's best for the world if all Americans are sitting ducks and if the Russians have veto power over U.S. nuclear defense decisions. So, in May 1993, just a few months after Clinton's inauguration, Defense Secretary Les Aspin announced that the government was scrapping SDI. The contract for development and deployment, which was ready for signing when the Clintonistas came to power, was simply round-filed. Though the Clinton White House did allow research to continue on a reduced basis, it had no intention of building SDI.

Thanks to Bill Clinton, we are going bare in a world that is bristling with nuclear weapons. Though the world is unquestionably a *better* place now that the Soviet Union is gone, it is not necessarily a *safer* place—a fact that the liberals in the White House can't seem to figure out. For example, in May 1995, a high-ranking Clinton policy maker, Deputy Undersecretary of Defense Jan Lodal, went to Capitol Hill and said, "There is currently no threat that requires the United States to defend itself. It will, moreover, take many years for one to materialize. In the event a country like Iran does eventually acquire the means of delivering its weapons of mass destruction by long-range ballistic missiles, then and only then would the administration begin to put a limited U.S. antimissile defense system in place. If such a system was inconsistent with the limitations imposed on U.S. missile defenses by the 1972 Anti-Ballistic Missile Treaty, we would first seek Russia's permission to field it."

This statement reflects Bill Clinton's own fantasyland, head-in-the-sand view of the world. Dire threats to U.S. soil could materialize at any moment in any one of a dozen places around the world. One of the most significant threats is in Russia itself—a politically unstable, nuclear-armed nation presided over by an emotionally volatile drunk (Boris

Yeltsin), with a fire-breathing, ultranationalist, strangelovian crackpot (Vladimir Zhirinovsky) just waiting in the wings. If Russia suddenly changes hands, shall we then go hat-in-hand to Mr. Zhirinovsky and say, "May we have your permission to build SDI now, pretty please?"

You have to wonder what's going on in the mind of a president who thinks it's okay for everybody else in the country to be vulnerable to incineration, but who decides to put up concrete barricades on Pennsylvania Avenue so he can feel safe! Wouldn't it be a good idea to put just a few dollars back into the SDI pot so that we could *all* feel safer?

Fortunately, there are a lot of Republicans who think so.

A CHEAP SDI

The Republican blowout of November 1994 has given the Congress an opportunity to do what previous Congresses and President Clinton have failed to do: Defend America. Particularly among freshman members of Congress, there seems to be an understanding that the post-Cold War world is still an extremely dangerous place, and America should leave no stone unturned in its quest to secure itself against foreign enemies.

At the moment, the United States may face little threat from a massive Russian attack (though thousands of Russian missiles are still pointed our way). There are, however, many other areas of mounting nuclear tension in the world. For one thing, all those old Soviet missiles and warheads are possibly being sold by cash-strapped Russia, or even by rogue ex-Soviet military officers, to countries like Iraq, Iran, Libya, Syria, China, and North Korea. And then there are the advanced weapons technologies our own Defense Department is handing out around the world!

Frank Gaffney, director of the Center for Security Policy and a frequent guest on my show, points out that the United States is rapidly transferring high-tech lethal technology to—of all places—China! "The Clinton Defense Department," he writes, "is fixedly pursuing a politically driven sales campaign providing the communist Chinese virtually any and all militarily relevant technology it seeks. Indeed, congressional sources report that, of all the contentious issues in the fiscal 1996 defense authorization bill, the Pentagon lobbied hardest against legislation that would cut off department funding for a joint U.S.-Chinese Defense Conversion Task Force that has provided political cover for wanton American tech transfers to China."[2] The Chinese, meanwhile, are engaged (along with the Russians and North Koreans) in transferring advanced missile technology to states such as Iran, Iraq, Pakistan, and Brazil. If Saddam Hussein could have fired ICBMs at Washington, D.C., during the Gulf War, don't you think he would have?

And there are other dangers beside the danger of deliberate attack. There has always been the possibility that the Russians, the Chinese, or, for that matter, even the United States, would launch an accidental or unauthorized attack. (Remember *Dr. Strangelove, Fail Safe,* and *Twilight's Last Gleaming?*) An SDI-style defense system could be used not only to defend America but to "recall" an accidental or rogue launch. Even as few as a dozen Patriot-style ground-based interceptors could prevent disaster from such a limited-scale accident or attack.

Ultimately, however, our goal should be to build a massive, impenetrable SDI shield over the United States. This goal could be accomplished by basing large numbers of interceptors on both coasts and in Hawaii. Problem: This basing plan would violate Bill Clinton's beloved ABM Treaty.

Currently, plans are under way (thanks to the Republicans in Congress) to upgrade the Navy's AEGIS fleet air defense system. Built at a cost of about $50 billion, AEGIS is a complex, yet flexible, program of satellites, ground-based sensors, launchers, and missiles designed to render the Navy's far-flung armada immune to surprise attack. Obviously, a system that can watch the skies and defend a fleet should be able to do the same for land masses. For a mere $200 million—that's 4/10 of one percent of the total cost of AEGIS—the system is being upgraded to defend against aircraft, cruise missiles, and ballistic missiles. You might think, "Great! SDI at last!"

Wrong. The Clinton administration's National Security Committee directs the deployment of this system and plans to see that only a so-called "upper tier" system is built—that is, a system capable of defending only our front-line forces and our allies. It will not protect American soil. As Gaffney points out, it is actually conceivable that a situation could arise in the not-too-distant future where Iraq might fire missiles at the U.S. and Israel, or North Korea might fire missiles at the

U.S. and Japan—and a Navy commander would have the ability to shoot down only the missiles aimed at our allies! The missiles aimed at American soil would sail unharmed to their targets, courtesy of Bill Clinton.

The very survival of America as this millennium draws to a close may well come down to who we elect to the White House and Congress. We have the technological know-how to build highly effective ground-based and space-based defense systems. Defense analysts believe that for a mere $2 billion to $3 billion, spread out over five years, we could have a virtually impenetrable nuclear shield in place by the year 2000—a shield capable of stopping any missile, short-range, medium-range, or even long-range ICBMs. We have the ability. All we lack is the will and the common sense to do it.

In order for America to be defended, all of us here at Ground Zero need to get involved. We need to put people in office who are committed to national defense. And we need to tell our elected representatives that we expect them to provide for the common defense through their legislation, their policies, and their floor votes. Republicans such as Floyd Spence, Curt Weldon, and my good friends Duncan Hunter and Robert Dornan are working hard to get America the defense it deserves. Strangely and unfortunately, other Republicans are fighting against strategic defense programs that are not only workable and necessary but affordable as well.

House speaker Newt Gingrich once described himself as "a hawk—but a cheap hawk." I think most of us in the conservative wing identify with that description. Fortunately, a truly effective missile shield *can* be purchased for America at Kmart prices. But we have to act now. It is absolutely stupid to continue researching (as the Clinton administration has done) what can already be built with off-the-shelf technology. It's time to stop tinkering and fiddling and writing reports. It's time to put Russia on notice that MAD policies between the U.S. and the defunct U.S.S.R. no longer apply. It's time to start building SDI.

Most of all, it's time to make Ronald Reagan's most visionary dream come true: a world in which nuclear war is no longer a possibility.

PART 3

INDISPENSABLE MEN

◆

Reflections on My Father—and on Being a Father

CHAPTER 14

Typical Gipper

THE QUESTION came up frequently from callers on my show: "Why doesn't your dad make as many public appearances as he used to?" The question had an answer—but it was a painful answer, one I couldn't give on the air.

Ronald Reagan's last major public appearance was on February 6, 1994, his eighty-third birthday, at a Republican party fund-raiser in his honor in Washington, D.C. After a number of party luminaries rose and gave tribute to the man who had defeated the Evil Empire and restored America's confidence in itself, Ronald Reagan himself stood up to speak. He gave his usual sparkling performance, full of humor, fond reminiscences, and that quiet but passionate belief in the goodness of America that has become the Reagan trademark. It was a fun moment for all of us in the Reagan family—but it was also a bittersweet moment. We saw the shadow in which he stood as he gave that speech, a shadow no one else in that room could see.

The people who came that night to honor Ronald Reagan didn't know how tough that speech was for him. He delivered it in classic Reagan style—an easygoing performance with all the usual laugh lines and applause lines. Only those who were closest to my father knew that he had to go into triple-overtime to prepare for that speech. Only those who were closest to my father knew how tough his 1992 speech at the Republican National Convention in Houston had been. And only those who were closest to my father knew the reason why: he has a progressive and incurable neurological disorder called *Alzheimer's disease.*

Some months before, my father's personal physician had run some routine tests that indicated a neurological problem. Further tests at the Mayo Clinic in late 1993 confirmed the diagnosis: He was entering the early stages of Alzheimer's. It was a subject I had never wanted even to think about. Suddenly I, and all the adult members of my father's family, had to think long and hard about this disease. We began reading *The 36-Hour Day* by Nancy L. Mace (Johns Hopkins University Press, 1991), a book about the problems of living with and caring for a loved one with Alzheimer's.

Of course, it's quite common for people, as they enter their senior years, to forget an appointment and occasionally to blank out on some fact or even the name of a friend. During the normal aging process, people just naturally lose brain cells and mental function slows down. But sometimes forgetfulness becomes more acute, more chronic. In many cases, it becomes clear that something more devastating than the normal aging process is at work. Besides memory loss, Alzheimer's symptoms include disorientation, personality change, and impaired judgment.

Though Alzheimer's disease primarily targets people in their senior years, it sometimes strikes people in their forties or fifties. In fact, the disease was first identified in 1906 by the German pathologist Alois Alzheimer during an autopsy of a fifty-five-year-old patient. Ninety years after the disease was first identified, there is no known cause or cure. It kills 100,000 people every year, making it the fourth leading cause of death in our country (after heart disease, cancer, and strokes). About half of all people who reach my father's age have some degree of Alzheimer's. The Food and Drug Administration has recently approved a drug called tacrine, which may relieve symptoms in certain patients. Though the cause of the disease is unknown, researchers know that it attacks the nerve cells of the frontal and temporal lobes of the brain and is accompanied by a number of physical abnormalities, such as:

- Decreases in neurotransmitting chemicals (such as acetylcholine and serotonin) in the brain.
- Neurofibrillary tangles—fibrous structures within the nerve cells.

- Neuritic plaques, composed of degenerating nerve-cell elements and amyloid protein.
- Accumulation of aluminum deposits in the brain.

Once the diagnosis of Alzheimer's was made in my father's case, our family naturally went into a protective mode. We shielded him from publicity and carried the secret of his diagnosis within ourselves. It was a great and painful burden. Then, in October 1994, the family became aware that a periodical had gotten hold of the information about my father's condition. You know the kind of periodical I'm talking about. You also know the way such publications tend to treat these kinds of stories.

So Ronald Reagan decided to be what he's always been: a leader. He made a choice to lay it all on the table. He sat down at his desk and composed a two-page "Letter to the American People" in his own hand:

My Fellow Americans,

I have recently been told that I am one of the millions of Americans who will be afflicted with Alzheimer's disease.

Upon learning this news, Nancy and I had to decide whether as private citizens we would keep this a private matter or whether we would make this news known in a public way.

In the past, Nancy suffered from breast cancer and I had my cancer surgeries. We found through our open disclosures we were able to raise public awareness. We were happy that as a result many more people underwent testing. They were treated in early stages and able to return to normal, healthy lives.

So now, we feel it is important to share it with you. In opening our hearts, we hope this might promote greater awareness of this condition. Perhaps it will encourage a clearer understanding of the individuals and families who are affected by it.

At the moment I feel just fine. I intend to live the remainder of the years God gives me on this earth doing the things I have always done. I will continue to share life's journey with my beloved Nancy and my family. I plan to enjoy the great outdoors and stay in touch with my friends and supporters.

Unfortunately, as Alzheimer's disease progresses, the family often bears a heavy burden. I only wish there was some way I could spare Nancy from this painful experience. When the time comes I am confident that, with your help, she will face it with faith and courage.

In closing, let me thank you, the American people, for giving me the great honor of allowing me to serve as your President. When the Lord calls me home, whenever that may be, I will leave with the greatest love for this country of ours and eternal optimism for its future.

I now begin the journey that will lead me into the sunset of my life. I know that for America there will always be a bright dawn ahead.

Thank you, my friends. May God always bless you.

Sincerely,
Ronald Reagan

That letter was released to the public on Saturday, November 5, 1994—a very difficult and emotional weekend for Nancy and for all of us who called Ronald Reagan father—Maureen, Ron, Patti, and me. But that letter also gave us a sense of relief: At last we were free to talk openly about a matter we had kept private for the past year. We would have liked the world to remember Ronald Reagan as he was—vigorous and dignified, a man of wit and good sense, a man of strength who made America strong. We wondered if Alzheimer's disease might cloud that image. We needn't have wondered. My father had faced this challenge like he had faced every other challenge of his life. He had given his country one more example of American can-do courage and optimism under great adversity.

It turned out that the timing of my father's announcement was fortuitous: November is National Alzheimer's Awareness Month—and ironically, it was Ronald Reagan who first signed that designation into law in 1983. The response of my father's many friends was exemplified by a comment from his former speechwriter, Ken Khachigian: "Typical Gipper. It was an act of courage for him to come forward with this." And George Bush issued a statement from his Houston office, commending his former boss for his courage and for "sharing this private matter with the American people. Barbara and I are thinking of our good friends, Ron and Nancy, and we wish them well."

Even those who were diametrically opposed to the principles and beliefs of Ronald Reagan were moved to salute him in this hour. On Saturday afternoon, President Clinton was about to address a large Democratic party gathering when he received the news of the announcement. He went out before the group and said, "I'm going to ask you to do something we normally wouldn't do at a Democratic rally." Then he read my father's letter. A stunned murmur went through the crowd. "I disagreed with President Reagan on a lot of things," he concluded, "but one thing you can't disagree with: he is a decent, courageous American. He has always fought with a sense of optimism and spirit. . . . I want every one of you in this room now to give Ronald Reagan a hand and wish him God-speed." And they applauded my father, loudly and long.

Monday the seventh rolled around. It was a big day in many ways. Colleen and I were celebrating our nineteenth wedding anniversary—though we were not in the most celebratory of moods. That day was also the eve of the 1994 midterm election—what would turn out to be the biggest Republican landslide in history.

It wasn't easy doing my show that night. I knew there would be a lot of callers who wanted to talk about my father's illness. As hard as it was to deal with this issue on the air, it was good to speak with so many well-wishers, so many people who appreciated what my father had done for this country in his eight years as president.

But I also wanted to stay focused on the country's future, and the need to bring change to the Congress of the United States. I opened my show with the statement, "If you do what you always did, you'll get what you always got." I knew we had to stay focused on reversing the liberal policies that threatened to bankrupt our nation morally and economically. And I knew exactly what kind of tribute would most please Ronald Reagan as he set out upon what he called "the journey that will lead me into the sunset of my life." If the country would go to the polls and vote for a new "Reagan revolution" for the '90s, that would be enough. So, for the most part, that's what we talked about on *The Michael Reagan Talk Show* the night of November 7, 1994—not the sunset of Ronald Reagan's life but the bright dawn that Ronald Reagan still envisioned for America.

Yet there was one moment I had to go through, one story I had to tell on the air. I knew it would be hard and I wasn't sure I could get through it without choking up. But I said a silent prayer, then opened my heart and began to talk.

"My eleven-year-old daughter, Ashley," I said, "will have a copy of the letter my father handwrote to the country to have with her forever, and so will her brother, Cameron. Ashley was hit very hard by this news over the weekend. She's known that her grandpa has not been as quick as he once was. After all, he's eighty-three years of age, and you expect people of that age to lose a step now and again. So that's how we've dealt with it with Ashley over the past year—'Your grandpa's getting older, honey, and he's slowing down a bit.'

"But when you have someone like Ronald Reagan in your family, a lot of life's events find their way into the public arena. So, over the past weekend, Ashley heard a lot of talk about her grandpa's illness in the media. She listened to the news reports and she heard one doctor explaining what Alzheimer's is and how it makes people forgetful.

"Each of us in the Reagan family has struggled in his or her own way to deal with this terrible disease which has no cure. But of all of us, I think Ashley is the winner, the one with the right attitude, the right perspective when it comes to getting the best you can from your remaining years with a loved one who has this disease. After watching some of the coverage on television, she walked into the kitchen where her mother and I were standing, and she said to Colleen and to me, 'You know, Mom and Dad, I'm going to love Grandpa even if he doesn't know who I am.'"

My voice broke down at that moment, and I went to a commercial break. I couldn't help thinking that Ashley is not the only granddaughter going through this experience, since four million people are afflicted nationwide with this disease.

But I also couldn't help thinking that if anyone can go through an experience like this with courage and character, optimism and faith, thinking more of others than of himself, Ronald Reagan will. And he will help a lot of people in the process.

Typical Gipper.

Note: The Ronald and Nancy Reagan Research Institute, an "institute without walls" dedicated to the study of Alzheimer's disease, cooperates with the nonprofit Alzheimer's Association to fund scientific inquiry into the causes, treatment, and eventual cure of this disease. For information or to make a tax-deductible donation to benefit Alzheimer's research, education, and respite care, contact your local chapter of the Alzheimer's Association; or contact the Alzheimer's Association national office at 919 N. Michigan Avenue, Suite 1000, Chicago, IL 60611-1676; telephone 1-800-272-3900.

CHAPTER 15

On the Inside at Last

IF MY KIDS were to write a book about their dad, it wouldn't be anything like my previous book, *On the Outside Looking In.* In fact, they'd probably call it *On the Inside, Trying to Get Out.* In contrast to my own childhood, which was largely a struggle to get my busy show-business parents to spend time with me, my kids probably wish their dad would give them more space! I have a rule that I refuse to break or even bend for anyone: I do not do weekends with anybody but my family. You don't have enough money to get me to leave my family for a weekend.

I don't say that to pat myself on the back, because there are times when I take it too far. Kids have their own lives and their own friends, and sometimes I forget that. So when I make plans to take Cameron and Ashley out to a ballgame or to Disneyland for the weekend, then find out that they both have plans to spend the day with their school friends, I have been known to—well, to go slightly ballistic. I mean, I take it personally! I take it as rejection! And there's a reason for this.

My parenting style is in many ways a reflection of my childhood—and by "reflection," I mean a reverse image, like you would see in a mirror. My parents—Ronald Reagan and Jane Wyman—were divorced when I was young. They were both extremely busy with their careers, and I spent my school years in boarding school, so I just didn't get very much time and attention from them.

I'm not saying my parents *never* spent time with me. Sometimes my dad would pick me up and take me to the ranch for a weekend. But we always did the things *he* wanted to do, like riding horses. He didn't really understand that there were things *I* wanted to do, like going to a ballgame.

I really believe that most of us parents, to a greater or lesser degree, have a hard time really listening to our kids and understanding their point of view. We tend to parent our kids through the lens of our own childhood. We try to make up for what we didn't get as children. If you didn't get that Lionel electric train you wanted when you were ten years old, your son will probably get the biggest, most expensive train set in town for Christmas—whether he wants one or not. We all bring guilt, hurt, regret, and needs from childhood into our adulthood—and into parenthood. This is our baggage, and one way or another, we usually end up dumping our baggage on our kids. And that's what I often found myself doing with Cameron and Ashley.

Ashley may have a sleep-over at a friend's house for the weekend. Meanwhile, Cameron's taking off on a camping trip. And me? I'm left thinking, *Hey! What gives? I'm trying to do all the things with you kids that my mom and dad didn't do with me! They were often too busy for me—and now you're too busy for me, too?* It all centers around feeling rejected and abandoned, just like when I was a kid. And as a result, I find myself getting angry—an anger that is really out of proportion to the situation.

That's when my wife, Colleen, steps in: "Remember who the parent is!" she says. She's really cute—and she's right! I forget who the parent is and what parenting is all about. Spending time with my kids is about *what my kids need,* not my needs and what I didn't get when I was a kid. If the kids need to be with their friends for a weekend, it's not because they don't like their dad. It's because they're healthy kids who have good friends and plenty of activities to keep them busy. And that's the way it should be. If I love my kids, I have to give them some room to grow and to be themselves.

I'm still learning what being a dad is all about.

THE INDISPENSABLE FATHER

I hope the women reading this book won't be offended if I take a few pages to talk it over with dads. Feel free to listen in, ladies—in fact, you may know a dad who needs to hear what I'm about to say, so feel free to buy an extra copy of this book for him! Understand, it's not that I undervalue motherhood; in fact, I may have Colleen write a chapter for moms in my next book! But I think dads in our society need both a word of encouragement and a kick in the pants—and that's what this chapter is all about.

Fatherhood has taken quite a drubbing over the past few decades. In the "old days"—say, before Woodstock—society used to support parents in their effort to raise decent, civilized, upright kids. Today, a good father and mother must parent *against* society. Virtually everything you do and say to your kids is part of an overall effort to bulletproof them against a morally hostile culture. It's not just that television and movies and MTV are trying to drench their minds with sex and drugs. The assault on our kids is much more insidious, massive, and pervasive than that. Our society is literally trying to tear down the safe, nurturing enclosure of the *family* that we, as parents, are trying to build around our kids.

We are told that the concept of "family" is anything we want it to be, that fathers aren't necessary, that "family values" is an obsolete and meaningless term. The wise, caring, strong, involved father of the old black-and-white TV sitcoms—men like Ward Cleaver, Jim Anderson, and Andy Taylor—have been replaced by TV fathers who are stupid, rude, apathetic, and weak. I mean, just look at how fatherhood is portrayed on shows like *Married With Children* and *The Simpsons*!

During the 1992 campaign, Vice President Dan Quayle was crucified for daring to suggest that families need fathers. In his famous "Murphy Brown speech" at the Commonwealth Club in San Francisco in May of that year, he cited a number of sobering facts:

- In 1991, only 48 percent of black families were two-parent families versus 68 percent in 1967.
- In 1989, two-thirds of black children were born to mothers who had never been married, versus 28 percent in 1965.

What was the social cost of these trends toward fatherlessness in America? For one thing, rapidly increasing poverty:

- In 1951, the unemployment rate for black youths between ages sixteen and nineteen was 9.2 percent. By 1965, the rate had jumped to 23 percent. By 1980, 35 percent.

- In 1992, the poverty rate among two-parent families was a mere 5.7 percent; among families headed by a single mom, the rate was a whopping 33.4 percent, or one-third.

The pattern is clear, as Quayle went on to explain: "The intergenerational poverty that troubles us so much today is predominantly a poverty of values." Quayle was critical of the CBS sitcom *Murphy Brown* for portraying unwed motherhood in a rosy, unrealistic, even glamorized way. It was only a single sentence in a twenty-five minute speech—but the media elite were quick to latch onto the issue as yet another opportunity for Quayle bashing—the twisted inference being that when Dan Quayle and other conservatives talk about "family values," they are really attacking poor people, unwed mothers, and minorities.

We conservatives are always having to defend ourselves against idiotic charges that we "hate" this or that group or that we "attack" certain classes of people. Again and again, we have to punch through the haze of lies and distortions in order to state what should be obvious to all: We conservatives are not into class warfare. We don't want to put this group or that group down.

The fact that I believe every family needs a father doesn't mean I am down on single mothers. After all, I was raised by a single mother! And I think Jane Wyman did a pretty good job raising Michael Reagan. Single mothers have a tough job, and I admire and honor all those parents who have taken on the difficult job of raising their children alone. But there's a big difference between glorifying the condition of single parenthood, as *Murphy Brown* does, and praising single parents for the tough job they are forced to shoulder. Single parenting is sometimes the only option a parent has, but no matter how you slice it, a single-parent home is not the best environment for kids. The fact that not every kid can have a dad does not negate the fact that every kid needs a dad and should, ideally, have a dad.

Boys need fathers to teach them what manhood is all about—how to work, build, provide, and protect. A boy learns how a man is supposed to treat a woman by watching how Dad relates to Mom. A good father validates the emerging man within the boy and empowers the boy to reach toward the goal of ideal manhood. When fathers fail to perform these functions for their sons—and especially when those fathers are out of the picture entirely—the results are often disastrous. Statistics show that 70 percent of long-term prison inmates—including 72 percent of adolescent murderers and 60 percent of all rapists—grew up in fatherless homes.

Girls also need fathers to model a healthy image of manhood. A good father exhibits positive traits for his daughter to seek when she enters courtship. A father who is affirming and appropriately affectionate with his daughter enables her to feel confident and good about herself. A teenage girl with high self-esteem is better equipped to "just say no" to peer pressure, drugs, and sex. Girls with low self-esteem—and particularly girls who were starved for love by their fathers—are more likely to give in to a scheming boy who says, "I *really* love you; now prove that you love me too." She has a void inside her where a father's love should be, and in her desperation to fill that void, she falls for the first guy with a fast line and an active sex drive—and when he's through using her, she's left feeling more empty, more unlovable than ever before.

So fathers are indispensable to both sons and daughters. Even when a marriage breaks up, kids need their dads—and dads should always be there for their kids. Unfortunately, there is a very ugly phrase that we hear too often these days: "deadbeat dad." How did such a great, warm, noble word like *dad* become linked with that awful adjective *deadbeat*? In part, because there are a lot of dads who have *earned* the right to be called deadbeats! If a man can't get along with his ex-wife, that's one thing—but depriving the kids just to get back at their mom is another thing altogether. There's nothing lower than a man who turns his back on his children and refuses to provide for them, divorce or no divorce. Men who would do that to their own kids are the main reason that 75 percent of children in single-parent families experience poverty at some point during the first ten years of their lives.

But divorced dads have something even more important to offer their kids than a regular child-support check: *themselves*. Even if you only get to see your kids every other weekend, you still have something absolutely crucial to give them: Your time. Your affirmation. Your values. Your example. Your guidance and support. Your love. Yes, it's important to provide for kids in a material way, even after the marriage is over. But kids don't just need a check. They need a *dad*.

Fathers are indispensable.

FACING THE PAST

I'm grateful for a film like Disney's *The Lion King*—especially in an age when fathers seem to be under assault and in decline. It's a story about fatherhood—how crucially important fathers are in shaping character, values, and self-image in their children. It is particularly a story about fathers and sons—how they make each other proud, how they disappoint each other, how they misunderstand each other, how they affirm and forgive each other, and how they ultimately need each other.

On a personal level, I find it impossible not to admire the wise, strong fathering of Mufasa—and it is equally impossible not to identify and empathize with the pain, self-doubt, and guilt of Mufasa's son, Simba. Much of the film revolves around Simba's youthful struggle to discover his own identity in the shadow of a great king—a struggle that, for obvious reasons, resonates in my own being. I know what is going on inside young Simba when he romps alongside his father, struggling to keep up, and asking, "Dad, we're pals, right? And we'll always be together?" I understand what Simba was feeling when he came to a moment of crisis in his life and concluded, "I know what I have to do, but going back means I'll have to face my past. I've been running from it so long."

I went back and faced my own past, the past I had been running from for so long, when I wrote *On the Outside Looking In*. It was a learning and changing experience for me, because when I completed that book, I had a much different outlook on myself, my past, and my parents than the outlook I had started out with. One of the most unexpected and healing aspects of the entire writing process was the part it played in my relationship with my father. A whole new depth of communication and understanding opened up between Dad and me, as he described in the foreword he wrote for the paperback edition of the book:

> As I walked Michael to his room, we began talking. It was a conversation we should have had years and years ago; too much had been left unsaid

on both our parts—but the important thing is that we finally did have the chance to open up to each other, Michael to unburden himself of years of doubt and self-recrimination, I to say things I always assumed he knew. Traveling back in my mind to Michael's babyhood, seeing again his impish, angelic smile and recalling his unlimited energy, I now realize that many adopted children do see themselves as different. Maybe not telling Michael about his adoption at the earliest possible age was a mistake. . . . But, as a parent then, I didn't know how Michael felt inside. To me, he was my adorable little son, and from the moment he first smiled at me, I never recalled he was adopted. I loved him as I did my other children.

Being a father forty-five years ago was a much different role than it is today, and I sometimes envy the freedom Michael has to show affection to my grandchildren, Cameron and Ashley. Back then, a man went to work and left the childrearing to the mother, much as it was when my mother raised me. Fathers didn't spend the amount of quality time with their children that today's fathers do, and they weren't always free to hug their sons or say I love you. In Michael's case, that was compounded by a divorce and by the fact that both his parents had very demanding careers. . . .

We, as parents, must always strive to communicate with our children, to let them know there is nothing they cannot tell us, to let them know our love will always be with them. . . . Michael, whatever happens, always know I love you![1]

Facing your past isn't easy. It hurts. It still hurts me to remember that I was molested by a day camp counselor when I was young. It hurts to recall my parents' divorce when I was seven years old and to remember how it felt when the only world I had ever known was split in two. It hurts to remember the day some kids at school told me I was a "bastard" because I was adopted.

It hurts to know that my birth mother followed my life and kept scrapbooks with clippings of my childhood and adolescence, and that she died just two years before I located her. It hurts that I never got to meet her and let her read *On the Outside Looking In,* a book I really wrote for her. It hurts to think of how I practically killed myself, racing boats at eighty miles an hour, trying to prove myself, desperately racing for the love and approval of my father—a love I didn't realize was there all along.

But it's much better to face the past, with all its pain, than to hide from it or deny it. As the Bible says, only the truth will really set you free.

In any family, fathers and sons have a special relationship—a relationship that goes through testing, pain, and triumph. Fathers and sons make each other proud, but they also disappoint and misunderstand each other. If they are able to endure the hurt courageously, if they are able to face the past honestly, they can come through the disappointment and misunderstanding. They can forgive each other, embrace each other, and make the bonds of love even stronger than ever before.

Dad, I love you too. Whatever happens, always know I love you.

A FEW NOTES FROM A FATHER-IN-PROCESS

I don't claim to be an expert on fatherhood. I'm just trying to be as good a dad to my kids as I can, making my share of mistakes, but finding a lot of satisfaction in the learning and growing process. I've made some notes—not on the aspects of fatherhood that I have mastered but on the issues and goals I'm still working on. Here are some notes on fatherhood from a father-in-process:

Build traditions with your kids.

I think it's important to do things with kids that they will remember and that they will want to take with them and pass on to their own children. Some traditions I'm building with Cameron and Ashley include Christmas and Easter traditions, annual family reunions with Colleen's family in Nebraska, family and father-son conferences at Hume Lake Christian Camp, going shopping with Ashley (she always knows what she wants—and she knows I'm an easy touch), going dove hunting every Labor Day with Cameron, taking the kids to Dad and Nancy's Santa Barbara ranch for horseback riding, and so forth.

Express affection to your kids.

Child development experts tell us that both boys and girls need to feel their father's affirming touch, from birth right on into adolescence. Children who grow up without a father's touch tend to have a lot of problems with self-acceptance and emotional security. A hug or an arm around the shoulders or some wrestling or tickling on the living-room floor tells a child, "I like to be close to you, I accept you, you're okay."

Practice integrity.

That means being the same kind of person in private, when nobody's looking, as you are in public. That means setting an absolute goal of always telling the truth, always keeping your word, even when it's costly or embarrassing to do so. That means building not only a *reputation* (which can be faked), but also building *character* (which is real and enduring). As basketball star A. C. Green says in *Victory: The Principles of Championship Living,* "We reap what we sow. Whatever we do in private, or don't do, will come to light in public. . . . To be a champion you need a firm foundation [or] cracks will eventually show up."[2]

Your children are around you all the time, and they watch you to see if your words and your actions match. "Do as I say, not as I do," is a prescription for raising kids who will one day reject you and your values. The best way to raise healthy, upright kids is to be a healthy, upright man and allow your kids to pattern themselves after your example.

Make sure you have mentors and close friends in your life.

In my church, I'm involved with Promise Keepers through New Men, Inc., and I seek out counsel, advice, and encouragement from other men, such as my pastor, Jack Hayford, and my friend, Bob Phillips, director of Hume Lake Christian Camps. We all need mentors and guides—other men who will ask us the tough questions and hold us accountable, men who will support us and pray for us and stand by us through the hard times.

For example, I ask my own mentors and friends to pray for me and hold me accountable in the area of humility. My radio show is growing rapidly, and I get a lot of positive strokes from a lot of people. It would be easy to let it go to my head, especially given the fact that I suffered major self-esteem problems as a child and grew up craving attention, affirmation, and positive strokes. As the show grows, as the influence and the reach of my voice grows, I don't want Mike Reagan to change. So I ask my friends to watch my life and to pray for me—and if you're a praying person, I ask you to pray for me too.

It's a goal I have set after watching my father over the years. He has been praised and lionized and magnified in the public mind—and I think his accomplishments on the world stage certainly merit that praise. But speaking as someone who has watched him up close, I can tell you that Ronald Reagan never changed from being Ronald Reagan. Hollywood fame didn't change him. Political fame didn't change him. Achievements, awards, and speeches in his honor didn't change him. A special place in the history books didn't change him. The real greatness of Ronald Reagan has always been his humility. That's not a trait that is highly prized or even recognized in this era of inflated egos and media hype— yet it is the humility of Ronald Reagan that truly sets him apart as a leader among leaders.

Just a few months ago, as I write these words, I was sitting and talking with Dad at the house in Bel-Air, and we were reminiscing together about his career in politics. As we talked, we realized that thirty years earlier, almost to the day, he had announced his candidacy for governor of the state of California. That announcement marked his entry into politics. "At that point in your political career," I noted, "you had no idea what lay ahead of you."

His eyebrows lifted as he glanced at me with a merry smile and said, "How did I do?"

"Pretty good, Dad," I replied, chuckling. "You did all right."

That's the example I have set before myself. I want always to be a man who maintains a sense of proportion and perspective about himself. I never want to be anything more than just plain Mike Reagan. And if I ever start to change or become full of myself and overinflated, I'm counting on my close friends and mentors to put me back in my place.

Take time to be a mentor to kids—not just to your own kids but to kids who don't have a father.

Children without fathers are more likely to live in poverty, to commit crimes, to join gangs, to use drugs, to grow up to become career criminals. Why? Poverty alone is not the answer. In fact, poverty is a symptom, not a root cause. The real source of juvenile crime is that fatherless children grow up hurting, angry, and lacking the moral control and inner strength a good father models. If we truly want to attack the *source* of crime in our society, men must make a decision to target fatherless boys with their strength and caring.

When the Anacostia/Congress Heights Partnership started a Little League program in a gang-infested section of Washington, D.C., a lot of people predicted the program would fall flat on its face. "Kids in the 'hood don't care about Little League," said the voice of conventional wisdom. "They won't show up!" Well, conventional wisdom was wrong. The kids not only showed up in staggering numbers, they showed up two hours early, they played their hearts out during practice, and they hung around after practice just to be close to their coaches. Was it because they loved baseball so much? No, it was because these mostly fatherless kids wanted to experience the company and affirmation of adult men. They were starved for fathering. They wanted to stand in the shadow of someone who patted them on the back, pointed them in the right direction, and affirmed the emerging men inside them.

Any man can have a powerful, positive influence on a fatherless child—by coaching a team, teaching a Sunday school class or youth group, leading a Scout troop, serving with a Big Brothers program, or even adopting a fatherless child. Any man with character, life experience, and a big heart can cast a shadow for some needy child to stand in and measure himself by. A man who is willing to do that for a child takes a little piece of this hurting world in his hands—and changes it for the better.

Work hard at your marriage.

If I could only leave one thing to my children, it would be an understanding of what it takes to make a marriage work. My kids go to school with dozens of kids from one-parent families or from families that have completely disintegrated, and they can see that those other kids have been damaged by what they've been through. Those kids have emotional problems. They have behavior problems. They have a diminished capacity for trust. Many of their emotional problems will follow them well into adulthood. I really believe that the best thing a dad can do for his kids is to focus on his marriage and really love his wife. That's harder than it sounds, even in the best marriages.

So many people go into marriage through the front door, but they keep an eye on the back door, the escape hatch, and the first time things get tough, they say, "That's it! I'm outta here! I guess we didn't love each other after all. I just don't feel the love anymore." Hey, the kind of love it takes to make a marriage work isn't a *feeling,* it's a *decision.* If you really love your kids, then you will do whatever it takes to work things through and hold the marriage together. You'll get counseling, you'll go to marriage seminars, you'll stay up until two in the morning talking it out, you'll do *anything* and *everything* to make that relationship healthy so that your kids will grow up feeling emotionally secure. If you love your kids, you don't give up on the marriage.

So often I hear people say, "Marriage is 50-50." No, it's not. Marriage is 100-100. Both partners have to put out 100 percent, and sometimes more. If you think marriage is 50-50, you're constantly trying to draw a line down the middle of your relationship, you're constantly bickering over who's keeping up her half or who's overstepping his half. It's a prescription for failure. When both sides accept 100 percent of the responsibility for the relationship, the relationship can work. Sometimes, to keep a marriage running smoothly, you have to swallow some pride, accept some blame, even when you don't feel it's your fault. That's a lot easier when you own 100 percent of the responsibility for the relationship instead of just your half.

So much of the credit for keeping our family together through the tough times goes to Colleen—to her character, her faith, and her midwestern values. Thank God I married above me! I tell my son again and again that when he is finally ready to be married, he needs to marry a girl from the Midwest. If he can't find one out here in California, he needs to get on a plane and fly to the center of the country, and the first midwestern single girl he runs into, he should grab her and marry her.

The family is the most important unit in our society. If it breaks down, everything else falls apart. If we, as a nation, make a decision to strengthen and protect the American family, we will be doing the best thing possible to strengthen and protect America itself.

Pray.

It was prayer that got Colleen and me through that grueling experience when I first took my show national. The long commute, the intense focus, the bouncing paychecks, the phone calls from creditors—it was incredibly tough on the marriage, on me, on her, and on the kids. I remember many nights, driving up the coast after the show, wearing my baseball cap, with tears in my eyes, wondering how I was going to make it, wondering if I was doing the right thing. I was mentally and physically exhausted from making that drive every day. Colleen was practically living the life of a single mom. I was frustrated because my family is number one with me—but in order to build my show so we could all have a future, I had to put my family in the backseat for a couple years, and that tore me apart. It was prayer that held my family together and prayer that held Michael Reagan together. It was my prayers, Colleen's prayers, and the prayers of a lot of good praying friends.

I believe an earthly father has a lot to do with shaping a child's mental and emotional image of the Heavenly Father. Kids who have loving, involved, affirming fathers tend to see God as loving, forgiving, and actively present in their lives; kids with abusive fathers tend to see God as harsh and scary; kids with remote, absent fathers tend to feel abandoned by God. So I'm convinced that a good father needs to spend a lot of time in prayer, talking to God and listening to God, getting to know Him, building God's character into his own life, so that he can better exemplify a wise and loving Heavenly Father to his own children.

One of the most satisfying things about being a parent is watching the spiritual growth of my two kids. It seems as though my daughter, Ashley, has always had the love of the Lord. She's one of a kind. She has my temper and temperament, but she really has that deep, special love for God that Colleen has.

For a long time, I gave her an allowance of $5. One day, I went to her and said, "Ashley, you're getting older, and I think with everything you do to help out the family, you've earned a raise in your allowance. So I'm going to increase it to $7.50 a week." And she said, "You know, Dad, I really don't need that much allowance. I think I'd rather give that extra $2.50 to the church every Sunday." And she does. If, for some reason, she doesn't make it to church on a given Sunday, she gives me the money and says, "Dad, make sure you give my money to the church." That's my Ashley.

And let me tell you about my son, Cameron. Every year, our family goes to Hume Lake Christian Camp. Back in 1988, Cameron and I attended a father-and-son event called Fisherman's Conference. It was a great weekend, during which the speaker, Ron Walters, challenged us as fathers and sons to a deeper commitment to Christ and to a lifestyle of honesty, integrity, and godly manhood. On Saturday night, there was an altar call in which we were invited to come forward and sign a pledge to seal the commitment. I thought it would be nice for Cameron and me to go forward together, so I leaned over to my son and said, "Let's go, Cameron."

Cameron, being ten years old at the time, gave me a horrified look and whispered back, "In front of all these people? You've gotta be nuts, Dad!"

"No," I said, "do it for me, son. I think it would really be a nice thing to do together."

With eyes wide, looking like the proverbial deer in the headlights, he pleaded, "Don't embarrass me like this, Dad!"

I nudged him. "C'mon!"

"Okay!" he groaned, hanging his head in surrender. "I'll do it." He slowly got up out of his chair and trudged up the aisle with me, looking like he was on his way to the gallows.

Once in front, we took the little commitment card and filled it out. There was a place for me to sign and a place for Cameron. We tore off the stub and handed it to my friend Bob Phillips, who was collecting the stubs. The other half of the card was ours to keep as a reminder of the commitment we made that night, April 30, 1988. I keep it in my Bible to this day. After we had done this, Cameron and I went back to our seats. I thought it was a great father-son moment for Cameron and me, although Cameron didn't seem affected by it one way or the other (except that I had embarrassed him right into the ground).

That night, we went to our cabin, where we shared a big king-size bed. I turned out the lights and we snuggled in close. It was quiet and dark, and I was beginning to drift off to sleep. Then Cameron broke the silence. "Dad?" he said.

"Yeah?"

"How long has Hume Lake Christian Camp been here?"

"Oh," I said, "twenty, thirty years at least."

"Do you think this place will be here, like, twenty years from now?"

"Probably," I replied. "Why'd you want to know?"

"That was really nice tonight," he said. "Maybe someday I'll be able to walk my son forward like you walked me forward tonight."

Cameron didn't know it, but I just kind of puddled up right there and whispered, "Wow! Thank you!" to the Lord. I keep that memory stored in my mind as one of the great moments with my son, Cameron.

There's a lot of satisfaction in what I do for a living—talking to lots of people every night on the radio, sounding off on the issues of the day, helping people to get a handle on their government, interviewing the movers and shakers and history-makers. But my greatest satisfaction in life doesn't come from my work—not even close! My greatest satisfaction in life comes from having a great wife, great kids, and a great place to come home to. When I hear Cameron or Ashley call me *Dad,* I think, *Man, it doesn't get any better than this! I'm on the inside at last!*

PART 4

MAKING WAVES

◆

What to Do Till the Next Millennium Arrives

CHAPTER 16

Making Waves

THINK WHAT you want: I'm triskaidekaphobic. In other words, I have a major aversion to the unlucky number 13.

Superstitious? Me? You bet! I've been superstitious ever since my boat-racing days. I would *never* set foot in a boat with the number 13 painted on the hull. No way, nohow, no sir!

Another bad luck sign for me: the color green. And that's a problem when you're racing a boat sponsored by Seven-Eleven, with that big green logo on the side! If I ever had to race a boat with any green on it, I'd wear a red cap to counteract the green. If I couldn't wear the cap on my head, I'd tuck it under my shirt. Most boat racers I know are superstitious—most of the ones who are still alive, anyway.

You think superstition is bunk, do you? Well, let me tell you about a couple of Florida boat racers who thought the same way. These two fellas bought a brand-new racing boat—a beautiful thirty-eight-foot Wellcraft Scarab—and the first thing they did to that boat was violate her hull with a big black number 13! These guys were really out to prove that superstition is bunk! As soon as the paint dried on the hull, they took that Scarab out on the water for its maiden run. They opened up the throttle and started wave-hopping at 85 knots or so—and they promptly flipped it. Both men were killed. You tell me: Is triskaidekaphobia really "bunk"?

Though the drivers were killed, the boat survived pretty much intact. So who do you think was the next person to drive that boat? Would you believe—Mike Reagan? That's right. In fact, I set a couple speed records in that boat. But you can be sure of this: Before I even touched the boat, I made dead-sure every speck of that ugly black 13 was buffed off the hull! Yet, even though there was no green, no number 13, no bad luck sign anywhere on my boat, my first race in it—a 1,027-mile dash from New Orleans to the St. Louis Arch—was plagued with bad breaks.

RUNNING INTO SHALLOW WATER

For years, I had raced against other boats, but this was a race against the clock—straight through with no rest stops, no sleep, only brief stops for refueling. There were three of us—my navigator, my throttle man, and myself. We set off from New Orleans at about three o'clock in the afternoon on July 19, 1982. The finish line was at least a full day away.

The race was called "The W. R. Grace Challenge Cup" after the principal corporate sponsor, but it soon became known as the "Assault on the Mississippi." I had managed to sign up almost $400,000 in corporate sponsorships, which would go to benefit the U.S. Olympic Committee. The publicity surrounding the event was awesome. A host of dignitaries crowded the starting line—George Bush, the vice president of the United States; Bill Simon, former treasury secretary under Gerald Ford and chairman of the U.S. Olympic Committee; my corporate sponsors, Peter Grace of the W. R. Grace Company (and later head of the Grace Commission on cutting federal waste during my father's administration), Augie Busch, of the Anhauser Busch brewing company, and J. W. Marriott, Jr., of Marriott Hotels; and many others. ABC Sports had TV cameras covering the event from all angles, and the Budweiser bus was following our route from New Orleans to St. Louis. In my mind, the whole world was watching me, waiting to see if the son of the president of the United States would break the Mississippi River speed record—or if he would wash out.

The pressure I felt as the race began was almost intolerable. Every ounce of my self-esteem was riding on that boat. The record I was going after had stood since 1929, and in all that time, more than a thousand attempts had been made to break it—all unsuccessful. There would be a victory dinner at the finish line, and the keynote speech of the event would be delivered by none other than my father, the president of the

United States. In my mind, if I broke the old record, I would be a hero. But if I failed to break the record—or worse, if I failed to finish the race—I would be a failure, a loser, a zero.

A lot of racers on long-distance runs have more than one driver. That's legal. There's nothing that says you can't change a driver from time to time—but I couldn't afford that luxury. I knew that the moment I came out of the driver's seat and let somebody else take the wheel, that's when the news cameras would all start clicking, and the caption would read, "Reagan's son is just along for the ride; Mike Reagan takes it easy while the *real* driver drives." I wasn't going to let the press portray me as some kind of wuss. I'd drive the entire race, all day and all night, just to make sure the news camera could never get a picture of someone else behind the wheel.

Speedboat racing is not something you do sitting down. When you are skimming waves at eighty or ninety knots, you can break parts of your anatomy or even get killed. You stand up the whole way, and you use your legs as shock absorbers. The boat spends most of its time airborne, hopping from crest to crest. Every time the boat smacks the water, your body absorbs tremendous gee-forces—and if you don't time it just right, you can snap a knee. It's tiring and grueling, and you get beat up and thrashed around a lot in the process.

The first leg of the race seemed to go fairly well and we were making good time. But by nightfall, I knew I was going to have trouble. My first big problem was my navigator. He was a riverboat captain and supposedly knew every inch of the mighty, muddy Mississippi. He probably would have worked out just fine if we were taking a leisurely riverboat ride upriver—but this was a grueling, punishing, all-day, all-night speedboat endurance race. This squirrely navigator of mine thought he was tougher than John Wayne; he didn't need to eat, he didn't need to drink water, he didn't need to refurbish himself. He wouldn't admit that his wits were dulled or that he didn't know where he was, and we repeatedly found he was running us into shallow water—a very dangerous place to be at 85 knots or more.

Lights are almost useless at night. By the time a tree or a rock pops up in your lights, it's too late to avoid it. We had radar on the boat, but radar doesn't pick up everything. It will pick up a riverboat but not a floating log or a big snag. So boat racing at night is pretty much an act of sheer blind faith.

Once during the night, my throttle man, Johnny Mann, leaned over and elbowed me, yelling in my ear, "How well do we know our navigator?"

"I don't know," I said. "I just met him last night."

Johnny's eyebrows shot up. *"You just met him last night?!"*

"Yeah. Why do you want to know?"

"Because we just missed a tree by about a foot."

"That's nice to know," I said. "Thanks for the information." And we kept on going.

UP THE MISSISSIPPI WITHOUT A PADDLE

Early the next morning, we fueled up in Memphis. At our previous fuel stop, the crew had overfilled the tanks, which caused us some problems, so our Memphis crew wanted to be extra careful not to overfuel us. That proved to be our next big problem: They didn't give me enough fuel to make it to the next stop.

Two hours out of Memphis, I knew we were in deep yogurt. Our navigator had gone completely tilt on us; he sank down into his seat in the back of the boat and disappeared for the rest of the trip. So much for our tough-guy riverboat captain. Johnny and I were on our own—which was fine with me, because it was clear that my navigator had lost all sense of where we were on that river.

But the big problem I had was that I was running out of gas. I was halfway between Memphis and our next fuel stop, and there was nothing in sight—just the river and a lot of trees. We had gone miles without seeing a single shack, house, or boat dock along the river. You talk about being up the creek! Here I was, up the biggest creek on the North American continent, running on fumes, and not even a paddle to push with when the fumes gave out. I couldn't believe this was happening. I could accept it if we had just hit a rock and the boat exploded and we got killed. It would be a failure, but it would be a *heroic* failure. But how was I doing to live with it if I just plain *ran out of gas*? That would be embarrassment and humiliation on top of failure! Well, no way! I wasn't going to let that happen. I was going to get to St. Louis and break that record if I had to get out and carry that boat on my head!

Fortunately, it didn't come to that, because just then Johnny pointed to the riverbank up ahead. "What's that?" he asked. We got closer, and soon Johnny had his answer: It was a launch ramp, and just off to the side was a little shed. So I nosed the boat into the mud at the riverbank, alongside the ramp. Then I jumped out, dashed up the ramp, and found a road. That road led to another road, where there was a little store with a phone booth around the side. I thought, "Unbelievable!"

I ran to the phone, called our bus and let my project coordinator, Eddie Morenz, know where we were and the trouble we were in. From the bus, Eddie immediately started radioing around for fuel. He found a driver who had a fuel truck with some extra marine fuel, and he told the driver to get over to the launch ramp where we were beached. Then he found a little outboard shop not far away that had just enough two cycle motor oil to get us to our next stop (you have to mix oil and gas in an outboard motor). The bus roared up to the little outboard shop, and Eddie jumped out and bought all the motor oil they had on hand. Then he dashed back onto the bus, and in a few minutes the bus pulled up to the boat ramp. We got the boat refueled—and I mean it was *just barely* enough fuel to get us to our next stop—and we were on our way.

As we were pulling away, I looked back and saw J. W. Marriott, Jr., the chairman of Marriott Hotels, running down the boat ramp, waving his arms and yelling. *He wanted to get in the boat!* I had already lost an hour scavenging fuel, and I still had a record to break. I sure wasn't going back to pick up passengers. I signaled Johnny to open up the throttle, and we were outta there!

By the time we reached the Arch in St. Louis, we had knocked sixty-one minutes off the old record. The time of the run—including time spent hunting for fuel—was twenty-five hours, ten minutes. My record was later broken—but I was the first person to break the previous record in more than fifty years, and I was the first to break that record on the very first attempt.

The "Assault on the Mississippi" was a success, raising a record amount of money for the U.S. Olympic Committee. To me, however, the achievement was intensely personal. I had been racing for approval and affirmation, especially from my father. I felt that if I broke the record and did something great for charity and got my name in the papers, my dad would be proud of me. On this night, at the Victory Banquet honoring me and August Busch III as Olympic Sportsmen of the Year, I knew that my dad would say to me, in front of a crowd of witnesses, the words of praise and affirmation I had waited a lifetime to hear.

There was a meal, followed by some toasts and introductions, and finally my dad, the president of the United States, got up to speak. I listened through a haze of fatigue as my dad began his speech. After all, I had been up for about forty hours without even a catnap. The next thing I knew, I was being nudged awake. Applause was ringing in my ears, and Bill Simon was leaning toward me, nudging my elbow and speaking into my ear. "That was great what your dad said about you," he said. "You must be proud."

I just nodded and smiled. I had no idea what my dad had said about me. I had waited years for that moment, and when it finally came I had slept through it all!

DRIVEN TO RACE

After the "Assault on the Mississippi" came the "Assault on the Great Lakes" in 1983. Again, I had my friend Johnny Mann at the throttle of that trusty, formerly unlucky Wellcraft Scarab—but this time I had a reliable navigator, Steve Lyshon, to chart my course. I needed all the help I could get, because this was a race against the clock across 605 nautical miles of the worst water I've been on in my life. It was twelve hours of sheer torture for man and machine, pounding through six-foot swells from Chicago, up Lake Michigan, then down Lake Huron to Detroit. Our bodies absorbed a force of twenty-five gees every time the hull pounded into a wall of water—that is, every couple seconds for twelve hours straight. Steve, my navigator, had blurred vision by the end of the run. The gelcoat on the bottom of the boat was cracked by the strain. Our radar and just about every other piece of machinery on the boat had quit functioning by the end of the race.

When the wind kicks up on the Great Lakes, it's like racing in a bathtub. There's no room for the wave action to disperse, so the waves pile up against the shores, then roll back at you. There's no predictable wave pattern that allows you to get used to a rhythm. There's just this fierce, jolting, jarring, erratic pounding from all directions. It's a very tough way to race a boat.

There were spotter planes over me during the race, and the guys in those planes kept saying, "They're crazy! It's too rough down there! They oughta pull off!" I kept going. I had to. I absolutely had to. Maybe people would have understood if I had just pulled over and tried it again another day. But I was sure I would be labeled a quitter. When your name is Reagan and the cameras are watching you, you don't want to wimp out and say, "It's too rough today, I'm gonna sit this one out." So I kept going. And I made it to Detroit. In the process, we raised $50,000 in sponsor pledges to benefit the U.S. Olympic Committee.

My next race, in June 1984, took me from Ketchikan, Alaska, down the Inside Passage, to Seattle, Washington. Johnny was again my throttle man, and my navigator was ABC newscaster Tom Jarriel, who was also covering the race for *20/20*. In the course of that run, we raised a quarter of a million dollars for the Cystic Fibrosis Foundation. Not long after that, I raced from L.A. to San Francisco, breaking the water speed record by three hours (the previous record was eleven hours; we did it in eight) and raising still more money for the U.S. Olympic Committee.

Why did I do it?

Because I wanted people to like me. I wanted to be a hero. I wanted my dad to pat me on the back and say, "Great job, Mike. Now you are really, officially a Reagan."

I was *driven* to race. I started racing professionally in the 1960s, gave it up in the '70s and sold boats for a while, then went back to racing in the '80s—supposedly for charity, but in fact I was trying to fill up an aching hole in my life. Though I didn't understand it at the time, I was racing for love, approval, affirmation, and validation. I never found any of those things out on the water, but that's what I was racing for. And I was determined either to find those things out there, among the waves and the spray, or die trying.

Boat racing is fun—but it's also a deadly serious business. In fact, I once disintegrated a boat. I was racing in the Speed Classic Circuit at Offut's Bayou near Galveston, Texas, in 1969. I was in the lead, doing 117 m.p.h. in a brand-new twenty-foot Raysoncraft when the boat suddenly left the water and chined in—which means it came into the water on its side. The fiberglass hull blew in on one side. Water sucked in and exploded the boat, throwing debris and plumes of spray about 45 feet in the air. Somewhere in that billow of water and fiberglass shrapnel was Michael Reagan, flying and flopping like a rag doll. I had to be fished out of the water by a rescue boat, and I'll tell you, I was hurting in places I didn't even know I had before.

I was lucky. I've had many friends in the sport who weren't so lucky. But you don't go into racing thinking about the danger. You've got plenty of other people—friends and family members—who think about the danger for you. If you go into a race fretting about the danger, you should never race. If you think about losing or getting hurt or getting killed, you're not a winner.

LIFE IS A BOAT RACE

Some people learned it all in kindergarten. Not me. Everything I needed to know about life I learned in boat racing. Well, maybe not everything, but almost everything. When I went into a race, I would always pile pressure onto myself to make it. I could have brought along a fresh driver, but I chose to do all the driving myself. I could have quit when the water and the weather turned nasty, but I chose to go on. I could have stopped trying when I ran out of gas or when I was just so bone-weary I could hardly stand up, but I chose to hang in there.

I'm not making myself out to be a hero. I went on not because I was so courageous but because I was less afraid of dying than of being called a quitter. I always piled pressure on myself to finish the race: *You will not quit, Mike. Quitting is not an option for you. You will stay at the wheel until the job is done.* And somehow I was always able to flail my way through the six-foot swells and the exhaustion and the crumbling circumstances, and I would get to the other end—often setting a new record in the process.

I figured out that the same laserlike focus, the same drive, the same stubborn sense of purpose that got me through those races could also get me through life. I learned one very simple principle from boat racing: *I learned to finish.* If I hadn't learned to finish, I wouldn't have a national radio show today. If I hadn't learned to keep going when the boat was running out of fuel, when my navigator had quit on me, when the waves were cracking my hull, I wouldn't have kept going when I was commuting 262 miles round-trip every day and getting paid in baseball caps.

There were days I came home from the studio feeling as tired, beat up, thrashed, and trashed as I had after a thousand-mile boat race. That's when I discovered those deep, God-given reserves of inner strength that we all have but don't realize we have until our backs are against the wall. Somehow, I managed to set my face against the wind and waves of my circumstances—and I kept on going. *I learned to finish.*

People today need to hear how to achieve their dreams. Like I say on my show: There are those who make it happen, those who watch it happen, and those who wonder what happened. For many years, I watched and I wondered. But now I'm making it happen. I'm making waves.

I started out making waves on the lakes and rivers of America. Now I'm making waves from sea to shining sea—electromagnetic airwaves radiating from broadcast towers across the country, which translate into political shockwaves, rattling the corridors of power and influence. And that's the way I like it.

I love it when Bill Clinton and Bryant Gumbel and Dick Gephardt holler like stuck pigs about "hate speech on the airwaves"—just because the truth is told. I love it when bad ideas like the Conference of States and the Clinton Healthcare Plan get shut down after we spotlight them on *The Michael Reagan Talk Show.* I love it when conservatives win by landslides, when Democrats switch to the Republican party *en masse,* when people across the country recognize liberal hypocrisy despite the best efforts of the liberal establishment and the dominant media to disguise the truth. It all just shows that you and I and a lot of other people are out there, smiling and dialing, romping and stomping, making things happen, making waves.

CHAPTER 17

Ronald Reagan's Third Term

OVERNIGHT, THE earth shifted underneath Capitol Hill. The political power structure in Washington, D.C., changed polarity. The government of the United States was wrested from the hands of one political ideology and placed in the hands of a completely opposite ideology. In many countries, you cannot change the government without getting people killed. But on January 4, 1995, the most dramatic political change in living memory swept through the corridors of power—but instead of being seized by panic and uncertainty, America threw a party!

I was there. I saw it with my own eyes. And in some ways, I still can't believe it.

I hadn't originally planned to be in Washington for the first day of the 104th Congress. But in December of 1994—a month after the astounding November 8 landslide that gave both houses of Congress to the Republicans for the first time in forty years—I got a call from Jon Christensen. Jon is the freshman congressman-elect from Nebraska and a heckuva great guy. "Mike," he said, "you've got to come to Washington for the swearing-in. You were a big part of what happened on November 8, and you've got to be a part of January 4."

I quickly agreed to be there, and I arranged through Sandy Sanders (who had been my advance man during my father's campaigns) to make the arrangements for my schedule in Washington, D.C. My producer, Paul Wilkinson, went with me, as did Andy Beal of MediaFAX Technolo-

gies in Sacramento. Andy publishes my newsletter and was then operating a fax network that supplied legislative news to my listeners via an
800 number (the fax operation has since been replaced by my Internet
website).

I was glad to have Paul with me, since he had spent three years on
Capitol Hill as a congressional staffer and a stint with the Bush
administration before joining *The Michael Reagan Talk Show*. He
really knew his way around the city of Washington. But me? Hey, I
knew my way around the processes and the political games of Washington, D.C., but I didn't know the *city* at all (people are often
surprised to learn that, in the entire eight years of my dad's administration, I only visited Washington twice, and only spent three nights
at the White House).

I arrived in Washington on Tuesday afternoon, the 3rd, in time for the
reception for Newt at the Old Post Office. After that, Paul, Andy, and I
went over to the Freshmen Gala—a big party with about four thousand
people packed into one ballroom, with plenty of music, dancing, and food.
On the way into the ballroom, Jon Christensen told me the freshman
class had a surprise for me. I found out what the surprise was when
Congressman Dick Chrysler from Michigan brought me forward and
presented me with my Majority-Maker pin, making me an honorary
member of the 104th Congress—an honor that was bestowed only on
two people, Rush Limbaugh and me. I still wear that pin whenever I put
on a suit and tie and do anything political. After the presentation, I gave
the keynote speech for the evening. The mood was festive and it was a
little hard to get people to quiet down for my speech, so I kept my
remarks brief and light.

At nine o'clock, I did my show from the studios of Standard News, and
the message that came through again and again, from caller after caller,
was a sense of excitement and hope: We were on the brink of the ultimate
fulfillment of the Reagan Revolution, which had begun fourteen years
earlier with my father's inauguration in January 1981. The newly elected
congressional class were the ideological heirs of Ronald Reagan. Because of the Twenty-second Amendment, Ronald Reagan was only
allowed to serve two terms. But if anything deserved to be called "Ronald
Reagan's third term," the 104th Congress was it!

GEE, THIS IS REALLY NEAT!

The next day, Wednesday the 4th, was the *big* day. It began with a lot of running around: morning phone interviews with affiliates KVI in Seattle and WXYT in Detroit and a taped interview with the BBC about the international implications of the Republican revolution. Then the three of us caught a cab to the Hill and sat around and schmoozed with Representative David Dreier—a California congressman who had guest-hosted my show a few times—in his office in the Cannon Building. We took the tunnel under Independence Avenue to the Capitol building and wandered through the Capitol basement, where dozens of radio talk-show hosts from around the country were broadcasting to their local audiences from microphones on card tables.

In the hallways of the Capitol and the House office buildings, we ran into many of the people I had gotten to know through my show—Congressman Steve Stockman from Texas, Ohio Democrat and all-around good guy James Trafficant, Republican legislative counsel Peter Davidson. I also stopped former Seattle Seahawks wide receiver (now Oklahoma congressman) Steve Largent as he was walking through the Cannon Building with his wife and kids. Steve had been on my show twice, but never when I was hosting, only when David Dreier sat in for me. So I shook his hand and said, "Steve, you don't know me, but I'm Mike Reagan and you've been on my radio show. Maybe you can come on again sometime when Dave Dreier lets me host my own show!"

Also that morning, I waited in the cattle call to have my picture taken with Newt Gingrich in his new (recently de-Foley-ated) speaker's office in the Capitol. What a zoo that was! Then it was back to Dreier's office to rest and regroup.

My big goal for the day was tracking down a ticket to the House gallery for the swearing-in ceremony. I tried to cajole Dreier into getting one for me. "Hey, each member only gets one guest ticket to give away," Dave replied, "and I gave my only guest ticket to my dad." I told Dave how insensitive I thought that was—looking out for his dad instead of me! "But Mike," he replied, "my dad's a loyal Mike Reagan listener in Kansas City!" Well, that made it a little better—but I still didn't have a ticket.

"Mike," said Paul, my producer, "why don't you just go on over to the Capitol? Even without a ticket, I'm sure you'll run into a member of Congress who can get you in." So I took Paul's advice. While Paul and Andy stayed in Dreier's office to watch the event on TV, I went over to the Capitol. About fifteen minutes or so before the historic event was to begin, I turned one of the hundreds of corridors of the Capitol building and found myself nose to nose with one of Newt's aides. "Mike!" she said, "I've been looking for you! Here's your ticket to the gallery!" I mean, what were the odds of me and the lady with the ticket bumping into each other like that?

So I went into the gallery, and what a seat I had! I was right next to Republican National Committee chairman Haley Barbour and his wife, and just behind and above me was Peggy Noonan, whose resume includes having written for both Dan Rather and Ronald Reagan. I looked around and waved at people I hadn't seen since the Reagan era. Over there was Al Hunt and the rest of the Capitol Gang. And over on that side of the aisle were Dick Gephardt, Pat Schroeder, Barney Frank, Chuckie Schumer, Major Owens, Kweisi Mfume—all firmly ensconced right where they belonged: in the minority. Among them, grinning like a Republican, was my old "blue-dog Democrat" buddy and frequent guest-host Billy Tauzin, the Ragin' Cajun. And there, on the good guys' side of the aisle, were my friends Bill Archer, Dick Armey, Helen Chenowyth, John Kasich, Tom Delay, Duncan Hunter, J. D. Hayworth, David Dreier, Randy "Duke" Cunningham, Chris Cox, Phil Crane, Bill McCollum, and more.

You might think a guy whose dad was president of the United States would greet all of this hoopla and ceremony with a big yawn—but not me! I was thinking, *Gee, this is really neat!* I was in awe during Newt's speech and throughout the solemn moment of the swearing in. I had been to both of my dad's inaugurations, and those were great days, in particular because I had worked so hard on my dad's campaigns. But this was different. For the first time in my life, I was a part of a great, historic event not because I was related to somebody but because I had earned my way there through the years of struggle on my radio show.

Back in the '80s, I had never been close to the politicos who surrounded my dad. To them, I was just a bump in the road, Reagan's kid, "Oh, him." They didn't give me the time of day and I didn't give them the time of day. Now there I was, sitting in the gallery, overlooking this august body, and I was thinking, *I'm rubbing shoulders with people who used to be around my dad—and I'm here on my own terms.* It was one of the first times in my life I was not being introduced as Ronald Reagan's son. I was Michael Reagan, talk-show host.

The new conservative majority had come about in large part because I, and others like me, had done what the dominant media had refused to do: I had helped make people knowledgeable about the processes of their government. We in talk radio had gained the trust of the American people through the quality of information we gave out on the air and because the values we spoke about had been proven right.

But in the midst of all that excitement and anticipation, a cloud came over my thoughts. What about the people out there in America? What if the change we are witnessing today is three thousand miles wide but an inch deep? This new Congress is revved up and ready to change America—but it will take time to undo forty years of neglect, pandering, and political chicanery. The people in this room are dedicated to balancing the budget and restoring fiscal sanity to the government—but what if the American people don't have the patience to let the 104th do its job? What if people aren't willing to accept slower growth in entitlements and social spending? What if the liberals successfully demagogue the issues (as they have often done in the past) and manage to paint these idealistic, committed conservatives as a bunch of heartless scrooges who hate children and old people?

I also worried about these freshmen congressmembers. The new Republican majority wasn't used to the leadership role, and leading is a whole different ballgame from being in the minority. The Republicans were used to opposing bad policy and bad legislation; did they have the street smarts to generate good policy and good legislation and to move their ideas through the system and past a barrage of liberal attacks, biased media coverage, and presidential vetoes?

But when the moment for the swearing in of the new Congress finally arrived and those new members of Congress rose to their feet, raised their right hands, and took the solemn oath of their office, one emotion crowded out all else: hope. The 104th Congress represented the best chance this country had yet known of fulfilling the dreams of the original Reagan revolution in the 1980s.

"Republicans and Democrats— They're All the Same!"

How many times have you heard someone say there really is no difference between the Democrats and the Republicans? If I've heard it once, I've heard it a bazillion times, both on and off the show. And there was a time when that statement had a lot of truth to it. For proof positive, here's a story I bet you've never heard before:

You may remember that, back in the dark old days of the 102nd Congress, the rascals of *both* parties voted themselves a pay raise in the wee hours of a cold November night—hoping nobody would notice. Soon afterward, they passed another, even more dastardly piece of legislation, this time making their pay raises *automatic* (they only had to vote if they wanted to *stop* the automatic pay raise!). Of course, the motive behind the automatic pay raise was strictly humanitarian and altruistic: Congress members didn't want to expose their constituents to the unpleasantness of watching their elected representatives gorge themselves at the public trough.

Along comes the 1990 congressional election season, and these Congressmembers of both parties have a problem: What if the pay raise becomes a campaign issue? What if the public decides to "throw all the rascals out"? So the Republican National Committee and the Democratic National Committee got together. The good ol' boys from both sides of the aisle went out, tossed back a few brews together, and cut a secret deal behind closed doors. Here's the deal: Neither side would make a campaign issue out of the pay raise. "This thing is embarrassing to both sides," they said, "so let's just leave it alone. If your challengers don't make the pay raise an issue against our incumbents, our challengers won't make it an issue against your incumbents." As an enforcement mechanism, they agreed that if any challenger brought up the pay raise against an incumbent, the party would cut off all campaign funds to that challenger.

Next, we go to the state of Georgia, where a Republican incumbent fights for his political life against a strong Democratic challenger. Pundits give this longtime Republican congressman no chance of winning. Suddenly, his Democratic challenger commits the unpardonable sin: He starts bashing the Republican incumbent for supporting the midnight pay raise! The challenger apparently doesn't know about the agreement between the DNC and the RNC! Suddenly, in the home stretch of the campaign, the Democratic challenger's funding completely dries up. No money—no media! Meanwhile, the Republican incumbent gets piles of money from the RNC and completely buries the Democrat with a massive media blitz. On election day, the Republican incumbent squeaks past his challenger by a tissue-thin margin of nine hundred votes. If the Democrat had kept his mouth shut about the pay raise, he almost certainly would have won.

That Republican incumbent is now the Speaker of the House of Representatives. His name is Newt Gingrich. He is in the House of Representatives today because a secret, closed-door deal was cut in 1990 between the DNC and the RNC. He is there because in 1990, there really was not much difference between Republicans and Democrats.

But times have changed. The Congress has changed. The Republican party has changed.

The 104th Congress is a different breed of cat from every other Congress before it. The biggest difference, of course, is the freshman class. Like an army of "Mr. Smiths" straight out of an old Jimmy Stewart movie, these citizen-legislators marched into Washington and announced from Day One that the days of politics-as-usual are over. In its first 100 days, in keeping with the Contract with America, the new majority completely changed the way Congress does business—and it did so with 622 fewer staff employees, three fewer committees, and no secret back-room deals!

A side-by-side, week-by-week comparison says it all. Here's what the first 100 days of the new 104th Congress look like, compared with the first 100 days of the old 103rd:

Week One

Democrat-controlled 103rd: Congress is sworn in on January 5, then immediately recesses for a two week vacation.

Republican-led 104th: The very first day, January 4, Republicans pass the most sweeping congressional reforms in history:

Committees and staff are dramatically cut, and Congress is required to abide by the same laws it passes for the rest of the country.

Week Two
Democrat-controlled 103rd: Congress is *still* on vacation. Meanwhile, the crime probe of Democrat Ways and Means Committee chairman Dan Rostenkowski is expanded.

Republican-led 104th: Republican Ways and Means Chairman Bill Archer gavels hearings on Welfare Reform and Family Tax Relief. On January 17, both houses of Congress pass a law requiring the Senate and the House to obey the same employment laws as those that govern the private sector.

Week Three
Democrat-controlled 103rd: The 103rd finally convenes but generates no newsworthy activity. Elsewhere in Washington, Clinton attorney general nominee Zoe Baird withdraws her name because of nannygate problems, and President Clinton issues an executive order that liberalizes abortion policy.

Republican-led 104th: House committees complete work on a new Balanced Budget Amendment and unfunded mandates reform, while beginning work on a tough new Crime Bill. On January 23, President Clinton signs the Congressional Accountability Act, which the House passed on the very first day of business.

Week Four
Democrat-controlled 103rd: No noteworthy legislative action in the Congress. President Clinton lifts the ban on gays in the military.

Republican-led 104th: On January 24, President Clinton delivers his State of the Union address to a joint session of Congress and announces his own "new covenant" with the American people. Perhaps he forgot that Jesus Christ already gave us a New Covenant, and we don't need another one.

Meanwhile, the 104th races onward, approving the Balanced Budget Amendment. The Senate passes the Unfunded Mandates Act. Secretary of State Warren Christopher comes to the Hill and warns a House panel that the Contract with America threatens to bring U.N. peacekeeping missions to a halt. The Illegal Immigration Control Act, which would deny most federal benefits to illegals, is introduced in the House. An *L.A. Times* poll finds that 63 percent of respondents support cutting federal subsidies to the arts and public broadcasting.

Week Five
Democrat-controlled 103rd: Still no major legislative action in the Congress. The Clinton White House, however, has been busy: Another attorney general nominee, Kimba Wood, is forced to withdraw her name because of nannygate problems. President Clinton creates a "welfare reform" commission but appoints no members to it (clearly demonstrating the depth of his commitment to reforming the welfare state).

Republican-led 104th: The House continues charging ahead, approving the Unfunded Mandates Reform Act and a measure giving the line-item veto to the president. Republican Conference Chairman John Boehner announces a top-to-bottom review of affirmative action policy and law in the United States.

Week Six
Democrat-controlled 103rd: Congress takes another vacation.

Republican-led 104th: The House approves the National Security Revitalization Act, plus several new crime bills.

Week Seven
Democrat-controlled 103rd: President Clinton breaks his pledge of a middle-class tax cut, instead announcing a new economic plan calling for the most massive tax increase in U.S. history. Democratic leaders in the Congress promise to deliver on the tax hike; raising taxes is the one thing the 103rd Congress knows how to do.

Republican-led 104th: The House approves a 25 percent healthcare deduction for the self-employed.

Week Eight
Democrat-controlled 103rd: President Clinton lobbies hard for a $16.2 billion "stimulus package"—all tax-and-spend, and no spending cuts.

Republican-led 104th: The House approves an emergency defense spending bill to shore up a military that has sagged under

Clinton administration neglect—and unlike previous Congresses, the House *offsets* this spending by cutting other areas of the budget. The House also defies President Clinton's veto threat, approving a one-year moratorium on new federal regulations.

Week Nine

Democrat-controlled 103rd: Another slow week in Congress. President Clinton announces on MTV that he wears briefs instead of boxer shorts, and he announces a planned government take-over of the student loan program.

Republican-led 104th: The House passes a series of tort (lawsuit) reform measures intended to bring some common sense to our civil legal system and curb frivolous litigation. The House also passes a regulatory reform package designed to limit government intrusion into business activity and property ownership. On March 2, the Senate demonstrates that it lags behind both the House and the American people: The Balanced Budget Amendment is defeated by just two votes.

Week Ten

Democrat-controlled 103rd: Another dull news week on the Hill. The White House, meanwhile, approves the use of tanks against a religious group in Waco, Texas, even though it refuses to send tanks to protect U.S. soldiers in Somalia.

Republican-led 104th: On March 9, House Republicans unveil a plan for major middle-class and business tax cuts; on March 14, Ways and Means approves $188 billion in tax cuts—the first Republican tax bill to reach the floor of the House in more than a decade! Meanwhile, the House continues its drive for lawsuit reform with legislation to make it more difficult to bring securities fraud suits against U.S. businesses.

Week Eleven

Democrat-controlled 103rd: Democrats in the House do what Democrats do best: they approve the largest taxing and spending budget resolution in American history.

Republican-led 104th: The House sends the Unfunded Mandates Reform Act to President Clinton for a signature, approves a record $17 billion spending cuts package, and begins debate on a massive overhauling of the welfare state.

Week Twelve

Democrat-controlled 103rd: No major action on the Hill. President Clinton orders immediate resignations of all thirty-two U.S. attorneys nationwide in order to disrupt investigations of Whitewater and powerful Congressman Dan Rostenkowski.

Republican-led 104th: The House approves the Contract with America's welfare reform bill, as promised. President Clinton signs the Unfunded Mandates Reform Act into law.

Week Thirteen

Democrat-controlled 103rd: Several former Democrat House members plead guilty to charges related to the House Post Office scandal.

Republican-led 104th: The House holds the first-ever debate and vote on congressional term limits. Though term limits is the only point in the Contract with America to be defeated, the Republicans keep their pledge to bring the issue forward for a vote. Senate majority leader Bob Dole promises to keep the issue alive. Meanwhile, House Republicans link a $189 billion tax-cut package to the balanced budget plan. Newt Gingrich asks the networks for a half hour of prime-time TV to report the achievements of the 104th Congress to the American people—a privilege previously accorded only to the chief executive.

Week Fourteen

Democrat-controlled 103rd: Senate Republicans narrowly block passage of the Democrats' budget-busting tax-and-spend "stimulus package."

Republican-led 104th: The House passes family tax relief and tax incentives—exactly as promised. Included: $189 billion in tax cuts, the "crown jewel of the Contract," according to Newt Gingrich. The Contract with America is completed one week ahead of schedule, on April 5, day 92 of the 104th Congress. On April 7, Speaker Gingrich addresses the nation to declare the House's 100-day agenda to be successfully completed.

Can it really be said anymore that there is "no difference" between Republicans and Democrats? You've seen the evidence. You be the judge.

Next, Newt Gingrich was sworn in as speaker of the House, and minority leader Dick Gephardt passed the gavel to the new speaker. Immediately afterwards, a cheer went up, and the House floor broke out in celebration. The celebration lasted all of about two minutes; then it was down to business. There was a lot of work to do, and the 104th Congress proceeded to do it.

During its first day in office, the new Republican majority kept its promise to change the way Congress does business and to cut government down to size. Often with huge bipartisan majorities, the new House passed a number of sweeping in-house reform measures, including the Congressional Accountability Act, requiring Congress to abide by its own laws. Next, the House voted to limit committee and subcommittee chairmen to three terms and the speaker of the House to four terms, and to end proxy voting in committee (from now on, you have to be present to vote). Measures were passed to end waste and inefficiency, including the first full public accounting of House finances in history. The House voted to eliminate three committees, twenty-five subcommittees, one-third of committee staff slots, and funding for all special-interest organizations. Moreover, the House voted to require a three-fifths supermajority to raise income taxes and implemented a commonsense budgetary process. It was the official end of "current services baseline budgeting" (that form of budgetary smoke-and-mirrors that liberals had long used deceptively to label spending increases as "cuts").

And all of this happened on the very first day!

THE ADVENTURE BEGINS

That night, the three of us were back at the Standard studios, doing my show from 9:00 to midnight (so it could air at its usual West Coast time of 6:00 to 9:00 P.M.). Then we went over to Grover Norquist's house, which is just six or seven blocks from Capitol Hill.

Grover is a very well-connected conservative and head of Americans for Tax Reform (he's the one who convinced Bob Dole to sign the Taxpayer Pledge), and he was having a party for all the freshmen members of Congress. Occasionally a congressmember would drop in for a few minutes, then dash off. (Because of all the Contract with

America business that had been promised for the first day, the work on the House floor was going on into the wee hours of the morning.) The three of us hung out at Grover's for about half an hour, talking to people like Peggy Noonan and Michael Barone of *U.S. News and World Report* and the *National Journal.* There was a TV on in one of the rooms, and CNN was covering the legislative action that was still happening up on the Hill, just a few blocks away. I looked at Paul and said, "You know, things are still really hot on the floor. Let's get back to the Capitol. We were there for the opening; let's be there for the closing."

So Paul, Andy, and I jumped in the cab and headed over to the Hill to see the end of "the longest day." The cab deposited us near the House side of the Capitol at nearly 1:00 A.M. As we got out of the cab and sprang up the steps, we ran into two congressmembers from San Diego County, Republican freshman Brian Bilbray and Democrat Bob Filner, who were doing a press interview together. They joined us as we went into the building, and Bilbray said, "Where are you going?"

"We're going downstairs," I said, "to see if we can get into the majority cloakroom."

"Well, ride with us," said Bilbray, and we hopped onto the members' elevator. When the doors opened, Bilbray and Filner went in one direction and we went in another. Paul guided us to the cloakroom—a plain, unmarked wooden door with a peephole (this, I suppose, is where you find the "government of the peephole, by the peephole, and for the peephole" we keep hearing about—sorry, I couldn't resist). I knocked on the door. Within seconds the door swung wide open and there was Congressman Duncan Hunter. "Hey, Reagan!" he roared, "come on in!" He grabbed me by both shoulders and pulled me inside, shutting the door and leaving Paul and Andy out in the corridor.

Over my shoulder, I heard the familiar gravelly baritone of "B-1 Bob" Dornan—the congressman from the Disneyland district in California, a frequent guest-host on my show, and my old boss back in my days as a congressional aide. Instantly, he had me in a big bear-hug from behind and was shaking my brain loose from its moorings. In front of me was Randy "Duke" Cunningham—and I guess Duke hadn't had anything to eat all day, because he immediately stuffed my tie into his mouth and started eating it!

"Guys, guys," I said, "excuse me, but my staff is still outside the door!" So Duke opened the door and let Paul and Andy into the cloakroom.

The cloakroom is located right off the House floor, and it's a place where members and committee staff who have legislation under consideration can go to hang out, kick back, relax, gather information, plan strategy, and so forth. There are chairs and sofas, refrigerators, phone booths, food tables, and a TV set. At that ungodly hour, the cloakroom was a crazy swirl of heady celebration and glassy-eyed exhaustion. In one corner, Dave Macintosh, a freshman from Indiana, was going over some books and papers, looking very sober, taking every floor vote very seriously. The veterans in the room tended to be looser, more excited, more exuberant now that these freshmen had made them part of the new majority.

Ironically, we had to watch TV to see what was going on just on the other side of the wall separating the cloakroom from the House floor. Only members and staff are allowed on the floor. At about 2:20 A.M., they finally cleared the last piece of business and the day's proceedings were gaveled to a close by Speaker Gingrich. A big cheer went up. The new Congress had hit the ground running and accomplished a lot on its first day. Everybody we saw was completely wiped out. We were wiped out. It had been an incredibly long day—but it had been one of the best, most memorable days any of us had gone through.

As tired as we were, we hung around for a while and greeted members as they came off the House floor. At about three o'clock in the morning, the three of us finally made our way from the Republican to the Democrat side, past the minority cloakroom and down a row of stairs toward the exit. As we were coming down the stairs, we encountered Maxine Waters, the liberal Democrat from Los Angeles. I held the door for her and said, "Representative Waters, this is a special moment. I'm sure this is the first time a Reagan has ever held the door for you, and it may never happen again." She smiled and went to her cab, and we went to ours.

One of the most awesome days in American history had just come to a close. But the adventure of "Ronald Reagan's third term" was just beginning.

CHAPTER 18

The New Reagan Revolution

PEOPLE OUTSIDE of talk radio—especially the pundits and poo-bahs of the dominant media culture—keep scratching their heads, trying to figure out why conservative talk radio is going through the roof. This phenomenon has often been dismissed as a fad or a phase America is going through—yet it shows no sign of stopping or even slowing. So people all over the print and broadcast media are trying to figure out what talk-show hosts have, why talk radio is so influential, what we are doing to unleash so much conservative passion and activism in America—and they keep missing the point. They conclude (wrongly) that the problem must be that there just isn't enough of the other side, the liberal side, on the air.

Sure, that must be it. National Public Radio isn't enough. Pacifica Radio isn't enough. NBC, ABC, CBS, PBS, and CNN aren't enough. We need more liberals on talk radio! They act as if there has been a palace coup in radioland, and the conservatives have put all the liberals up against the wall and done away with them. They don't understand that it's the marketplace at work.

Liberal talk-show hosts aren't on the air because people, by and large, don't want to listen to liberal talk-show hosts. One of the icons of liberal talk, none other than Larry King himself, tried moving his late-night talk show into the time slot I occupy. He bombed!

Now we have a new crop of liberals coming into talk radio. There's

Gary Hart, the former Democratic presidential candidate who got caught on the island of Bimini with a blonde in his lap. There's Mario Cuomo, the liberal former governor of New York. There's Lowell Weicker, former senator and governor from Connecticut, who announced his entrance into the talk-radio fray by saying that conservative talk-show hosts are dangerous and dishonest. So Weicker is going to save America by giving us the *liberal* facts. He's going to roll back the Second Reagan Revolution by going on the air and extolling the virtues of higher taxes and more government spending. Well, good luck, Lowell—you're gonna need it.

A 24-HOUR, TWO-WAY INTERCHANGE

Bill Clinton and other liberals have accused the new Republican majority in Congress of being "antigovernment" because these Republicans want to shrink the bureaucracy. The liberals actually believe the bureaucracy *is* the government. We conservatives know better. We truly love our government, because we know that the true government of the United States of America is "We the People." The bureaucracy exists only to serve the People—not to bully them or to run their lives. I believe one of the reasons I was honored as a "Majority-Maker" by the 104th Congress is that, through my program, I have helped "We the People" become more involved than ever in our own self-government and self-determination. My show has served as a meeting place, a town hall, where the American Congress and the American people have met in a great two-way dialogue. And out of that dialogue has come enormous, positive change.

Over the past few years, my show has become much more than a three-hour nightly talk show. Today, it is a twenty-four-hour-a-day information interchange, three hours of which is audio. The rest of the time, you can access my show via my newsletter, *The Michael Reagan Monthly Monitor*, and my Internet website at *http://www.reagan.com*. From my website you can gather fact-filled information on the latest issues, House and Senate bills, think-tank studies, and liberal idiocy—and from my website you can write and send e-mail to me and my staff, to your own congressmember or senator, or to the White House—and we've made it incredibly easy. If, for any reason, you can't hear my show in your area, you can hear the show in RealAudio over the Internet. No other radio talk show offers you this kind of connecting point between you and your government.

And there's another important way I put you in touch with your government through my show: Did you ever notice who guest-hosts my show when I'm away or on vacation? You hardly ever hear so-called "best of" reruns of my show (which I consider the next worst thing to dead air). I refuse to allow *The Michael Reagan Talk Show* to spin its wheels. So I have guest hosts who are intimately connected with your government. I have Republican congressmembers like Bob Dornan, David Dreier, J. D. Hayworth, and Bill McCollum come in and host the show. And I also have (get this!) *Democratic* congressmembers like Gary Condit and Billy Tauzin come in (all right, Tauzin's a Republican now—but he was a Democrat when he hosted my show). I've had presidential candidate Pat Buchanan hosting my show, and I've had the heads of major think tanks on my show—people like Grover Norquist from Americans for Tax Reform, Amy Moritz from National Center for Public Policy Research, and Edmund Peterson and Phyllis Berry-Myers from Project 21. Why do I have these people sitting in for me when I'm away? Not only because I want you to hear what they have to say, but because *I want them to hear what YOU have to say!* I want to do all I can to encourage a robust, two-way dialogue between you and your government!

So if you tune into my show, and you don't hear my voice behind the mike, don't think the show has stopped moving forward. Realize that I have put yet another political leader in the hot seat—and I am turning that person over to you! I expect you to do your job, to call in, and to give him or her an earful and a good grilling!

One time, I was talking about a budget bill being debated on the House floor even as my show was on the air. I did something that sends cold chills down the spines of radio station program directors and general managers: I told my listeners to turn on C-SPAN and watch the debate! I talked about the importance of the budget debate and the issues being decided. Then I gave out the names of members who were for the bill, those who were against, and those who were riding the fence. If those fence-riders would just get their fannies off the fence, I said, then we would get a very important piece of legislation passed.

Get Plugged in . . .
to the Reagan Information Interchange

My radio show is three audio hours of a non-stop, 24-hour, two-way information interchange. To find *The Michael Reagan Talk Show* on a station in your area, download the latest station list from my Internet website at *http://www.reagan.com*, or write us via U.S. Snailmail at:

> The Michael Reagan Talk Show
> P.O. Box 6061-405
> Sherman Oaks, CA 91413

And hey, give me a call! Whether you agree with me or disagree, let's talk it over on the air! Just sit back, smile, and dial toll-free at:

1-800-468-MIKE (1-800-468-6453)

To order my newsletter, *The Michael Reagan Monthly Monitor*, call my good friends at MediaFAX Technologies. You may order a subscription online from my Internet website at *http://www.reagan.com*, or order by phone. All major credit cards are accepted, and the call is free:

The Michael Reagan Monthly Monitor — 1-800-895-9898

If you have a computer and a modem, you can find a wealth of information at my Internet website—the latest information on congressional legislation, bill updates, vote trackers, hot topics, discussion forum, links to other vital conservative websites, speeches by Ronald Reagan, station list, staff page, my e-mail box, and much, much more! You can even listen to my show in RealAudio over the Internet! So when you're surfing the web, surf on over to:

> *http://www.reagan.com*

Keep in touch!

Less than twenty minutes later, a call came in from Congressman Nick Smith of Michigan, one of those I had named on the air as a "fence-rider." He was calling from the majority cloakroom, and his first words when he got on the air were, "Hey, Mike! Tell my constituents I'm voting *yes* on this bill!" That's just one example among many of how the movers and shakers in Washington, D.C., are increasingly using *The Michael Reagan Talk Show* as a tool for communicating with their constituents.

So what can *you* do? How can you join the *new* Reagan revolution—a revolution of smaller government, lower taxes, and individual and family empowerment? You can get involved. Here's how:

1. Be informed. Listen to *The Michael Reagan Talk Show,* subscribe to *The Michael Reagan Monthly Monitor,* plug in to the Michael Reagan Information Interchange on the Internet, and stay on top of what your government is doing *for* you—and *to* you. Watch C-SPAN—and compare what you see with your own eyes with the sliced, diced, edited, slanted version of events that Tweedle-Dan, Tweedle-Peter, and Tweedle-Tom serve up on the big three networks. If you must watch the networks, watch them with a jaundiced, skeptical eye, and realize that you are watching filtered news. The networks will treat nonstories, puff-pieces, and liberal press releases as major stories—then ignore other truly major news as if it never happened. They will insert opinion into what they call "news," and they will splice soundbites and videobites to reshape reality into something that conforms to their agenda.

If you truly want to be informed, *read.* As I say again and again on my show, *readers are leaders.* In my callow, shallow youth, I was a TV-watcher, a lazy thinker, and I didn't know what I believed in. Reading wasn't that easy for me, and I just didn't take the time. But all that changed for me about ten years ago. I figured out that if I wanted to make it in talk radio, I needed to know what was going on around me. So I became not just a reader but a *voracious* reader, a Eureka Power-Vac of information, sucking the marrow out of seven or eight newspapers a day, plus numerous books and magazines, not to mention all the faxes and e-mail I get.

I think all the reading I do these days is God's way of getting me back for all the lazy reading habits I had when I was younger. Every once in a while, I get a chance to chat with someone who knew me back in the 1970s or '80s, who thought of me as a spoiled know-nothing if they thought of me at all, and now they say, "Mike! I knew you back when and I *never* would have figured you to become a national radio talk-show host! Now you're the number one nighttime talk-show host and you're emceeing a reception for Lady Margaret Thatcher and you're being introduced by Ed Meese at a Heritage Foundation fund-raiser. *What in the world happened to you?*" I became a *reader,* that's what happened. And readers are leaders.

2. *Become an activist.* Keep in regular contact with your elected representatives and let them know what you think about the various issues and pieces of legislation that affect your life and your future. Write letters to the editor and call in to local and national radio talk shows. Make your thoughts known and your voice heard. Vote. Support conservative candidates and causes with your donations. Get involved at the grassroots level, stuffing envelopes and walking precincts for your local candidates.

Turn your friends and neighbors on to my show, my website, and my books. Engage them in a friendly, cordial dialogue about why government should be smaller, why well-intentioned programs like welfare and affirmative action do more harm than good, why high taxes destroy initiative and hinder economic growth for us all.

Run for office: Your local school boards, your city and county governments, your state government, and your Congress all need *citizen legislators*—not career politicians but ordinary people with common sense and life experience, people who can change the way government does business.

3. *Keep it brief.* When writing or faxing, write as concisely as possible—preferably keeping your communication to a single page. Focus on one issue per letter (congressmembers often assign different staff members to different issues, and single-subject letters have a better chance of getting to the people who get things done). Don't worry that your letter may not be personally seen by your representative. All constituent mail is read by someone, usually a staff member, and if your letter can persuade the congressman's staff expert to your position on a certain issue, then you have very likely persuaded the congressman as well!

4. *Keep it legible.* Typewritten letters and faxes are the most effective ways to communicate. Don't make your congressmember or congressional aide have to decipher your fancy penmanship or your muddy, scrunchy fax. Don't use attention-getting gimmicks to make your letter "stand out"; it will only make your letter look like the work of a nut! Letters should be businesslike and easy to read. Faxes should be sent in the "high resolution" or "fine" mode.

5. *Be courteous and positive.* Avoid exaggerations or threats such as, "If you don't vote my way, you'll never get reelected!" Instead, make your thoughts clear and precise, and support them with one or two good reasons. And what about those preprinted mass-mailing postcards that different groups send you to sign and send to your representative? Congress members don't exactly ignore them—but a dozen preprinted cards won't pack as much persuasive wallop as a single, well-thought-out letter from a constituent. Consider rewording the message of the pre-printed card in your own way, using your own thoughts and your own passion, and sending on your own stationery.

6. *Send an e-mail message.* Congressmembers are increasingly becoming accessible via the Internet, so you may want to consider this fast, effective way of communicating with your legislators. For an up-to-the-minute list of all members of Congress, including those with e-mail addresses, download the list from my website at *reagan.com.* Also, you can compose and send electronic mail to your representatives from my website.

7. *Limit your contacts to your own representatives and senators.* When congressional offices receive communication from outside their own districts, they almost always forward it to the office of that citizen's representative or senator, stamped RESPECTFULLY RE-FERRED—NOT ACKNOWLEDGED. That means, no one in the office you sent it to took the time to look at the substance of your letter. On some occasions you may want to write a member of Congress who doesn't represent you—for example, if that person chairs a committee that oversees a piece of legislation that is very important to you. If you must write a member who is not your legislative representative, mark your correspondence and the envelope with the words DO NOT REFER in large letters. But understand that congressmembers are naturally going to be more sensitive to the concerns of those who vote in their district.

8. *When telephoning, call early.* That means you should call before 9:00 A.M. Eastern time, because back in Washington, they clear their phone messages at 9:00 when they show up for work. If a vote is coming down on a certain day, and you want to be heard on that issue, you'd better get your message in before 9:00 A.M. that day. If you're on the West Coast like me, you may have to set your alarm to get up early in the morning. If you call after 9:00, your message will be old news by the time your representative gets it. You can call your representative's local office and save the cost of a call to Washington, but you should call a day in advance of a vote or other action, because it takes that long for the message to be forwarded.

9. *Be specific.* Occasionally, someone complains that *The Michael Reagan Talk Show* is "too technical" because I "always give out those HR numbers." But I give out those numbers for a reason: I want you to get results when you talk to your congressmember. So when you listen to my show, keep a pad and pencil handy, because you never know when I might throw a bill number or a phone number at you. Your representative appreciates it when you call with clear, explicit information about specific bills and even specific parts of a bill. Together, you and I have already done the brain surgery for them, so they can go right to that bill, look up the section you are concerned about, then go out and cure the problem on the floor of the House or Senate.

If a legislator gets a letter or call from someone who talks in general terms about "the antiterrorism bill," he or she may ignore it. There may be half a dozen different "antiterrorism bills" in conflict with each other, and saying you are for or against "the antiterrorism bill" may be absolutely meaningless. But when you write or call to express a strong opinion on HR1710, you immediately have the attention of someone on the Hill. When a constituent cares enough to be informed about a specific bill, the member of Congress knows that the constituent is going to notice how he or she votes on that bill. In many cases, the member of

Congress has not read the bill and may not even be aware that the bill exists—until *you* call.

Here's an example of why it pays to be specific: Remember the so-called "Crime Bill" of 1993—the one with midnight basketball and the assault weapons ban, the one that was supposed to hire 100,000 new policemen in America? Bad as it was, the bill—which passed in the Democrat-controlled 103rd Congress—could have been much worse. While the bill was being debated, we began talking on my show about a little-known provision in that bill, Section 5110. That provision would have authorized the Treasury Department to go to Hong Kong and hire Royal Hong Kong Police (RHKP) officers and bring them to America as federal narcotics agents. (Maybe that was where Clinton got his claim of hiring 100,000 new policemen; we obviously weren't going to get American cops to work for the kind of money provided in the bill, so he was planning to import cops from the Third World!)

As I dug into the facts behind Section 5110, I learned that many RHKP officers were themselves involved in the drug trade; they had joined the Hong Kong police force in order to play both sides of the fence! Even though the corruption in the RHKP was known and had been disclosed in congressional testimony, Section 5110 was quietly slipped into the bill on the Senate side. Because there was no fiscal impact to the amendment, it didn't have to go to the floor for a separate vote; it could slide right through on the back of the Clinton crime package without any debate or public scrutiny!

In addition to talking about it on my show, I called David Dreier's office and spoke to one of his staffers. "You need to let David know," I said, "that there's a ridiculous provision in the crime bill that's coming over to the House side." I described it to the staffer, and he was incredulous.

"You can't—! How could—! This couldn't possibly—! You're putting me on! Hiring cops from the other side of the world to chase drug traffickers in America? That's nuts! That's absolutely luuuuuudicrous! Who would put that in a bill?! Are you sure you didn't dream this?!"

"Look up Section 5110."

He was gone for a while, and I could hear the sound of pages turning a little ways from the phone, along with a muttered, "Section 4990 . . . 5000 . . . 5100 . . . " And suddenly, as if he was shouting right in my ear, I heard, "Ohmigosh! It *is* in the bill!"

And soon afterwards, it was stripped *out* of the bill. Even though we couldn't stop the Clinton Crime Bill, we were able to make a bad bill a little better because I could go to a member of Congress and talk about a specific provision.

10. *Last but not least, remember to keep in touch with your state legislators as well as your congressmembers.* As the Congress begins returning more power to state and local governments, it becomes all the more important for citizens to remain aware of—and involved with—legislative action that is taking place closer to home. It would be tragic to succeed at the congressional level only to have everything undone at the state and local levels. If you listen to my show and log on to my website on a regular basis, you can be sure to catch a lot of important information that is happening in various state-houses, as well as on the national stage. Also, pay attention to the local talk shows on the same station where you hear my show. These hosts often cover local events and legislation that you should be aware of and that may not be adequately reported in your local newspaper or on TV.

(Credit where credit is due: Many of the preceding suggestions were adapted from "A Guide for Effective Communication," written by my producer, Paul Wilkinson, for the June 1995 issue of *The Michael Reagan Monthly Monitor.* Paul worked on the Hill as a congressional staffer for three years before joining *The Michael Reagan Talk Show* team—so he knows whereof he speaks!)

STAY TUNED!

Why has my show become such a powerful link between people and their government? It's not because I have the great oratorical or persuasive skills of Ronald Reagan; I don't. It's not because I have a six-hundred-station network like Rush Limbaugh; I don't. I believe it's because I look for the events nobody else is talking about, the issues nobody else wants to really get into. My listeners count on me to give them the information, the statistics, the stories to back up their beliefs. They count on my show to break the important news affecting their lives and their government, and they trust my credibility.

Many talk-show hosts actually make a policy of *not* giving out phone numbers, fax numbers, and bill numbers. "This is an entertainment show," they huff. "That stuff's too technical for our audience." Well, I have more faith in my audience than that—and the fact that my show continues to grow and my audience has made its presence felt again and again in Washington, D.C., and in all fifty statehouses proves I am right.

I have one of the most active, involved, and informed radio audiences around. And that scares the left. They saw what happened across America on November 8, 1994, they know that talk radio had a big hand in it, and they are terrified. That's why they have been trying to demonize conservative talk-show hosts, conservative talk-radio listeners, and conservatives in general. They're afraid—afraid of the truth, afraid of change, afraid of losing power and control over the American agenda.

I have the best job in the world. There's nothing I'd rather do than host this radio show. I don't even look at it as work. It's fun. But it's also serious business. The world is changing, America is changing, and together, you and I are making change happen! The *new* Reagan Revolution is just beginning—a revolution of smaller government and greater freedom to pursue the American Dream, a revolution to finally realize Ronald Reagan's dream for America's next millennium. And you and I are a part of that revolution.

As rock-and-roller (and conservative activist) Ted Nugent says, "If you ain't makin' waves, you ain't paddlin'." So let's keep paddlin', you and I. Let's keep making waves. Till the next book, you've got my number and you know where to find me.

Keep in touch. Stay positive, stay focused, stay involved.

And most of all, stay tuned!

NOTES

Chapter 2. If the Press Doesn't Want the Job, I'll Do It

1. Quoted by Ambrose Evans-Pritchard in the *Washington Times*, July 17-23, 1995, 4.
2. Quoted in the *Washington Times*, March 13, 1991.
3. Rowan Scarborough, "Leftist press? You guessed right," *The Washington Times* (National Weekly Ed.), April 29, 1996, p. 1,15.

Chapter 3. *Whose* Hate Talk?

1. Quoted by Jack B. Coffman, "Clinton Urges Outcry Against Words of Hate," *St. Paul Pioneer Press*, April 25, 1995, 1A.
2. "Hate Talk," Creators Syndicate, April 26, 1995.
3. "Strong Language," *Washington Post*, April 28, 1995.
4. "History's Lesson: Words Matter," *New York Times*, May 8, 1995.
5. *Time*, May 8, 1995.
6. Proverbs 8:13b.
7. Amos 5:15.
8. Romans 12:9.

Chapter 5. The Arkansas Flu

1. Christopher Ruddy, *Vincent Foster: The Ruddy Investigation*, (Fair Oaks, CA: Western Journalism Center), pp. 151-152.

Chapter 6. Vince Foster: The Mystery Unravels

1. Ruddy, *Vincent Foster: The Ruddy Investigation*, p. 15.
2. Editorial: "Whitewater Torture," *Akron Beacon Journal*, Sunday, August 13, 1995, p. A18; William Safire, "A Hubbell Plea," *Akron Beacon Journal*, Tuesday, December 6, 1994, p. A9; William Safire, "Clinton's Shuffling," *Akron Beacon Journal*, Sunday, August 14, 1994, p. A19.
3. Ruddy, *Vincent Foster: The Ruddy Investigation*, p. 68.
4. Ruddy, p. 112.
5. Ruddy, pp. 3-5, 94-95.

6. Ruddy, pp. 22-23; also "Nussbaum Withheld Key Diary," *The Washington Times,* National Weekly Edition, September 25-October 1, 1995, p. 1.

7. Ruddy, p. 22.

8. Ruddy, pp. 22-23. Also "Clinton Records Were Taken," *Boston Globe,* Tuesday, December 21, 1993, p. 3; "Nussbaum Out as Aide to Clinton," *Boston Globe,* Sunday, March 6, 1994, p. 1.

9. Ruddy, p. viii.

10. Ruddy, pp. 114-116.

11. Ruddy, pp. 87-91.

12. R. Emmett Tyrrell, Jr., "Penetrating the Cloud Cover over Mena," *The Washington Times,* National Weekly Edition, April 3-9, 1995, p. 31.

13. On February 16, 1994, a Rose Law Firm employee testified before the Fiske grand jury that he was ordered to destroy documents from the files of Vince Foster ("Aide at Law Firm Tells Panel that He Shredded Foster Papers," *Charlotte Observer,* Friday, March 4, 1994, p. 1A; also Bill Clinton has admitted the truth of a March 7, 1994 *Washington Times* report that Hillary Rodham Clinton ordered documents shredded in Arkansas, saying, "Law firms dispose of their documents all the time," ignoring the fact that *these* documents were not stored at the law firm, but in the Clinton residence (Fred Barnes, "White House Watch: Drips," *The New Republic,* March 28, 1994, electronically retrieved on America OnLine).

Chapter 7. A Close Call for the Constitution

1. Quoted by Don Fotheringham in "Con-Con Call," *The New American,* March 6, 1995, 21-22.

2. Ibid., 25.

3. Ibid., 22.

Chapter 8. What a ONE-derful World It Will Be!

1. Quoted in *Washington Times,* March 20-26, 1995, 30.

Chapter 9. A Trillion Here, a Trillion There—of Our Money!

1. Quoted by *Investor's Business Daily,* May 15, 1995.

2. Source for defense spending statistics in this chapter: Senator Dan

Coats (R-Indiana), in a speech on the floor of the U.S. Senate, December 19, 1995.

Chapter 10. What's So Progressive About the Progressive Tax?
1. Grover Norquist, "Perspective: Flat Tax," *The Michael Reagan Monthly Monitor,* November 1995, 14; emphasis added.
2. Ibid., 12; emphasis in the original.

Chapter 11. Why Not Promote the GENERAL Welfare?
1. Ronald Reagan, *An American Life* (New York: Simon & Schuster, 1990), 68-69.
2. Ibid., 66-67.

Chapter 12. Within Reach: Dr. King's Dream
1. Molly Ivins, "Affirmative action terms and realities," Creators Syndicate, July 23, 1995.
2. Thomas Sowell, "Race hustlers and the politics of selling out," *Washington Times,* October 23-29, 1995, 30.

Chapter 13. In a Nuclear War, We're Sitting on Ground Zero
1. *Washington Times,* March 13-19, 1995.
2. Frank J. Gaffney, Jr., "Politics vs. U.S. security," *Washington Times,* July 10-16, 1995, 34.

Chapter 15. On the Inside at Last
1. Ronald Reagan, "Foreword," *On the Outside Looking In,* Michael Reagan (New York: Zebra Books, paperback edition, 1989), 8-10.
2. A. C. Green, *Victory: The Principles of Championship Living* (Orlando: Creation House, 1994), 155.